FINDING THE EMOTION IN NAMES

CYNTHIA WHISSELL

Order this book online at www.trafford.com
or email orders@trafford.com

Most Trafford titles are also available at major online book retailers.

Note for Librarians: A cataloguing record for this book is available from Library
and Archives Canada at www.collectionscanada.ca/amicus/index-e.html

Printed in Victoria, BC, Canada.

ISBN: 9781-4269-115-8-3

*Our mission is to efficiently provide the world's finest, most comprehensive book publishing
service, enabling every author to experience success. To find out how to publish your book, your
way, and have it available worldwide, visit us online at www.trafford.com*

Trafford rev 08/12/09.

 www.trafford.com

North America & international
toll-free: 1 888 232 4444 (USA & Canada)
phone: 250 383 6864 ♦ fax: 812 355 4082

I would like to dedicate this book to some of my favorite names

(and their owners).

This is for Mavros, Rebecca, John, Paul, and Matthew.

ABOUT THE AUTHOR

Dr. Cynthia Whissell has been teaching and conducting research at Laurentian University in Sudbury, Ontario, Canada, for four decades. She regularly instructs in courses at the undergraduate (B.A.) and graduate (M.A., Ph.D.) levels. These courses focus on the topics of emotion, language, and research design and analysis. Cynthia is a member of the Psychology department and also teaches in two graduate interdisciplinary departments (Human Development and Human Studies).

Cynthia's research on sounds and the emotion in names led to the publication of several scientific articles and also to this book. Finding the emotion in names (by analyzing the sounds in them) was a favorite lecture topic for students in classes and also for members of the general public who wanted to know more about names.

FOREWORD

Every name is made up of sounds, and the sounds that we use in names are not chosen by accident. They are meaningful: they tell us about the emotions or feelings contained in the names that influence name-givers (parents) when they choose names for their children. This book is about ways of measuring and revealing the emotions that are hidden in names. Are the sounds in a name Cheerful? Tough? Gentle? Unpleasant? The Table of Names and Emotions in this book answers these and other important questions.

In the first pages of this book, I explain how we know that the sounds in names are tied to feelings. In the remainder of the book, I provide a Table of Names and Emotions: this Table scores over 1200 popular US and Canadian names in terms of the emotions or feelings in their sounds. The most popular current boys' and girls' names are included in the table. In addition to picturing emotions, the entries in the Table tell you how masculine or feminine a name sounds, and also how easy it would be for children to pronounce the name.

Here is a sample entry from the <u>Table</u>:

BELINDA

Cheerfulness	××××××
Activity	×××
Toughness	××××××
Unpleasantness	××××××××

Sadness	××××××××××××××××
Passivity	××××××
Gentleness	××××××
Pleasantness	×××××××××××

Masculine sounds/emotions are medium high.
Feminine sounds/emotions are very high.
Pronunciation is more difficult.

This book also gives you some insight into the key sounds which make a name Cheerful, Tough, Sad, or Gentle. For example, **l** is a Gentle sound while **r** is a Tough one. If you are inventing your own name, you can use the <u>Guide to Sounds</u> to obtain a sense of the emotions in the name.

The scores in the <u>Table of Names and Emotions</u> and the sound-feelings in the <u>Guide to Sounds</u> are all based on research. For those interested in the background of this work, I have included a bibliography. While enjoying the book, please remember that names are not personality tests, and that they tell us more about name-givers (parents!) than about name recipients.

INTRODUCTION: NAMES AND EMOTIONS

Why Might You Want to Read this Book?

This book is about people's first names, and the emotions that are related to the sounds in them. You might want to read it because you are interested in names and want to know more about them. You might also be choosing a name for your child, and looking for information to help you make your choice. As well, you might want to look up names in the <u>Table of Names and Emotions</u> at the end of the book to see what emotions each name expresses. Finally, you might want to know how feminine or masculine a name sounds, or how easy it is to pronounce. Whatever your reason, this book will help you understand more about names, sounds, and emotions, and how they interact; it will help you discover the emotions in names.

Names are Important

Names are important to us because they are ours for an entire lifetime. They are labels by which we are known. However, they are not arbitrary labels and they are not chosen at random, nor do some names sound as good or as fitting to us as others. Psychologists have identified the teenage years as those during which young people struggle to establish their identities. Many teenagers attempt to change their identities by changing their names – sometimes drastically, to a totally different name and other times to a different form of their own name. Mary can transform into Jen, or she can become Mariah, only slightly changing her usual name. Peter can become P-Dog or Pete. You probably know at least one young person who has insisted that he or she be known, from one particular day forward, by a different name – one that suits him or her better than the "old" name.

Names have special meaning to us at the brain level, too. We hear our own names so often in important contexts that the brain treats them differently than it treats most other words or even other names. It is almost impossible to hear someone calling your name without paying attention to him or her – if only for a moment. Our names command our attention, since they have more meaning for us than most other words we know. We can hear our own names spoken in a tone of voice so low that any other word spoken at that level would be inaudible. Even someone whispering our name when we are asleep is often enough to wake us up, when a blaring TV wouldn't cause us to budge.

In many tribes and cultures (we can find them by looking back in history or to other regions of the world today), the naming of individuals is considered to be very important: knowing somebody's name is supposed to give you power over that person. By a twisted logic, if your name is Joe, you would want to be called Frank, because someone knowing you name (Joe) would give that person power over you. Of course, if you are called Frank for a while, that also becomes your name. Your attention can then be commanded by the name Frank, as well as by the secret name Joe, so there's no escaping the power of names over people.

Some societies have very complicated rules about the naming of children, while, in others, the process of naming is steeped in superstition. Even in societies with few superstitious beliefs about naming, such as those in North America, parents name their children with considerable care. Names have to sound and feel right, and convey the right message. They also have to have positive associations. A child's mission in life is to live up to his or her name; nobody would suggest that giving a name to a child is a trivial exercise. Using a relative's name is considered an honour for both the child and the relative in many cultures. When names are "copied" from relatives, they tend to be names that parents like: if not, they might end up as middle names instead of first ones.

Names do not necessarily reflect the personality of the child to whom they are given, because they are often chosen long before the child is born. What they do represent is the ideals and emotions of the name-givers – the child's parents. Most parents have some choice when it comes to naming their children, and they exercise this choice by selecting carefully from among the names available to them – invented names, family names, saints' names, or names belonging to popular figures.

Not all Names are Equally Popular

Names change in popularity across time, and this is so true that you can almost estimate the age of a person from his or her name. How old would you think a Walter is? A Mildred? Would a girl born more than 50 years ago have been named Madison? Or Ashley? If you hear of someone called Florence, might you not assume that she is quite old? What about Ronald, Donald, and Noah? Although some names have been popular for a very long time and continue to be so (Mary and William, for example), there are distinct fashions in naming. The researcher, Stanley Lieberson, has shown that these fashions – these rises and falls in popularity – are related to many different socioeconomic factors such as divorce rates, education rates, and racial or ethnic group membership. In my research, I demonstrate that name popularity is related to name sounds, which, in turn, are related to emotions or feelings.

Popular baby names for different years (in the US) are posted on the website http://www.ssa.gov/OACT/babynames/index.html. These names have been gathered from Social Security information and were originally collected by Michael Shackleford. A fascinating system for checking on how the popularity of a name changes is The Baby Name Wizard – Name Voyager (http://babynamewizard. com/namevoyager/lnc0105.htm) prepared by Laura Wattenberg. According to this site, the names Mildred, Walter, and Florence were all more popular 100 years ago than they are today, so anyone having these names would be quite old. The names Ronald, Donald, and Carol were popular in the middle of the last century so people with those names would be a little over half a century old. Madison and Ashley have been popular names during the last 20 years. Noah is an example of a name which has gained in popularity only in recent years.

Names and Sounds

All names are made up of sounds. If you write a name such as Mary, it is made up of four letters. When you say it out loud, it is made up of four basic sounds, **m**, an **a** sound, **r**, and a long **e** sound. The name Joe is also made up of a collection of sounds. Although it has three letters, the name only includes two sounds, the **j** sound and an **o** sound. The name Ashley includes the beginning **a** sound, the **sh** sound, the **l**, and the long **e** sound at the end which is represented by the letters **e** and **y** together. The saying of names out loud is important to our understanding of the emotions in them, as you will see later.

Some Sounds Work Better for Some Names than Other Sounds

All sounds do not work equally well in all names. If I were writing a children's story book with a story that included a delicate fairy and a grumpy troll, I would want to use names for my characters that had the right sounds in them. Of the two names, Gurd and Leemal, which do you think describes the fairy and which the troll? There is almost 100 percent agreement among those surveyed that Gurd should be the troll's name and Leemal the fairy's name. Why? Because of the different sounds used in them.

G, **r**, **d** are troll-sounds while **l**, long **e**, and **m** are fairy sounds. Gurd and Leemal are invented names, not real ones, and the only clue we have as to which name should belong to a fairy and which to a troll are the sounds in the names. The sounds obviously give us enough information to allow many of us to make the same choice. Imagine that we are making up more fictional names – this time for a young, impatient, medieval scholar and his older, wiser, patient professor. Who would be Melthos and who would be Portag? Why? What about a large lumbering elephant and a small energetic mouse? Who would be Chichik and who Horozon?

Masculine and Feminine Names

All names, both real and invented, are made up of sounds and these sounds tell us about emotions. A group of researchers (K.W. Cassidy and colleagues, who published their findings in the *Journal of Experimental Psychology* in 1999) have shown that both real names and invented names can be easily classified as masculine names or feminine names. The researchers were able to write a computer program that could learn to distinguish masculine names from feminine ones with the help of the sounds in them and some other information (for example how long the name was and how it ended). The computer program had no previous experience with names, so to it every name was a new or invented one. Yet after a small amount of training, it could tell the difference between men's and women's names. The researchers concluded that the emotion or feeling in the sounds of the names is one clue to the gender assignment of the name – to knowing if the name is more masculine or feminine. Unfortunately, they had no way of measuring the emotion or feeling in name sounds.

In my own research, I have found that people can take names made up of letters chosen in random patterns and assign a sex to the names: they agree with each other in saying that a name "sounds masculine" or "sounds feminine". This research was published in the journal *Perceptual and Motor Skills* in 2001. I have also used a computer program which created a formula to successfully guess the sex of a real name. This program was correct 80 percent of the time on samples of thousands of names. Four out of every five times the program (which had no background knowledge of names) could look at the sounds and emotions in names along with some additional information (length of the name; ending sounds) and guess correctly whether the name belonged to a man or to a woman.

When We Make Sounds We Use Our Muscles

Research of many different kinds has suggested that the way in which we form sounds influences our understanding of them. One theory of speech, called the motor theory of speech perception, emphasizes the movements of our facial and throat muscles as we form sounds and claims that these movements are crucial to our understanding of speech.

People who are hard of hearing can be taught to speak; because they cannot hear themselves make sounds, they are taught on the basis of the muscle movements we normally use to produce sounds. They can also learn to interpret speech by lip reading. When sounds are not available, the muscle movements of the face and lips serve as important clues to what is being said.

We use our breathing apparatus and our vocal cords along with our tongue, lips, and teeth to produce sounds. Our understanding of the sounds happens partly because of the actual noises that we create, but also because of the muscle movements that we go through in order to create them. Letters and the sounds they represent are forever linked with these muscle movements. When we look at the emotions conveyed by sounds, we will see that many of them are related to muscle movements.

A Match between Muscle Movements and Emotions

Imagine that a photographer is helping a group of people to pose for a photograph. As her final instruction, she may ask them to say "Cheese!" She does this because saying "cheese" produces a very desirable result – a smile. Holding on to the long **e** sound in the middle is especially helpful in creating the smile. Try it and see. If the photographer had asked her subjects to say "Chips!" instead of "Cheese!" she would have found some very funny expressions in her group photo. The word "chips" does not create a smile; neither does the word "alone" nor the word "yuck." The muscles we use in sounding out these words produce different facial expressions. The muscles also feel different in ways that a photographer might not notice because she cannot see the insides of our mouths and throats.

Here is a demonstration that you can try. Put on a big smile. Now say the words "cheese," "chips," "alone," and "yuck." Which word fit best with the smile? Which words were hardest to say correctly while smiling? Now put on a sad look: turn down your mouth and relax your jaw. Repeat the exercise. Which word matched the sad expression best? How easy was it to say "Cheese!" while looking sad? Did the sound of the word change as you spoke it while trying to hang on to a sad look? Finally, imagine feeling sick, and think of yourself as about to throw up. Which word best matches this particular feeling? You can also try this demonstration while looking at yourself in a mirror. You will plainly see, for example, that pronouncing the word "cheese" will break your sad expression – especially if you hold on to the middle e sound for a while. You will feel some funny muscle tensions when trying to say "alone" while holding on to a strong smile.

It is obvious that some of the muscle movements we use to produce sounds either **enhance** facial expressions of feeling or **interfere** with them. The word "cheese" enhances a smile, but interferes with a sad expression; the word "alone" does the exact opposite. The word "yuck" interferes with a smile, but enhances a feeling of yuckiness. The word "grim" might enhance an angry expression, but would not match all that well with a happy one.

Guesses about Emotions

How good are you at guessing the emotions in the sounds that make up names? Look at the list of eight invented names on the next page. These were created by throwing selected sounds together. Which names are tough and angry? Which are soft and gentle? About half of the sounds used fall into each category. To get a good start on your prediction, try saying each name out loud and see how you feel about it. Try to say it while smiling lovingly (to check if it is soft and gentle) or while frowning (to see if it is tough and angry). Try to decide if the name enhances or interferes with each of these facial expressions. Also think about how hard or soft your mouth feels when you say the name. Then make your guess, and circle one feeling in the table below. The answers are provided further on.

NAME	CIRCLE THE APPROPRIATE FEELING	
Gahm	Tough/Angry	Soft/Gentle
Theel	Touch/Angry	Soft/Gentle
Duhr	Tough/Angry	Soft/Gentle
Gahr	Tough/Angry	Soft/Gentle
Lahm	Tough/Angry	Soft/Gentle
Meeth	Tough/Angry	Soft/Gentle
Luth	Tough/Angry	Soft/Gentle
Reeg	Tough/Angry	Soft/Gentle
Ludh	Tough/Angry	Soft/Gentle
Duhg	Tough/Angry	Soft/Gentle

Here are the answers:

Theel, Lahm, Meeth, and *Luth* are soft and gentle names. They feel soft to say and can be said with a gentle smiling face.

Gahr, Reeg, Duhr, and *Dugh* are tough and angry names. They feel hard when spoken and are a good match for a grimmer facial expression.

Gahm and *Luhd* are "mixed" names – people will most likely disagree on how to classify these names because they contain mixed emotions. They contain some soft sounds and some harsh sounds.

The Importance of the Sound-Emotion Relationship

Sounds and emotions are related to one another, and this relationship is not limited to names. The sounds in any word produce emotions. Try saying "marshmallow" – how does this word feel in your mouth and throat? Soft and mushy? Now try saying "brick." How does that feel? Hard and tough? No wonder we don't build houses with marshmallows!

Although we are especially interested in names, the relationship between sounds and emotions applies to all words, not only to names. There are sound-emotions in "marshmallow" and in "Lianna" as well as in "brick" and in "Derek." (You would be correct in guessing that the first two words have soft emotions and the second two, tough ones.)

If we wished to be clear and logical about the argument relating sounds and emotions, we could present it in the following point-by-point form:

- Names are made up of sounds.

- When we say sounds out loud, we use our faces and throats.

- We also use our faces and throats to express our emotions.

- Saying some sounds out loud emphasizes some facial expressions of emotions. For example, saying "cheese" emphasizes a smile.

- Saying some sounds out loud interferes with some facial expressions of emotion. For example, saying "cheese" gets in the way of a frown or sad face.

- Because of the key role of the face and throat in both emotion and sound, and because of the evidence above, **we conclude that sounds have emotional meaning – that they are related to emotions and that they express and reveal emotions.**

Scoring the Eight Emotions in Names with the Help of a Computer Program

Following the logic presented in the last paragraph, I created a computer program which would score names in terms of the emotions which underlie their sounds. This program and the research which accompanied it are discussed in my other published work. The program scores names for eight emotions – Cheerfulness, Activity, Toughness, Unpleasantness, Sadness, Passivity, Gentleness, and Pleasantness.

When this program was applied to the name "Gurd", it produced the following scores:

Cheerfulness	1
Activity	3
Toughness	4
Unpleasantness	2
Sadness	1
Passivity	1
Gentleness	0
Pleasantness	0

Clearly Gurd is not a nice troll to know: he is maximally Tough and minimally Gentle and Pleasant. He is also quite Active, which would make him dangerous. The sounds in his names express these emotions.

According to the computer program, the emotions in the name Leemal look like this:

Cheerfulness	1
Activity	0
Toughness	0
Unpleasantness	0
Sadness	2
Passivity	3
Gentleness	4
Pleasantness	3

Leemal is almost the direct opposite of Gurd: her name includes sounds that suggest Gentle, Passive, and Pleasant emotions rather than their opposites. In fact, her name includes no Active, Tough, or Unpleasant sounds.

Given the emotions conveyed by the sounds in Gurd and Leemal, we should not be surprised when people nominate the first name for a troll (who is expected to be tough, unpleasant, etc.) and the second for a fairy (who is expected to be gentle, pleasant, and so on).

Some Fun Facts

I have been conducting research on names, emotions, masculinity, femininity, and pronunciation for several years. Here are some of the findings that show how the sounds in names and the emotions related to them provide us with meaningful information.

You already know that men's and boys' names contain more masculine sounds. They also tend to be shorter than women's and girls' names. Men's names include fewer vowels and more consonants (proportionally), and they seldom end in **a, ee, ie, or y,** which are common endings for girls' and women's names.

Differences between popular boys' and girls' names are not getting smaller – in fact they are getting larger year by year. This finding is based on a study of popular baby names for about the last 100 years. A currently popular boys' name, Jacob, has distinctly tough masculine sounds in it while a currently popular girls' name, Emma, presents a picture of gentleness.

Names given to newborn boys and girls respond to and reflect social, economic, and political influences. During wars, boys are given more Active names. During depressions, girls are given Tougher names. When the Consumer Price Index is high, parents give newborns of both sexes more emotionally positive names. Republicans tend to give boys very masculine names and girls very feminine ones. People from the state of California tend to give more gender-neutral names to their newborns. Parents from New England give their baby girls Tougher names than parents in other States.

Boys' names are easier to pronounce than girls' names, in part because they are shorter. For example, Ted is easier to pronounce than Jocelyn. Nicknames are easier to pronounce than full names, again partly because they are shorter, but also because they tend to drop harder sounds. Gabby is a shorter and easier to pronounce than Gabrielle, and Al is much easier to pronounce than Alexander.

Names given to heroes and heroines in fiction exaggerate the differences we have been describing in this book…hero's names are Tougher and heroine's Gentler and more Pleasant than real people's. (Leemal and Gurd's names mirror this kind of trend.)

Even names given to inanimate objects (fighter jets, for example) have emotional meanings. NATO fighter jets from many countries have names that are Cheerful but also very Active; examples are Tomcat, Vulcan, and Raven.

Since people love their pets, it should be no surprise that pets' names have emotions tied to them. In terms of their emotions and pronounceability, cats' names are more like girls' and women's names (for example, Miss Christine) while dogs' names are most like men's and boys' (for example, Max). Pets' names tend to be longer than people's names, but they are easier to pronounce (more like nicknames).

Name emotions also tell us something about the age of various names. In a small study that I performed with invented names, "old" names such as Malloth and Ethion contained more Passive and Sad sounds than "young" ones such as Jovak and Chapt.

A Guide to Sounds

Although the <u>Table of Names and Emotions</u> provides profiles for many, many names, it can not include all of them. One reason for this is that people are continually inventing new names or adapting old ones to new forms. If you want to know about the emotions or feelings in a name which does not appear in the book, you can use the <u>Guide</u> provided here. The <u>Guide</u> gives you a list of some of the key sounds which contribute to the emotions in names. The list is only a partial one (there are more than three dozen different sounds in English), but it does include most commonly used sounds such as **t**, **l**, **r**, **n**, and a variety of **e** sounds. The **s** sound does not appear in the <u>Guide</u> because it has no clear association to feelings.

You will notice that the <u>Guide</u> provides you with pronunciation examples. This is because a letter can be associated with many different sounds. For example in the <u>Guide</u> you will find a short **e** sound, a long **e** sound, and a gentle **e** sound. Some sounds are associated strongly with more than one feeling or emotion. For example, the **v** sound is tied to feelings of both Gentleness and Cheerfulness.

The way you use the <u>Guide</u> is simple and straightforward: the more sounds you use from a particular feeling, the more the name you are considering will reflect that feeling. Take a look at the <u>Guide</u> and then at the two examples which follow it.

Guide to Sounds

GENTLE SOUNDS

Consonants

l…as in laugh

light th…as in thumb

m…as in mat

v…as in vet

z…as in zoo

Vowels

aw…as in lawn

soft e…as in bet

long e…as in beet

CHEERFUL SOUNDS

Consonants

f…as in fork

j…as in jar

v…as in vet

ch…as in charm

Vowels

long e…as in beet

short e…as in bit

oi…as in boil

i…as in bide

a…as in father

Guide to Sounds

SAD SOUNDS	TOUGH SOUNDS
Consonants	Consonants
l…as in laugh	g…as in guy
heavy th…as in that	r…as in run
n…as in now	t…as in told
d…as in dog	p…as in put
b…as in blue	sh…as in shoot
Vowels	Vowels
long o…as in lone	short e…as in bit
ow…as in how	oi…as in boil
	oo…as in fool

Here is an example using the name Melthos, which was suggested earlier as the name of an older, wiser, patient scholar. Further below you will find an example using the name Portag, which was suggested for his younger, more impatient student. Each sound in the names was checked against the <u>Guide</u>: the associated emotions from the <u>Guide</u> are reported in parentheses.

MELTHOS includes:

- an **m** sound (m shows up in the Gentle box of the <u>Guide</u>),

- a soft **e** sound (Gentle),

- an **l** sound (Gentle and Sad),

- a light **th** sound (Gentle),

- an **o** sound (not exactly included in the <u>Guide</u>, but close to o in lone, Sad),

- and an **s** sound (no clear emotional connections).

- The sounds in the name Melthos are primarily Gentle, and also a little Sad.

PORTAG includes:

- a **p** sound (Tough),

- an **o** sound (like the one in lone, Sad),

- an **r** sound (Tough),

- a **t** sound (Tough),

- an **a** sound (like the one in father, Cheerful),

- and a **g** sound (Tough).

The sounds in the name Portag are mainly Tough. The one Sad and one Cheerful sound cancel each other out.

Profiling the Emotions in a Name

(What you Need to Know in Order to Read the <u>Table of Names and Emotions</u>)

Profiles provide a quick and easy way to interpret the emotions in names. They are based on the type of counts shown above for the names Gurd and Leemal, and they also take normal names into account because each name has been compared to an average of millions of names. The <u>Table</u> that forms the bulk of this book is made up entirely of profiles. This is what a profile looks like:

EMMA

Cheerfulness	×××
Activity	×
Toughness	×
Unpleasantness	×
Sadness	×
Passivity	×××××
Gentleness	×××××××××
Pleasantness	×

Masculine sounds/emotions are low.
Feminine sounds/emotions are medium.
Pronunciation is easier.

In interpreting profiles, you should be aware that:

- Profiles are pictures of the emotions in a name.

- Profiles use lines of exes instead of scores or numbers.

- Long lines for an emotion tell us that the name being profiled has a lot of that particular emotion in its sounds. *In the example above, Emma has many Passive sounds and even more Gentle sounds.*

- Short lines for an emotion let us know that the name being profiled has little of that particular emotion in its sounds. *In the example above, Emma has very few Active, Tough, Unpleasant, Pleasant or Sad sounds, and few Cheerful sounds.*

- The emotions conveyed by a name are revealed by its longest lines. *Emma is a Gentle and Passive name.*

- The lines of exes include a built-in comparison of each name to millions of others. If a name has a long line for a feeling, you know that it is higher than most North American names for that feeling. If it has a short line, then it is lower than most names.

- Sounds are classified according to masculine and feminine emotions. The first four lines in the profile represent masculine emotions (Cheerfulness, Activity, Toughness, and Unpleasantness); the last four represent feminine emotions (Sadness, Passivity, Gentleness, and Pleasantness). We also know that masculine-sounding names are shorter than feminine ones.

- Right below the emotion lines, you will see two lines of text which tell you how masculine or feminine the sounds and emotions in a name are. The values in these two lines range from Very Low to Very High. Please note that almost all names contain a mix of both masculine and feminine emotions. *Emma is low in terms of masculine sounds and medium in terms of feminine ones.*

- Some sounds (for example, **e** and **m**) are easy for children to pronounce. Others (for example **r** and **j**) are more difficult. Long names are more difficult to pronounce than short ones. The last line in the profile tells you how easily a name can be pronounced by young children. The values in this line range from Most Difficult to Easiest. *Emma is an easy name to pronounce.*

This is the information you need to help you interpret the profiles in the <u>Table of Names and Emotions.</u> You can use the table to look up names and to see which emotions are emphasized by each name. You can also discover if a name is loaded with masculine or feminine emotions (or both, or neither) in its sounds. You can find out how easily children can learn to pronounce the name.

Things to Watch Out For

The <u>Table of Names and Emotions</u> is based on research, but it does not claim to be perfect. Don't let this book bully you!! If you like a name, use it. Trust your own intuition and don't feel obliged to follow the book.

In particular do not let the masculinity and femininity scores suggest to you that a person is more or less masculine or feminine than he or she should be. THESE SCORES ARE NOT A PERSONALITY TEST. Remember that they represent how your parents felt when they named you, but they also represent fads and fashions. A currently fashionable boys' name (Ethan) is actually very feminine in its sounds. However, the real Ethans out there will have a wide variety of different masculine personalities. Please take a look at the <u>Table of Names and Emotions</u>, where you will see that most names have both masculine and feminine sounds in them. There is a great deal of overlap.

Because the names in this book are North American names, you will be able to find several names of Hispanic and French origin in the <u>Table of Names and Emotions</u>.

Often the <u>Table</u> includes both a name (such as Rebecca or Alexander) and also the nickname associated with it (Becky or Alex), so you will be able to find some individual profiles for nicknames or shortened name forms.

The <u>Table</u> includes profiles for slightly different spellings of the same name: for example, Linda and Lynda are both profiled. If you can't find the exact spelling of a name that want to know about, find a similar name or one that is pronounced in a similar way. This will give you some idea about your name. For example, Nicky, Nikki, Niki, and Neeki all have the same sounds in them, and would all have similar profiles. The same is true for Jully and Julie, and for Carrie and Kari.

The names in the <u>Table</u> come from various sources, including popular baby name web sites, a list of US Census names made available by David Word, and Michael Shackleford's lists based on Social Security applications. The program which I wrote to score names made use of some information from another program made available to the general public by John Wasser.

I hope you enjoy looking at the information in this book. If you are choosing a name for a baby or a character in a story, you might want to browse the names here and sharpen your ideas. The pronounceability information will help you understand that young children might find some names easier to say than others. The information about emotions will probably tell you some things about names that you already know, or at least suspect, but it might also surprise you.

Boys' and men's names are presented first, in alphabetical order, and girls' and women's names next.

BIBLIOGRAPHY

If you would like to do some more in-depth reading, here are some possible sources for you. I first list other researchers (in alphabetical order), and then give you a few examples of my own work.

OTHER RESEARCHERS

Cassidy, K. W., Kelly, M. H., & Sharon, L. J. (1999) Inferring gender from name phonology. Journal of Experimental Psychology: General, Volume 128, pages 362-381.

Fonagy, I. (1983-1991) La Vive Voix : Essais de Psycho-phonétique. Paris : Éditions Payot.

Jakobson, R., & Waugh, L. (1979) The Sound Shape of Language. Brighton, UK: Harvester Press.

Lieberson, S. & Bell, O. E. (1992) Children's first names: An empirical study of social taste. American Journal of Sociology, Volume 98, pages 511-554.

Tsur, R. (1992) What Makes Sound Patterns Expressive? The Poetic Mode of Speech Perception. Durham, NC: Dike University Press.

MY OWN WORK

Whissel, C. (1999) Phonosymbolism and the emotional nature of sounds. <u>Perceptual and Motor Skills</u>, Volume 89, pages 19-48.

Whissell, C. (2000) Phonoemotional profiling: A description of the emotional flavor of English texts on the basis of the phonemes employed in them. <u>Perceptual and Motor Skills</u>, Volume 91, pages 617-648.

Whissell, C. (2001) Sound and emotion in given names. <u>Names</u>, Volume 49, pages 97-120.

Whissell, C. (2001) Cues to referent gender in randomly constructed names. <u>Perceptual and Motor Skills</u>, Volume 93, pages 856-858.

Whissell, C. (2003) Pronounceability: A measure of language samples based on children's mastery of the phonemes employed in them. <u>Perceptual and Motor Skills</u>, Volume 96, pages 748-754.

Whissell, C. (2006) Emotion in the sounds of pets' names. <u>Perceptual and Motor Skills</u>, Volume 102, pages 121-124.

Whissell, C. (2006) Historical and socioeconomic predictors of the emotional associations of sounds in popular names. <u>Perceptual and Motor Skills</u>, Volume 103, pages 451-456.

Whissell, C. (2006) Geographical and political predictors of emotion in the sounds of favorite baby names. <u>Perceptual and Motor Skills</u>, Volume 102, pages 105-108.

MEN'S AND BOYS' NAMES

Men's And Boys' Names

AARON

Cheerfulness	xxx
Activity	xxx
Toughness	xxxx
Unpleasantness	xxxxx
Sadness	xxxxx
Passivity	xxxxxxx
Gentleness	xxxx
Pleasantness	x

Masculine sounds/feelings are low.
Feminine sounds/feelings are medium low.
Pronunciation is more difficult.

ADAM

Cheerfulness	x
Activity	x
Toughness	xxxx
Unpleasantness	xxxxx
Sadness	xxxxx
Passivity	xxxxxxxxx
Gentleness	xxxx
Pleasantness	x

Masculine sounds/feelings are medium low.
Feminine sounds/feelings are medium.
Pronunciation is easiest.

ADRIAN

Cheerfulness	xxx
Activity	xxxxxx
Toughness	xxxxxxxxxx
Unpleasantness	xxxxxxxx
Sadness	xxxxxxxxx
Passivity	xxxxxxxxx
Gentleness	x
Pleasantness	x

Masculine sounds/feelings are high.
Feminine sounds/feelings are medium.
Pronunciation is average.

ALAN

Cheerfulness	x
Activity	x
Toughness	x
Unpleasantness	x
Sadness	xxxxxxxx
Passivity	xxxxxxx
Gentleness	xxxx
Pleasantness	xxxxxx

Masculine sounds/feelings are very low.
Feminine sounds/feelings are medium high.
Pronunciation is easier.

ALBERT

Cheerfulness	xxx
Activity	xxxxxx
Toughness	xxxxxxx
Unpleasantness	xxxxxxxxx
Sadness	xxxxxxxxx
Passivity	xxxxx
Gentleness	xxxxxxx
Pleasantness	xxxxxx

Masculine sounds/feelings are medium high.
Feminine sounds/feelings are medium high.
Pronunciation is average.

ALBERTO

Cheerfulness	xxx
Activity	xxxxxxxxx
Toughness	xxxxxxxxxx
Unpleasantness	xxxxxxxxx
Sadness	xxxxxxxxx
Passivity	xxxxx
Gentleness	xxxxxxx
Pleasantness	xxxxxx

Masculine sounds/feelings are very high.
Feminine sounds/feelings are medium high.
Pronunciation is more difficult.

ALEJANDRO

Cheerfulness	xxxxxx
Activity	xxxxxx
Toughness	xxxxxxx
Unpleasantness	xxxxxxxxxxxx
Sadness	xxxxxxxxxxxxxxxxx
Passivity	xxxxxxxxxxxxx
Gentleness	xxxxxxx
Pleasantness	xxxxxx

Masculine sounds/feelings are very high.
Feminine sounds/feelings are very high.
Pronunciation is most difficult.

ALEX

Cheerfulness	xxx
Activity	x
Toughness	xxxx
Unpleasantness	xxxxx
Sadness	xxxxx
Passivity	xxxxxxx
Gentleness	xxxxxxx
Pleasantness	xxxxxx

Masculine sounds/feelings are low.
Feminine sounds/feelings are medium.
Pronunciation is more difficult.

ALEXANDER

Cheerfulness	xxxxxx
Activity	xxx
Toughness	xxxxxxxxxx
Unpleasantness	xxxxxxxxx
Sadness	xxxxxxxxxxxx
Passivity	xxxxxxxxxxxxxx
Gentleness	xxxxxxx
Pleasantness	xxxxxx

Masculine sounds/feelings are high.
Feminine sounds/feelings are very high.
Pronunciation is most difficult.

ALFRED

Cheerfulness	xxx
Activity	xxxxx
Toughness	xxxxxxx
Unpleasantness	xxxxxxxxx
Sadness	xxxxxxxxx
Passivity	xxxxxxx
Gentleness	xxxxxxx
Pleasantness	xxxxx

Masculine sounds/feelings are medium high.
Feminine sounds/feelings are high.
Pronunciation is more difficult.

ALFREDO

Cheerfulness	xxxxxx
Activity	xxxxxx
Toughness	xxxxxxx
Unpleasantness	xxxxxxxxxxxx
Sadness	xxxxxxxxxxxx
Passivity	xxxxxxxxxxx
Gentleness	xxxxxxxxxxx
Pleasantness	xxxxx

Masculine sounds/feelings are very high.
Feminine sounds/feelings are very high.
Pronunciation is most difficult.

ALLAN

Cheerfulness	x
Activity	x
Toughness	x
Unpleasantness	x
Sadness	xxxxxxxxx
Passivity	xxxxxxxxx
Gentleness	xxxxxxx
Pleasantness	xxxxxx

Masculine sounds/feelings are very low.
Feminine sounds/feelings are very high.
Pronunciation is easiest.

Men's And Boys' Names

ALLEN

Cheerfulness	xxx
Activity	x
Toughness	x
Unpleasantness	x
Sadness	xxxxxxxx
Passivity	xxxxxxxx
Gentleness	xxxxxxxxxx
Pleasantness	xxxxxx

Masculine sounds/feelings are low.
Feminine sounds/feelings are very high.
Pronunciation is easier.

ANDREW

Cheerfulness	xxx
Activity	xxx
Toughness	xxxxxx
Unpleasantness	xxxxxxxxx
Sadness	xxxxxxxxx
Passivity	xxxxxxx
Gentleness	x
Pleasantness	xxxxx

Masculine sounds/feelings are medium.
Feminine sounds/feelings are medium.
Pronunciation is average.

ALVIN

Cheerfulness	xxxxxx
Activity	xxx
Toughness	xxxx
Unpleasantness	x
Sadness	xxxxxxxx
Passivity	xxxxxx
Gentleness	xxxxxxxxxx
Pleasantness	xxxxxxxxxxx

Masculine sounds/feelings are low.
Feminine sounds/feelings are very high.
Pronunciation is average.

ANDY

Cheerfulness	xxx
Activity	x
Toughness	xxxx
Unpleasantness	xxxxx
Sadness	xxxxxxxxx
Passivity	xxxxxxx
Gentleness	xxxx
Pleasantness	xxxxxx

Masculine sounds/feelings are medium.
Feminine sounds/feelings are medium high.
Pronunciation is easiest.

ANDRE

Cheerfulness	x
Activity	xxx
Toughness	xxxxxx
Unpleasantness	xxxxxxxxx
Sadness	xxxxxxxxx
Passivity	xxxxxx
Gentleness	x
Pleasantness	x

Masculine sounds/feelings are medium high.
Feminine sounds/feelings are medium low.
Pronunciation is easier.

ANGEL

Cheerfulness	xxxxxx
Activity	xxx
Toughness	x
Unpleasantness	x
Sadness	xxxxxxxxx
Passivity	xxxxxxx
Gentleness	xxxxxxx
Pleasantness	xxxxxx

Masculine sounds/feelings are very low.
Feminine sounds/feelings are high.
Pronunciation is more difficult.

ANTHONY

Cheerfulness	xxxxxxxx
Activity	xxx
Toughness	x
Unpleasantness	x
Sadness	xxxxxxxx
Passivity	xxxxxx
Gentleness	xxxxxx
Pleasantness	xxxxxxxxxxx

Masculine sounds/feelings are low.
Feminine sounds/feelings are very high.
Pronunciation is easier.

ANTONIO

Cheerfulness	xxx
Activity	xxxxxx
Toughness	xxxxxxx
Unpleasantness	xxxxxxxxxxxx
Sadness	xxxxxxxxxxxxxxxxx
Passivity	xxxxxxxxxx
Gentleness	x
Pleasantness	x

Masculine sounds/feelings are high.
Feminine sounds/feelings are high.
Pronunciation is average.

ARMANDO

Cheerfulness	xxx
Activity	xxxxxx
Toughness	xxxxxxx
Unpleasantness	xxxxxxxxxxxx
Sadness	xxxxxxxxxxxx
Passivity	xxxxxxxxxx
Gentleness	xxxx
Pleasantness	x

Masculine sounds/feelings are high.
Feminine sounds/feelings are high.
Pronunciation is more difficult.

ARNOLD

Cheerfulness	xxx
Activity	xxxxx
Toughness	xxxxxx
Unpleasantness	xxxxxxxxxxxx
Sadness	xxxxxxxxxxxxxxxxx
Passivity	xxxxxxxxx
Gentleness	xxxx
Pleasantness	xxxxx

Masculine sounds/feelings are high.
Feminine sounds/feelings are very high.
Pronunciation is more difficult.

ARTHUR

Cheerfulness	xxxxxxxxx
Activity	xxxxxxxxx
Toughness	xxxxxxx
Unpleasantness	xxxxx
Sadness	x
Passivity	x
Gentleness	xxxx
Pleasantness	xxxxxx

Masculine sounds/feelings are very high.
Feminine sounds/feelings are very low.
Pronunciation is average.

ARTURO

Cheerfulness	xxxxxxxxx
Activity	xxxxxxxxxxx
Toughness	xxxxxxx
Unpleasantness	xxxxxxxxx
Sadness	xxxxx
Passivity	xxx
Gentleness	x
Pleasantness	x

Masculine sounds/feelings are very high.
Feminine sounds/feelings are very low.
Pronunciation is more difficult.

Men's And Boys' Names

AUSTIN

Cheerfulness	xxx
Activity	xxxxxx
Toughness	xxxxxxx
Unpleasantness	xxxxx
Sadness	xxxxx
Passivity	xxxxx
Gentleness	xxxx
Pleasantness	x

Masculine sounds/feelings are medium.
Feminine sounds/feelings are low.
Pronunciation is easier.

BARRY

Cheerfulness	xxx
Activity	xxx
Toughness	xxxx
Unpleasantness	xxxxxxxxx
Sadness	xxxxx
Passivity	xxx
Gentleness	xxxx
Pleasantness	xxxxxx

Masculine sounds/feelings are medium high.
Feminine sounds/feelings are medium low.
Pronunciation is easiest.

BEN

Cheerfulness	xxx
Activity	x
Toughness	x
Unpleasantness	xxxxx
Sadness	xxxxxxxxx
Passivity	xxxxx
Gentleness	xxxx
Pleasantness	x

Masculine sounds/feelings are medium low.
Feminine sounds/feelings are medium.
Pronunciation is easiest.

BENJAMIN

Cheerfulness	xxxxxxxxx
Activity	xxxxxx
Toughness	xxxx
Unpleasantness	xxxxx
Sadness	xxxxxxxxxxxx
Passivity	xxxxxxxxxx
Gentleness	xxxxxx
Pleasantness	x

Masculine sounds/feelings are medium.
Feminine sounds/feelings are very high.
Pronunciation is more difficult.

BERNARD

Cheerfulness	xxxxxx
Activity	xxxxxxxxx
Toughness	xxxxxxxxxx
Unpleasantness	xxxxxxxxxxxxx
Sadness	xxxxxxxxxxxx
Passivity	xxxxx
Gentleness	x
Pleasantness	x

Masculine sounds/feelings are very high.
Feminine sounds/feelings are medium.
Pronunciation is more difficult.

BILL

Cheerfulness	xxx
Activity	xxx
Toughness	xxxx
Unpleasantness	xxxxx
Sadness	xxxxxxxxx
Passivity	xxx
Gentleness	xxxx
Pleasantness	xxxxxx

Masculine sounds/feelings are medium.
Feminine sounds/feelings are medium.
Pronunciation is easiest.

BILLY

Cheerfulness	xxxxxx
Activity	xxx
Toughness	xxxx
Unpleasantness	xxxxx
Sadness	xxxxxxxxx
Passivity	xxx
Gentleness	xxxxxxx
Pleasantness	xxxxxxxxxxx

Masculine sounds/feelings are medium high.
Feminine sounds/feelings are high.
Pronunciation is easiest.

BOB

Cheerfulness	xxx
Activity	xxx
Toughness	x
Unpleasantness	xxxxxxxxx
Sadness	xxxxxxxxx
Passivity	x
Gentleness	x
Pleasantness	x

Masculine sounds/feelings are medium.
Feminine sounds/feelings are very low.
Pronunciation is easiest.

BOBBY

Cheerfulness	xxxxxx
Activity	xxx
Toughness	x
Unpleasantness	xxxxxxxxxxxx
Sadness	xxxxxxxxxxxx
Passivity	x
Gentleness	xxxx
Pleasantness	xxxxxx

Masculine sounds/feelings are medium.
Feminine sounds/feelings are medium.
Pronunciation is easiest.

BRAD

Cheerfulness	x
Activity	xxx
Toughness	xxxxxxx
Unpleasantness	xxxxxxxxxxxx
Sadness	xxxxxxxxx
Passivity	xxxxx
Gentleness	x
Pleasantness	x

Masculine sounds/feelings are very high.
Feminine sounds/feelings are low.
Pronunciation is easier.

BRADLEY

Cheerfulness	xxx
Activity	xxx
Toughness	xxxxxxx
Unpleasantness	xxxxxxxxxxxx
Sadness	xxxxxxxxxxxx
Passivity	xxxxxxx
Gentleness	xxxxxxx
Pleasantness	xxxxxxxxxxxx

Masculine sounds/feelings are medium high.
Feminine sounds/feelings are very high.
Pronunciation is most difficult.

BRANDON

Cheerfulness	x
Activity	xxx
Toughness	xxxxxxx
Unpleasantness	xxxxxxxxxxxx
Sadness	xxxxxxxxxxxxxxxxx
Passivity	xxxxxxxxx
Gentleness	x
Pleasantness	x

Masculine sounds/feelings are medium.
Feminine sounds/feelings are medium high.
Pronunciation is more difficult.

BRENT

Cheerfulness	xxx
Activity	xxxxxx
Toughness	xxxxxxx
Unpleasantness	xxxxxxxxxxxx
Sadness	xxxxxxxxx
Passivity	xxxxx
Gentleness	xxxx
Pleasantness	x

Masculine sounds/feelings are high.
Feminine sounds/feelings are medium.
Pronunciation is easier.

BRETT

Cheerfulness	xxx
Activity	xxxxxxxxx
Toughness	xxxxxxxxxx
Unpleasantness	xxxxxxxxxxxxxxxxx
Sadness	xxxxx
Passivity	xxx
Gentleness	xxxx
Pleasantness	x

Masculine sounds/feelings are very high.
Feminine sounds/feelings are very low.
Pronunciation is average.

BRIAN

Cheerfulness	xxx
Activity	xxxxxx
Toughness	xxxxxxx
Unpleasantness	xxxxxxxxx
Sadness	xxxxxxxxx
Passivity	xxxxx
Gentleness	x
Pleasantness	x

Masculine sounds/feelings are medium high.
Feminine sounds/feelings are low.
Pronunciation is easier.

BRUCE

Cheerfulness	x
Activity	xxxxxx
Toughness	xxxxxxx
Unpleasantness	xxxxxxxxx
Sadness	xxxxx
Passivity	x
Gentleness	x
Pleasantness	x

Masculine sounds/feelings are high.
Feminine sounds/feelings are very low.
Pronunciation is easier.

BRYAN

Cheerfulness	xxx
Activity	xxx
Toughness	xxxx
Unpleasantness	xxxxxxxxx
Sadness	xxxxxxxxx
Passivity	xxxxx
Gentleness	xxxx
Pleasantness	xxxxxx

Masculine sounds/feelings are medium.
Feminine sounds/feelings are medium.
Pronunciation is easier.

BYRON

Cheerfulness	xxx
Activity	xxx
Toughness	xxxx
Unpleasantness	xxxxxxxxx
Sadness	xxxxxxxxx
Passivity	xxxxx
Gentleness	xxxx
Pleasantness	xxxxxx

Masculine sounds/feelings are medium.
Feminine sounds/feelings are medium.
Pronunciation is easier.

CALVIN

Cheerfulness	xxxxxx
Activity	xxx
Toughness	xxxxxxx
Unpleasantness	xxxxx
Sadness	xxxxxxxx
Passivity	xxxxxxxx
Gentleness	xxxxxxxxxx
Pleasantness	xxxxxxxxxxx

Masculine sounds/feelings are medium.
Feminine sounds/feelings are very high.
Pronunciation is more difficult.

CARL

Cheerfulness	xxx
Activity	xxxxxx
Toughness	xxxxxxx
Unpleasantness	xxxxxxxxx
Sadness	xxxxx
Passivity	xxxxx
Gentleness	xxxx
Pleasantness	xxxxxx

Masculine sounds/feelings are very high.
Feminine sounds/feelings are medium.
Pronunciation is easier.

CARLOS

Cheerfulness	xxxxx
Activity	xxxxxxxxx
Toughness	xxxxxxx
Unpleasantness	xxxxxxxxx
Sadness	xxxxx
Passivity	xxxxx
Gentleness	xxxx
Pleasantness	xxxxxx

Masculine sounds/feelings are very high.
Feminine sounds/feelings are medium.
Pronunciation is more difficult.

CASEY

Cheerfulness	xxx
Activity	x
Toughness	xxxx
Unpleasantness	xxxxx
Sadness	x
Passivity	xxx
Gentleness	xxxx
Pleasantness	xxxxx

Masculine sounds/feelings are medium.
Feminine sounds/feelings are low.
Pronunciation is easiest.

CECIL

Cheerfulness	xxxxxx
Activity	xxx
Toughness	xxxx
Unpleasantness	x
Sadness	xxxxx
Passivity	xxxxx
Gentleness	xxxxxxx
Pleasantness	xxxxx

Masculine sounds/feelings are low.
Feminine sounds/feelings are medium.
Pronunciation is average.

CHAD

Cheerfulness	xxx
Activity	xxx
Toughness	xxxx
Unpleasantness	xxxxx
Sadness	xxxxx
Passivity	xxxxx
Gentleness	x
Pleasantness	x

Masculine sounds/feelings are medium.
Feminine sounds/feelings are very low.
Pronunciation is easiest.

Men's And Boys' Names

CHARLES

Cheerfulness	xxxxx
Activity	xxxxxxxx
Toughness	xxxx
Unpleasantness	xxxxx
Sadness	xxxxx
Passivity	xxxxx
Gentleness	xxxxxxx
Pleasantness	xxxxxxxxxxx

Masculine sounds/feelings are medium.
Feminine sounds/feelings are high.
Pronunciation is most difficult.

CHARLIE

Cheerfulness	xxxxxxxxx
Activity	xxxxxxxxx
Toughness	xxxx
Unpleasantness	xxxxx
Sadness	xxxxx
Passivity	xxx
Gentleness	xxxxxxx
Pleasantness	xxxxxxxxxxx

Masculine sounds/feelings are medium high.
Feminine sounds/feelings are medium high.
Pronunciation is average.

CHESTER

Cheerfulness	xxxxxxxxx
Activity	xxxxxxxxx
Toughness	xxxxxxx
Unpleasantness	xxxxx
Sadness	x
Passivity	xxx
Gentleness	xxxx
Pleasantness	x

Masculine sounds/feelings are high.
Feminine sounds/feelings are very low.
Pronunciation is more difficult.

CHRIS

Cheerfulness	xxx
Activity	xxxxx
Toughness	xxxxxxxxx
Unpleasantness	xxxxxxxx
Sadness	x
Passivity	xxxxx
Gentleness	xxxx
Pleasantness	xxxxx

Masculine sounds/feelings are very high.
Feminine sounds/feelings are low.
Pronunciation is easier.

CHRISTIAN

Cheerfulness	xxxxx
Activity	xxxxxxxxx
Toughness	xxxxxxxxx
Unpleasantness	xxxxxxxx
Sadness	xxxxx
Passivity	xxxxxxx
Gentleness	x
Pleasantness	x

Masculine sounds/feelings are very high.
Feminine sounds/feelings are very low.
Pronunciation is more difficult.

CHRISTOPHER

Cheerfulness	xxxxxxxxxxx
Activity	xxxxxxxxxxxxxxxxx
Toughness	xxxxxxxxxxxxxxx
Unpleasantness	xxxxxxxxxxxx
Sadness	x
Passivity	xxx
Gentleness	x
Pleasantness	x

Masculine sounds/feelings are very high.
Feminine sounds/feelings are very low.
Pronunciation is most difficult.

CLARENCE

Cheerfulness	xxxxxx
Activity	xxx
Toughness	xxxxxxx
Unpleasantness	xxxxxxxxx
Sadness	xxxxxxxxx
Passivity	xxxxxxxxxxx
Gentleness	xxxxxxxxxx
Pleasantness	xxxxxx

Masculine sounds/feelings are medium high.
Feminine sounds/feelings are very high.
Pronunciation is most difficult.

CLAUDE

Cheerfulness	x
Activity	x
Toughness	xxxxxx
Unpleasantness	xxxxxxxxx
Sadness	xxxxxxxxx
Passivity	xxxxxxxxx
Gentleness	xxxxxx
Pleasantness	xxxxxx

Masculine sounds/feelings are medium.
Feminine sounds/feelings are very high.
Pronunciation is easier.

CLAYTON

Cheerfulness	x
Activity	xxx
Toughness	xxxxxx
Unpleasantness	xxxxxxxxx
Sadness	xxxxxxxxx
Passivity	xxxxxxx
Gentleness	xxxx
Pleasantness	xxxxxx

Masculine sounds/feelings are medium.
Feminine sounds/feelings are medium high.
Pronunciation is more difficult.

CLIFFORD

Cheerfulness	xxxxxxxxx
Activity	xxxxxxxxxxx
Toughness	xxxxxxxxxxx
Unpleasantness	xxxxxxxxxxxx
Sadness	xxxxxxxxx
Passivity	xxxxxxxxx
Gentleness	xxxxxxx
Pleasantness	xxxxxx

Masculine sounds/feelings are very high.
Feminine sounds/feelings are very high.
Pronunciation is most difficult.

CLIFTON

Cheerfulness	xxxxxx
Activity	xxxxxxxxx
Toughness	xxxxxxxxxx
Unpleasantness	xxxxxxxxx
Sadness	xxxxxxxxx
Passivity	xxxxxxx
Gentleness	xxxx
Pleasantness	xxxxxx

Masculine sounds/feelings are very high.
Feminine sounds/feelings are medium high.
Pronunciation is most difficult.

CLINTON

Cheerfulness	xxx
Activity	xxxxxx
Toughness	xxxxxxxxxx
Unpleasantness	xxxxxxxxx
Sadness	xxxxxxxxxxxx
Passivity	xxxxxxxxx
Gentleness	xxxx
Pleasantness	xxxxxx

Masculine sounds/feelings are high.
Feminine sounds/feelings are very high.
Pronunciation is more difficult.

CLYDE

Cheerfulness	xxxxxx
Activity	x
Toughness	xxxxxxx
Unpleasantness	xxxxxxxxx
Sadness	xxxxxxxxx
Passivity	xxxxxxx
Gentleness	xxxxxxxxxxx
Pleasantness	xxxxxxxxxxxxxxxxx

Masculine sounds/feelings are medium.
Feminine sounds/feelings are very high.
Pronunciation is easier.

CODY

Cheerfulness	xxxxx
Activity	xxx
Toughness	xxxxxxx
Unpleasantness	xxxxxxxxx
Sadness	xxxxx
Passivity	xxxxx
Gentleness	xxxx
Pleasantness	xxxxxx

Masculine sounds/feelings are very high.
Feminine sounds/feelings are medium.
Pronunciation is easiest.

COREY

Cheerfulness	xxx
Activity	xxx
Toughness	xxxxxxx
Unpleasantness	xxxxxxxxx
Sadness	x
Passivity	xxxxx
Gentleness	xxxxxxx
Pleasantness	xxxxxx

Masculine sounds/feelings are high.
Feminine sounds/feelings are medium.
Pronunciation is easiest.

CORY

Cheerfulness	xxx
Activity	xxx
Toughness	xxxxxxx
Unpleasantness	xxxxxxxxx
Sadness	x
Passivity	xxxxx
Gentleness	xxxxxxx
Pleasantness	xxxxx

Masculine sounds/feelings are high.
Feminine sounds/feelings are medium.
Pronunciation is easiest.

CRAIG

Cheerfulness	x
Activity	xxxxxx
Toughness	xxxxxxxxxx
Unpleasantness	xxxxxxxxx
Sadness	x
Passivity	xxx
Gentleness	x
Pleasantness	x

Masculine sounds/feelings are very high.
Feminine sounds/feelings are very low.
Pronunciation is easier.

CURTIS

Cheerfulness	xxxxxx
Activity	xxxxxxxxx
Toughness	xxxxxxxxxxxxx
Unpleasantness	xxxxxxxxx
Sadness	x
Passivity	xxx
Gentleness	x
Pleasantness	x

Masculine sounds/feelings are very high.
Feminine sounds/feelings are very low.
Pronunciation is easier.

DALE

Cheerfulness	x
Activity	x
Toughness	xxxx
Unpleasantness	xxxxx
Sadness	xxxxxxxxx
Passivity	xxxxx
Gentleness	xxxx
Pleasantness	xxxxxx

Masculine sounds/feelings are medium low.
Feminine sounds/feelings are medium.
Pronunciation is easier.

DAN

Cheerfulness	x
Activity	x
Toughness	xxxx
Unpleasantness	xxxxx
Sadness	xxxxxxxxx
Passivity	xxxxxxx
Gentleness	x
Pleasantness	x

Masculine sounds/feelings are medium low.
Feminine sounds/feelings are medium low.
Pronunciation is easiest.

DANIEL

Cheerfulness	xxxxxx
Activity	x
Toughness	xxxx
Unpleasantness	xxxxx
Sadness	xxxxxxxxxxxx
Passivity	xxxxxxxxx
Gentleness	xxxxxxxxxxx
Pleasantness	xxxxxxxxxxxx

Masculine sounds/feelings are low.
Feminine sounds/feelings are very high.
Pronunciation is average.

DANNY

Cheerfulness	xxx
Activity	x
Toughness	xxxx
Unpleasantness	xxxxx
Sadness	xxxxxxxxxxxx
Passivity	xxxxxxxxx
Gentleness	xxxx
Pleasantness	xxxxxx

Masculine sounds/feelings are low.
Feminine sounds/feelings are very high.
Pronunciation is easiest.

DARRELL

Cheerfulness	xxx
Activity	xxx
Toughness	xxxxxxx
Unpleasantness	xxxxxxxxx
Sadness	xxxxxxxxx
Passivity	xxxxxxxxx
Gentleness	xxxxxxx
Pleasantness	xxxxxx

Masculine sounds/feelings are medium.
Feminine sounds/feelings are very high.
Pronunciation is more difficult.

DARREN

Cheerfulness	xxx
Activity	xxx
Toughness	xxxxxxx
Unpleasantness	xxxxxxxxx
Sadness	xxxxxxxxx
Passivity	xxxxxxxxx
Gentleness	xxxx
Pleasantness	x

Masculine sounds/feelings are medium.
Feminine sounds/feelings are medium.
Pronunciation is average.

Men's And Boys' Names

DARRYL

Cheerfulness	xxx
Activity	xxxxxx
Toughness	xxxxxxxxx
Unpleasantness	xxxxxxxxx
Sadness	xxxxxxxxx
Passivity	xxxxxx
Gentleness	xxxx
Pleasantness	xxxxxx

Masculine sounds/feelings are high.
Feminine sounds/feelings are medium high.
Pronunciation is more difficult.

DARYL

Cheerfulness	xxxxx
Activity	xxxxxxxxx
Toughness	xxxxxxxxxx
Unpleasantness	xxxxxxxxx
Sadness	xxxxxxxxx
Passivity	xxxxx
Gentleness	xxxx
Pleasantness	xxxxxx

Masculine sounds/feelings are very high.
Feminine sounds/feelings are medium.
Pronunciation is more difficult.

DAVE

Cheerfulness	xxx
Activity	x
Toughness	xxxx
Unpleasantness	xxxxx
Sadness	xxxxx
Passivity	xxx
Gentleness	xxxx
Pleasantness	xxxxxx

Masculine sounds/feelings are medium.
Feminine sounds/feelings are medium low.
Pronunciation is easier.

DAVID

Cheerfulness	xxxxxx
Activity	xxx
Toughness	xxxxxxxxx
Unpleasantness	xxxxxxxxx
Sadness	xxxxxxxxx
Passivity	xxxxxx
Gentleness	xxxx
Pleasantness	xxxxx

Masculine sounds/feelings are high.
Feminine sounds/feelings are medium high.
Pronunciation is average.

DEAN

Cheerfulness	xxx
Activity	x
Toughness	xxxx
Unpleasantness	xxxxx
Sadness	xxxxxxxxx
Passivity	xxxxx
Gentleness	xxxx
Pleasantness	xxxxxx

Masculine sounds/feelings are medium.
Feminine sounds/feelings are medium.
Pronunciation is easiest.

DENNIS

Cheerfulness	xxxxxx
Activity	xxx
Toughness	xxxxxxx
Unpleasantness	xxxxx
Sadness	xxxxxxxxxxxxx
Passivity	xxxxxxxxx
Gentleness	xxxx
Pleasantness	x

Masculine sounds/feelings are medium.
Feminine sounds/feelings are medium high.
Pronunciation is average.

DEREK

Cheerfulness	xxxxxx
Activity	xxxxxx
Toughness	xxxxxxxxxxxx
Unpleasantness	xxxxxxxxxxxx
Sadness	xxxxx
Passivity	xxxxxxx
Gentleness	xxxx
Pleasantness	x

Masculine sounds/feelings are very high.
Feminine sounds/feelings are medium low.
Pronunciation is average.

DERRICK

Cheerfulness	xxxxxx
Activity	xxxxxxxxx
Toughness	xxxxxxxxxxxxxxx
Unpleasantness	xxxxxxxxxxxx
Sadness	xxxxx
Passivity	xxxxx
Gentleness	x
Pleasantness	x

Masculine sounds/feelings are very high.
Feminine sounds/feelings are very low.
Pronunciation is average.

DON

Cheerfulness	x
Activity	x
Toughness	xxxx
Unpleasantness	xxxxx
Sadness	xxxxxxxxx
Passivity	xxxxxxx
Gentleness	x
Pleasantness	x

Masculine sounds/feelings are medium low.
Feminine sounds/feelings are medium low.
Pronunciation is easiest.

DONALD

Cheerfulness	x
Activity	x
Toughness	xxxxxxx
Unpleasantness	xxxxxxxxx
Sadness	xxxxxxxxxxxxxxxxx
Passivity	xxxxxxxxxxxxxx
Gentleness	xxxxxxx
Pleasantness	xxxxx

Masculine sounds/feelings are medium low.
Feminine sounds/feelings are very high.
Pronunciation is more difficult.

DOUGLAS

Cheerfulness	x
Activity	xxx
Toughness	xxxxxxx
Unpleasantness	xxxxx
Sadness	xxxxxxxxx
Passivity	xxxxxxxxx
Gentleness	xxxx
Pleasantness	xxxxxx

Masculine sounds/feelings are low.
Feminine sounds/feelings are medium high.
Pronunciation is average.

DUANE

Cheerfulness	xxx
Activity	xxxxxx
Toughness	xxxx
Unpleasantness	x
Sadness	xxxxx
Passivity	xxx
Gentleness	x
Pleasantness	x

Masculine sounds/feelings are medium.
Feminine sounds/feelings are very low.
Pronunciation is easier.

DUSTIN

Cheerfulness	xxx
Activity	xxxxxx
Toughness	xxxxxxxxx
Unpleasantness	xxxxxxxxx
Sadness	xxxxxxxxx
Passivity	xxxxxxx
Gentleness	x
Pleasantness	x

Masculine sounds/feelings are high.
Feminine sounds/feelings are medium low.
Pronunciation is average.

DWAYNE

Cheerfulness	xxx
Activity	x
Toughness	xxxx
Unpleasantness	xxxxx
Sadness	xxxxxxxxx
Passivity	xxxxx
Gentleness	x
Pleasantness	xxxxxx

Masculine sounds/feelings are medium.
Feminine sounds/feelings are medium.
Pronunciation is easier.

DWIGHT

Cheerfulness	xxxxxx
Activity	xxx
Toughness	xxxxxxx
Unpleasantness	xxxxxxxxx
Sadness	xxxxx
Passivity	xxx
Gentleness	xxxx
Pleasantness	xxxxxxxxxxxx

Masculine sounds/feelings are very high.
Feminine sounds/feelings are medium.
Pronunciation is easier.

EARL

Cheerfulness	xxx
Activity	xxx
Toughness	xxxx
Unpleasantness	x
Sadness	xxxxx
Passivity	xxx
Gentleness	xxxx
Pleasantness	xxxxxx

Masculine sounds/feelings are medium.
Feminine sounds/feelings are medium low.
Pronunciation is easiest.

EDDIE

Cheerfulness	xxxxxx
Activity	x
Toughness	xxxxxxx
Unpleasantness	xxxxxxxxx
Sadness	xxxxxxxxx
Passivity	xxxxxxx
Gentleness	xxxxxxx
Pleasantness	xxxxxx

Masculine sounds/feelings are high.
Feminine sounds/feelings are high.
Pronunciation is easier.

EDGAR

Cheerfulness	xxxxxx
Activity	xxxxxx
Toughness	xxxxxxxxxx
Unpleasantness	xxxxx
Sadness	xxxxx
Passivity	xxxxx
Gentleness	xxxx
Pleasantness	x

Masculine sounds/feelings are very high.
Feminine sounds/feelings are low.
Pronunciation is easier.

EDUARDO

Cheerfulness	xxxxxxxx
Activity	xxxxxxxxxxx
Toughness	xxxxxxxxxx
Unpleasantness	xxxxxxxxxxxx
Sadness	xxxxxxxx
Passivity	xxxxxx
Gentleness	xxxx
Pleasantness	x

Masculine sounds/feelings are very high.
Feminine sounds/feelings are medium.
Pronunciation is most difficult.

EDWARD

Cheerfulness	xxxxxx
Activity	xxx
Toughness	xxxxxxxxxx
Unpleasantness	xxxxxxxxxxxx
Sadness	xxxxxxxxx
Passivity	xxxxxxxxx
Gentleness	xxxxxx
Pleasantness	xxxxxx

Masculine sounds/feelings are very high.
Feminine sounds/feelings are very high.
Pronunciation is more difficult.

EDWIN

Cheerfulness	xxxxxxxx
Activity	xxx
Toughness	xxxxxx
Unpleasantness	xxxxx
Sadness	xxxxxxxxx
Passivity	xxxxxxx
Gentleness	xxxx
Pleasantness	xxxxxx

Masculine sounds/feelings are medium.
Feminine sounds/feelings are medium high.
Pronunciation is easier.

ELMER

Cheerfulness	xxxxx
Activity	xxx
Toughness	xxxx
Unpleasantness	x
Sadness	xxxxx
Passivity	xxxxxx
Gentleness	xxxxxxxxxx
Pleasantness	xxxxx

Masculine sounds/feelings are medium.
Feminine sounds/feelings are high.
Pronunciation is easier.

ENRIQUE

Cheerfulness	xxxxxx
Activity	xxx
Toughness	xxxxxx
Unpleasantness	xxxxxxxxx
Sadness	xxxxx
Passivity	xxxxxx
Gentleness	xxxxxx
Pleasantness	xxxxx

Masculine sounds/feelings are medium high.
Feminine sounds/feelings are medium.
Pronunciation is easier.

ERIC

Cheerfulness	xxxxx
Activity	xxxxxx
Toughness	xxxxxxxxx
Unpleasantness	xxxxxxxx
Sadness	x
Passivity	xxxxx
Gentleness	xxxx
Pleasantness	x

Masculine sounds/feelings are very high.
Feminine sounds/feelings are very low.
Pronunciation is easier.

ERIK

Cheerfulness	xxxxx
Activity	xxxxxx
Toughness	xxxxxxxxx
Unpleasantness	xxxxxxxxx
Sadness	x
Passivity	xxxxx
Gentleness	xxxx
Pleasantness	x

Masculine sounds/feelings are very high.
Feminine sounds/feelings are very low.
Pronunciation is easier.

ERNEST

Cheerfulness	xxxxx
Activity	xxxxxx
Toughness	xxxxxxx
Unpleasantness	xxxxx
Sadness	xxxxx
Passivity	xxxxx
Gentleness	xxxx
Pleasantness	x

Masculine sounds/feelings are medium.
Feminine sounds/feelings are low.
Pronunciation is average.

EUGENE

Cheerfulness	xxxxx
Activity	xxxxxx
Toughness	xxxx
Unpleasantness	x
Sadness	xxxxx
Passivity	xxx
Gentleness	xxxx
Pleasantness	xxxxxx

Masculine sounds/feelings are medium low.
Feminine sounds/feelings are medium low.
Pronunciation is average.

EVERETT

Cheerfulness	xxxxxxxxxxx
Activity	xxxxxxxxx
Toughness	xxxxxxxxx
Unpleasantness	xxxxxxxxxxxx
Sadness	x
Passivity	xxxxx
Gentleness	xxxxxxxxxxxxxx
Pleasantness	xxxxxxxxxxx

Masculine sounds/feelings are very high.
Feminine sounds/feelings are high.
Pronunciation is most difficult.

FELIX

Cheerfulness	xxxxxxxxx
Activity	xxxxxx
Toughness	xxxxxxx
Unpleasantness	xxxxx
Sadness	xxxxx
Passivity	xxxxxxx
Gentleness	xxxxxxx
Pleasantness	xxxxxx

Masculine sounds/feelings are medium high.
Feminine sounds/feelings are medium.
Pronunciation is average.

FERNANDO

Cheerfulness	xxxxx
Activity	xxxxxx
Toughness	xxxxxxx
Unpleasantness	xxxxxxxxx
Sadness	xxxxxxxxxxxxxxxxxx
Passivity	xxxxxxxxxxx
Gentleness	x
Pleasantness	x

Masculine sounds/feelings are high.
Feminine sounds/feelings are high.
Pronunciation is more difficult.

FLOYD

Cheerfulness	xxxxx
Activity	xxxxx
Toughness	xxxxxxx
Unpleasantness	xxxxx
Sadness	xxxxxxxx
Passivity	xxxxx
Gentleness	xxxx
Pleasantness	xxxxxx

Masculine sounds/feelings are very high.
Feminine sounds/feelings are medium.
Pronunciation is average.

FRANCIS

Cheerfulness	xxxxx
Activity	xxxxxxxxx
Toughness	xxxxxxx
Unpleasantness	xxxxx
Sadness	xxxxx
Passivity	xxxxx
Gentleness	x
Pleasantness	x

Masculine sounds/feelings are medium high.
Feminine sounds/feelings are very low.
Pronunciation is more difficult.

FRANCISCO

Cheerfulness	xxxxx
Activity	xxxxxxxxx
Toughness	xxxxxxxxxx
Unpleasantness	xxxxxxxxxxxx
Sadness	xxxxxxxx
Passivity	xxxxxxxx
Gentleness	x
Pleasantness	x

Masculine sounds/feelings are very high.
Feminine sounds/feelings are medium.
Pronunciation is most difficult.

FRANK

Cheerfulness	xxxxx
Activity	xxxxxxxx
Toughness	xxxxxxxxx
Unpleasantness	xxxxxxxx
Sadness	x
Passivity	xxxxx
Gentleness	x
Pleasantness	x

Masculine sounds/feelings are very high.
Feminine sounds/feelings are very low.
Pronunciation is average.

FRANKLIN

Cheerfulness	xxxxxxxxx
Activity	xxxxxxxxxxxx
Toughness	xxxxxxxxxxxxx
Unpleasantness	xxxxxxxxx
Sadness	xxxxxxxxx
Passivity	xxxxxxxx
Gentleness	xxxx
Pleasantness	xxxxxx

Masculine sounds/feelings are very high.
Feminine sounds/feelings are medium high.
Pronunciation is most difficult.

FRED

Cheerfulness	xxxxx
Activity	xxxxx
Toughness	xxxxxxx
Unpleasantness	xxxxxxxx
Sadness	xxxxx
Passivity	xxxxx
Gentleness	xxxx
Pleasantness	x

Masculine sounds/feelings are very high.
Feminine sounds/feelings are low.
Pronunciation is easier.

FREDDIE

Cheerfulness	xxxxxxxx
Activity	xxxxx
Toughness	xxxxxxxxxx
Unpleasantness	xxxxxxxxxxxxx
Sadness	xxxxxxxx
Passivity	xxxxxxx
Gentleness	xxxxxxx
Pleasantness	xxxxx

Masculine sounds/feelings are very high.
Feminine sounds/feelings are high.
Pronunciation is more difficult.

FREDERICK

Cheerfulness	xxxxxxxxxxx
Activity	xxxxxxxxxxx
Toughness	xxxxxxxxxxxxxxx
Unpleasantness	xxxxxxxxxxxxxxxxxx
Sadness	xxxxx
Passivity	xxxxxxx
Gentleness	xxxxxxx
Pleasantness	xxxxxx

Masculine sounds/feelings are very high.
Feminine sounds/feelings are medium.
Pronunciation is most difficult.

FREDRICK

Cheerfulness	xxxxxxxxx
Activity	xxxxxxxxxxxx
Toughness	xxxxxxxxxxxxxxx
Unpleasantness	xxxxxxxxxxxxxxxxx
Sadness	xxxxx
Passivity	xxxxxxx
Gentleness	xxxx
Pleasantness	x

Masculine sounds/feelings are very high.
Feminine sounds/feelings are medium low.
Pronunciation is most difficult.

GABRIEL

Cheerfulness	xxxxx
Activity	xxxxx
Toughness	xxxxxx
Unpleasantness	xxxxxxxxx
Sadness	xxxxxxxxx
Passivity	xxxxxxx
Gentleness	xxxxxxxxxxx
Pleasantness	xxxxxxxxxxx

Masculine sounds/feelings are high.
Feminine sounds/feelings are very high.
Pronunciation is more difficult.

GARY

Cheerfulness	xxx
Activity	xxxxxx
Toughness	xxxxxxx
Unpleasantness	xxxxx
Sadness	x
Passivity	x
Gentleness	xxxx
Pleasantness	xxxxxx

Masculine sounds/feelings are high.
Feminine sounds/feelings are very low.
Pronunciation is easiest.

GENE

Cheerfulness	xxxxxx
Activity	xxx
Toughness	x
Unpleasantness	x
Sadness	xxxxx
Passivity	xxx
Gentleness	xxxx
Pleasantness	xxxxxx

Masculine sounds/feelings are medium.
Feminine sounds/feelings are medium low.
Pronunciation is easiest.

GEORGE

Cheerfulness	xxxxxxxx
Activity	xxxxxxxxx
Toughness	xxxx
Unpleasantness	xxxxx
Sadness	x
Passivity	xxx
Gentleness	xxxxxx
Pleasantness	xxxxxx

Masculine sounds/feelings are medium high.
Feminine sounds/feelings are medium low.
Pronunciation is more difficult.

GERALD

Cheerfulness	xxxxxx
Activity	xxxxxx
Toughness	xxxxxxx
Unpleasantness	xxxxxxxxx
Sadness	xxxxxxxxx
Passivity	xxxxxxxxx
Gentleness	xxxxxxxxxxx
Pleasantness	xxxxxx

Masculine sounds/feelings are high.
Feminine sounds/feelings are very high.
Pronunciation is most difficult.

GILBERT

Cheerfulness	xxxxxx
Activity	xxxxxxxxxxxx
Toughness	xxxxxxxxxxxxxx
Unpleasantness	xxxxxxxxx
Sadness	xxxxxxxxx
Passivity	xxx
Gentleness	xxxx
Pleasantness	xxxxxx

Masculine sounds/feelings are very high.
Feminine sounds/feelings are medium.
Pronunciation is average.

GLEN

Cheerfulness	xxx
Activity	xxx
Toughness	xxxx
Unpleasantness	x
Sadness	xxxxxxxxx
Passivity	xxxxxx
Gentleness	xxxxxxx
Pleasantness	xxxxx

Masculine sounds/feelings are medium.
Feminine sounds/feelings are high.
Pronunciation is easier.

GLENN

Cheerfulness	xxx
Activity	xxx
Toughness	xxxx
Unpleasantness	x
Sadness	xxxxxxxxxxxxx
Passivity	xxxxxxxxx
Gentleness	xxxxxxx
Pleasantness	xxxxx

Masculine sounds/feelings are very low.
Feminine sounds/feelings are very high.
Pronunciation is easier.

GORDON

Cheerfulness	x
Activity	xxxxxx
Toughness	xxxxxxxxx
Unpleasantness	xxxxxxxx
Sadness	xxxxxxxxx
Passivity	xxxxxxx
Gentleness	xxxx
Pleasantness	x

Masculine sounds/feelings are medium high.
Feminine sounds/feelings are medium.
Pronunciation is more difficult.

Men's And Boys' Names

GREG

Cheerfulness	xxx
Activity	xxxxxxxx
Toughness	xxxxxxxxxx
Unpleasantness	xxxxx

Sadness	x
Passivity	xxx
Gentleness	xxxx
Pleasantness	x

Masculine sounds/feelings are very high.
Feminine sounds/feelings are very low.
Pronunciation is easier.

GREGORY

Cheerfulness	xxxxxx
Activity	xxxxxxxxxxxx
Toughness	xxxxxxxxxxxxx
Unpleasantness	xxxxxxxxx

Sadness	x
Passivity	xxxxx
Gentleness	xxxxxxxxxxx
Pleasantness	xxxxxx

Masculine sounds/feelings are very high.
Feminine sounds/feelings are medium.
Pronunciation is more difficult.

GUY

Cheerfulness	xxx
Activity	xxxxxx
Toughness	xxxxxxx
Unpleasantness	x

Sadness	x
Passivity	xxx
Gentleness	x
Pleasantness	x

Masculine sounds/feelings are medium high.
Feminine sounds/feelings are very low.
Pronunciation is easiest.

HAROLD

Cheerfulness	xxx
Activity	xxx
Toughness	xxxxxxx
Unpleasantness	xxxxxxxxxxxxx

Sadness	xxxxxxxxxxxxx
Passivity	xxxxxxxxx
Gentleness	xxxxxxx
Pleasantness	xxxxxx

Masculine sounds/feelings are medium high.
Feminine sounds/feelings are very high.
Pronunciation is most difficult.

HARRY

Cheerfulness	xxx
Activity	xxx
Toughness	xxxx
Unpleasantness	xxxxx

Sadness	x
Passivity	xxx
Gentleness	xxxx
Pleasantness	xxxxxx

Masculine sounds/feelings are medium.
Feminine sounds/feelings are low.
Pronunciation is easiest.

HARVEY

Cheerfulness	xxxxxxxxx
Activity	xxxxxx
Toughness	xxxx
Unpleasantness	xxxxx

Sadness	x
Passivity	x
Gentleness	xxxxxxx
Pleasantness	xxxxxxxxxxx

Masculine sounds/feelings are medium.
Feminine sounds/feelings are medium.
Pronunciation is average.

HECTOR

Cheerfulness	xxxxx
Activity	xxxxxx
Toughness	xxxxxxxxx
Unpleasantness	xxxxxxxx
Sadness	x
Passivity	xxxxx
Gentleness	xxxx
Pleasantness	x

Masculine sounds/feelings are very high.
Feminine sounds/feelings are very low.
Pronunciation is average.

HENRY

Cheerfulness	xxxxxx
Activity	xxx
Toughness	xxxx
Unpleasantness	xxxxx
Sadness	xxxxx
Passivity	xxxxx
Gentleness	xxxxxxx
Pleasantness	xxxxxx

Masculine sounds/feelings are medium.
Feminine sounds/feelings are medium.
Pronunciation is easier.

HERBERT

Cheerfulness	xxxxxx
Activity	xxxxxxxxx
Toughness	xxxxxxxxxx
Unpleasantness	xxxxxxxx
Sadness	xxxxx
Passivity	x
Gentleness	x
Pleasantness	x

Masculine sounds/feelings are very high.
Feminine sounds/feelings are very low.
Pronunciation is average.

HERMAN

Cheerfulness	xxx
Activity	xxx
Toughness	xxxx
Unpleasantness	x
Sadness	xxxxx
Passivity	xxxxxxx
Gentleness	xxxx
Pleasantness	x

Masculine sounds/feelings are very low.
Feminine sounds/feelings are medium low.
Pronunciation is easier.

HOWARD

Cheerfulness	xxx
Activity	xxxxxx
Toughness	xxxxxxx
Unpleasantness	xxxxxxxxxxxxx
Sadness	xxxxxxxxx
Passivity	xxxxx
Gentleness	x
Pleasantness	x

Masculine sounds/feelings are high.
Feminine sounds/feelings are low.
Pronunciation is average.

HUGH

Cheerfulness	x
Activity	x
Toughness	x
Unpleasantness	x
Sadness	x
Passivity	xxx
Gentleness	x
Pleasantness	x

Masculine sounds/feelings are very low.
Feminine sounds/feelings are very low.
Pronunciation is easiest.

Men's And Boys' Names

IAN

Cheerfulness	xxx
Activity	xxx
Toughness	xxxx
Unpleasantness	x
Sadness	xxxxx
Passivity	xxxxx
Gentleness	x
Pleasantness	x

Masculine sounds/feelings are medium.
Feminine sounds/feelings are very low.
Pronunciation is easiest.

ISAAC

Cheerfulness	xxx
Activity	xxx
Toughness	xxxxxxx
Unpleasantness	xxxxx
Sadness	x
Passivity	xxxxxxxxx
Gentleness	xxxx
Pleasantness	xxxxxx

Masculine sounds/feelings are medium.
Feminine sounds/feelings are medium.
Pronunciation is easiest.

IVAN

Cheerfulness	xxxxx
Activity	xxx
Toughness	xxxx
Unpleasantness	x
Sadness	xxxxx
Passivity	xxxxx
Gentleness	xxxx
Pleasantness	xxxxxx

Masculine sounds/feelings are medium.
Feminine sounds/feelings are medium.
Pronunciation is easier.

JACK

Cheerfulness	xxx
Activity	xxx
Toughness	xxxx
Unpleasantness	xxxxx
Sadness	x
Passivity	xxxxx
Gentleness	x
Pleasantness	x

Masculine sounds/feelings are medium.
Feminine sounds/feelings are very low.
Pronunciation is easiest.

JACKIE

Cheerfulness	xxxxxx
Activity	xxx
Toughness	xxxx
Unpleasantness	xxxxx
Sadness	x
Passivity	xxxxx
Gentleness	xxxx
Pleasantness	xxxxxx

Masculine sounds/feelings are medium high.
Feminine sounds/feelings are low.
Pronunciation is easiest.

JACOB

Cheerfulness	xxxxxx
Activity	xxxxxx
Toughness	xxxx
Unpleasantness	xxxxxxxx
Sadness	xxxxx
Passivity	xxxxx
Gentleness	x
Pleasantness	x

Masculine sounds/feelings are medium high.
Feminine sounds/feelings are very low.
Pronunciation is easier.

JAIME

Cheerfulness	xxx
Activity	xxx
Toughness	x
Unpleasantness	x
Sadness	x
Passivity	xxx
Gentleness	xxxx
Pleasantness	x

Masculine sounds/feelings are low.
Feminine sounds/feelings are very low.
Pronunciation is easier.

JAMES

Cheerfulness	xxx
Activity	xxx
Toughness	x
Unpleasantness	x
Sadness	x
Passivity	xxxxx
Gentleness	xxxxxxx
Pleasantness	xxxxxx

Masculine sounds/feelings are low.
Feminine sounds/feelings are medium.
Pronunciation is easier.

JAMIE

Cheerfulness	xxxxxx
Activity	xxx
Toughness	x
Unpleasantness	x
Sadness	x
Passivity	xxx
Gentleness	xxxxxxx
Pleasantness	xxxxxx

Masculine sounds/feelings are medium.
Feminine sounds/feelings are medium low.
Pronunciation is easier.

JARED

Cheerfulness	xxxxxx
Activity	xxxxxx
Toughness	xxxxxxx
Unpleasantness	xxxxxxxxx
Sadness	xxxxx
Passivity	xxxxx
Gentleness	xxxx
Pleasantness	x

Masculine sounds/feelings are very high.
Feminine sounds/feelings are low.
Pronunciation is more difficult.

JASON

Cheerfulness	xxx
Activity	xxx
Toughness	x
Unpleasantness	x
Sadness	xxxxx
Passivity	xxx
Gentleness	x
Pleasantness	x

Masculine sounds/feelings are very low.
Feminine sounds/feelings are very low.
Pronunciation is more difficult.

JAVIER

Cheerfulness	xxxxxxxxxxx
Activity	xxxxxx
Toughness	xxxx
Unpleasantness	x
Sadness	x
Passivity	x
Gentleness	xxxxxxx
Pleasantness	xxxxxxxxxxx

Masculine sounds/feelings are medium.
Feminine sounds/feelings are medium.
Pronunciation is more difficult.

JAY

Cheerfulness	xxx
Activity	xxx
Toughness	x
Unpleasantness	x
Sadness	x
Passivity	x
Gentleness	x
Pleasantness	x

Masculine sounds/feelings are low.
Feminine sounds/feelings are very low.
Pronunciation is easiest.

JEFF

Cheerfulness	xxxxxxxxxxx
Activity	xxxxxxxxx
Toughness	x
Unpleasantness	x
Sadness	x
Passivity	xxx
Gentleness	xxxx
Pleasantness	x

Masculine sounds/feelings are high.
Feminine sounds/feelings are very low.
Pronunciation is easier.

JEFFERY

Cheerfulness	xxxxxxxxxxxxxxxxx
Activity	xxxxxxxxxxxx
Toughness	xxxx
Unpleasantness	x
Sadness	x
Passivity	xxx
Gentleness	xxxxxxx
Pleasantness	xxxxxx

Masculine sounds/feelings are very high.
Feminine sounds/feelings are medium low.
Pronunciation is more difficult.

JEFFREY

Cheerfulness	xxxxxxxxxxxxxx
Activity	xxxxxxxxxxx
Toughness	xxxx
Unpleasantness	xxxxx
Sadness	x
Passivity	xxx
Gentleness	xxxxxxx
Pleasantness	xxxxxx

Masculine sounds/feelings are very high.
Feminine sounds/feelings are medium low.
Pronunciation is more difficult.

JEREMY

Cheerfulness	xxxxxxxxxxxx
Activity	xxxxxx
Toughness	xxxx
Unpleasantness	xxxxx
Sadness	x
Passivity	xxxxx
Gentleness	xxxxxxxxxxxxxx
Pleasantness	xxxxxxxxxxxx

Masculine sounds/feelings are medium high.
Feminine sounds/feelings are high.
Pronunciation is more difficult.

JEROME

Cheerfulness	xxxxxx
Activity	xxxxxx
Toughness	xxxx
Unpleasantness	xxxxxxxxx
Sadness	xxxxx
Passivity	xxxxxxx
Gentleness	xxxxxxx
Pleasantness	x

Masculine sounds/feelings are medium high.
Feminine sounds/feelings are medium.
Pronunciation is more difficult.

JERRY

Cheerfulness	xxxxxxxx
Activity	xxxxxxxx
Toughness	xxxxxxx
Unpleasantness	xxxxx
Sadness	x
Passivity	x
Gentleness	xxxx
Pleasantness	xxxxxx

Masculine sounds/feelings are very high.
Feminine sounds/feelings are very low.
Pronunciation is average.

JESSE

Cheerfulness	xxxxxx
Activity	xxx
Toughness	x
Unpleasantness	x
Sadness	x
Passivity	xxx
Gentleness	xxxx
Pleasantness	x

Masculine sounds/feelings are medium.
Feminine sounds/feelings are very low.
Pronunciation is easier.

JESSIE

Cheerfulness	xxxxxxxxx
Activity	xxx
Toughness	x
Unpleasantness	x
Sadness	x
Passivity	xxx
Gentleness	xxxxxxx
Pleasantness	xxxxxx

Masculine sounds/feelings are medium.
Feminine sounds/feelings are medium low.
Pronunciation is easier.

JESUS

Cheerfulness	xxxxx
Activity	xxx
Toughness	x
Unpleasantness	x
Sadness	x
Passivity	xxxxxx
Gentleness	xxxxxxx
Pleasantness	xxxxx

Masculine sounds/feelings are very low.
Feminine sounds/feelings are medium.
Pronunciation is more difficult.

JIM

Cheerfulness	xxxxxx
Activity	xxxxxx
Toughness	xxxx
Unpleasantness	x
Sadness	x
Passivity	xxx
Gentleness	xxxx
Pleasantness	x

Masculine sounds/feelings are medium.
Feminine sounds/feelings are very low.
Pronunciation is easiest.

JIMMIE

Cheerfulness	xxxxxxxxx
Activity	xxxxxx
Toughness	xxxx
Unpleasantness	x
Sadness	x
Passivity	xxxxx
Gentleness	xxxxxxxxxx
Pleasantness	xxxxx

Masculine sounds/feelings are medium.
Feminine sounds/feelings are medium.
Pronunciation is easier.

JIMMY

Cheerfulness	xxxxxxxx
Activity	xxxxxx
Toughness	xxxx
Unpleasantness	x
Sadness	x
Passivity	xxxxx
Gentleness	xxxxxxxxxx
Pleasantness	xxxxxx

Masculine sounds/feelings are medium.
Feminine sounds/feelings are medium.
Pronunciation is easier.

JOE

Cheerfulness	xxx
Activity	xxx
Toughness	x
Unpleasantness	xxxxx
Sadness	xxxxx
Passivity	xxx
Gentleness	x
Pleasantness	x

Masculine sounds/feelings are medium.
Feminine sounds/feelings are very low.
Pronunciation is easiest.

JOEL

Cheerfulness	xxxxxx
Activity	xxx
Toughness	x
Unpleasantness	xxxxx
Sadness	xxxxxxxxx
Passivity	xxxxxxx
Gentleness	xxxxxxx
Pleasantness	xxxxxx

Masculine sounds/feelings are medium.
Feminine sounds/feelings are high.
Pronunciation is average.

JOEY

Cheerfulness	xxxxx
Activity	xxx
Toughness	x
Unpleasantness	xxxxx
Sadness	xxxxx
Passivity	xxx
Gentleness	xxxx
Pleasantness	xxxxxx

Masculine sounds/feelings are medium.
Feminine sounds/feelings are medium low.
Pronunciation is easiest.

JOHN

Cheerfulness	xxxxxx
Activity	xxxxxx
Toughness	x
Unpleasantness	x
Sadness	xxxxx
Passivity	xxx
Gentleness	x
Pleasantness	x

Masculine sounds/feelings are medium.
Feminine sounds/feelings are very low.
Pronunciation is easiest.

JOHNNIE

Cheerfulness	xxxxxxxxx
Activity	xxxxxx
Toughness	x
Unpleasantness	x
Sadness	xxxxxxxxx
Passivity	xxxxx
Gentleness	xxxx
Pleasantness	xxxxxx

Masculine sounds/feelings are medium low.
Feminine sounds/feelings are medium.
Pronunciation is easier.

JOHNNY

Cheerfulness	xxxxxxxx
Activity	xxxxx
Toughness	x
Unpleasantness	x

Sadness	xxxxxxxx
Passivity	xxxxx
Gentleness	xxxx
Pleasantness	xxxxx

Masculine sounds/feelings are medium low.
Feminine sounds/feelings are medium.
Pronunciation is easier.

JON

Cheerfulness	xxx
Activity	xxx
Toughness	x
Unpleasantness	x

Sadness	xxxxx
Passivity	xxxxx
Gentleness	x
Pleasantness	x

Masculine sounds/feelings are low.
Feminine sounds/feelings are very low.
Pronunciation is easiest.

JONATHAN

Cheerfulness	xxxxxx
Activity	xxx
Toughness	x
Unpleasantness	x

Sadness	xxxxxxxx
Passivity	xxxxxxxxxx
Gentleness	xxxx
Pleasantness	xxxxxx

Masculine sounds/feelings are very low.
Feminine sounds/feelings are high.
Pronunciation is most difficult.

JORDAN

Cheerfulness	xxx
Activity	xxxxx
Toughness	xxxxxx
Unpleasantness	xxxxxxxxx

Sadness	xxxxxxxxx
Passivity	xxxxxxxxx
Gentleness	xxxx
Pleasantness	x

Masculine sounds/feelings are medium high.
Feminine sounds/feelings are medium.
Pronunciation is more difficult.

JORGE

Cheerfulness	xxxxx
Activity	xxxxxxxxx
Toughness	xxxx
Unpleasantness	xxxxx

Sadness	x
Passivity	xxx
Gentleness	xxxx
Pleasantness	x

Masculine sounds/feelings are very high.
Feminine sounds/feelings are very low.
Pronunciation is more difficult.

JOSE

Cheerfulness	xxx
Activity	xxx
Toughness	x
Unpleasantness	xxxxx

Sadness	xxxxx
Passivity	xxxxx
Gentleness	xxxx
Pleasantness	xxxxx

Masculine sounds/feelings are medium.
Feminine sounds/feelings are medium.
Pronunciation is easier.

JOSEPH

Cheerfulness	xxxxxxxx
Activity	xxxxxx
Toughness	x
Unpleasantness	xxxxx
Sadness	xxxxx
Passivity	xxxxxx
Gentleness	xxxxxxx
Pleasantness	xxxxxx

Masculine sounds/feelings are medium.
Feminine sounds/feelings are medium.
Pronunciation is more difficult.

JOSHUA

Cheerfulness	xxxxx
Activity	xxxxxxxxxxx
Toughness	xxxxxx
Unpleasantness	x
Sadness	x
Passivity	x
Gentleness	x
Pleasantness	x

Masculine sounds/feelings are medium high.
Feminine sounds/feelings are very low.
Pronunciation is more difficult.

JUAN

Cheerfulness	xxx
Activity	xxxxxx
Toughness	xxxx
Unpleasantness	x
Sadness	xxxxx
Passivity	xxxxx
Gentleness	x
Pleasantness	x

Masculine sounds/feelings are medium.
Feminine sounds/feelings are very low.
Pronunciation is easier.

JULIAN

Cheerfulness	xxxxx
Activity	xxxxxxxxx
Toughness	xxxxxxx
Unpleasantness	x
Sadness	xxxxxxxxx
Passivity	xxxxxxx
Gentleness	xxxx
Pleasantness	xxxxx

Masculine sounds/feelings are medium.
Feminine sounds/feelings are medium high.
Pronunciation is more difficult.

JULIO

Cheerfulness	xxxxxx
Activity	xxxxxxxxx
Toughness	xxxxxxx
Unpleasantness	xxxxx
Sadness	xxxxxxxxx
Passivity	xxxxx
Gentleness	xxxx
Pleasantness	xxxxxx

Masculine sounds/feelings are medium high.
Feminine sounds/feelings are medium.
Pronunciation is more difficult.

JUSTIN

Cheerfulness	xxxxxx
Activity	xxxxxxxxx
Toughness	xxxxxxx
Unpleasantness	xxxxx
Sadness	xxxxx
Passivity	xxxxx
Gentleness	x
Pleasantness	x

Masculine sounds/feelings are medium high.
Feminine sounds/feelings are very low.
Pronunciation is more difficult.

KARL

Cheerfulness	xxx
Activity	xxxxxx
Toughness	xxxxxxx
Unpleasantness	xxxxxxxx
Sadness	xxxxx
Passivity	xxxxx
Gentleness	xxxx
Pleasantness	xxxxxx

Masculine sounds/feelings are very high.
Feminine sounds/feelings are medium.
Pronunciation is easier.

KEITH

Cheerfulness	xxxxxx
Activity	x
Toughness	xxxx
Unpleasantness	xxxxx
Sadness	x
Passivity	xxx
Gentleness	xxxxxxx
Pleasantness	xxxxxxxxxxx

Masculine sounds/feelings are medium.
Feminine sounds/feelings are medium.
Pronunciation is easiest.

KELLY

Cheerfulness	xxxxxx
Activity	x
Toughness	xxxx
Unpleasantness	xxxxx
Sadness	xxxxx
Passivity	xxxxxxx
Gentleness	xxxxxxxxxx
Pleasantness	xxxxxxxxxxx

Masculine sounds/feelings are medium.
Feminine sounds/feelings are very high.
Pronunciation is easiest.

KEN

Cheerfulness	xxx
Activity	x
Toughness	xxxx
Unpleasantness	xxxxx
Sadness	xxxxx
Passivity	xxxxxxx
Gentleness	xxxx
Pleasantness	x

Masculine sounds/feelings are medium.
Feminine sounds/feelings are medium low.
Pronunciation is easiest.

KENNETH

Cheerfulness	xxxxxxxxx
Activity	x
Toughness	xxxx
Unpleasantness	xxxxx
Sadness	xxxxxxxxx
Passivity	xxxxxxxxxxx
Gentleness	xxxxxxxxxx
Pleasantness	xxxxxx

Masculine sounds/feelings are medium.
Feminine sounds/feelings are very high.
Pronunciation is more difficult.

KENT

Cheerfulness	xxx
Activity	xxx
Toughness	xxxxxxx
Unpleasantness	xxxxxxxx
Sadness	xxxxx
Passivity	xxxxxxx
Gentleness	xxxx
Pleasantness	x

Masculine sounds/feelings are high.
Feminine sounds/feelings are medium low.
Pronunciation is easiest.

Men's And Boys' Names

KEVIN

Cheerfulness	xxxxxxxxx
Activity	xxx
Toughness	xxxxxxx
Unpleasantness	xxxxx
Sadness	xxxxx
Passivity	xxxxxxx
Gentleness	xxxxxxx
Pleasantness	xxxxxx

Masculine sounds/feelings are medium.
Feminine sounds/feelings are medium.
Pronunciation is easier.

KIRK

Cheerfulness	xxx
Activity	xxx
Toughness	xxxxxxxxxx
Unpleasantness	xxxxxxxxx
Sadness	x
Passivity	xxxxx
Gentleness	x
Pleasantness	x

Masculine sounds/feelings are very high.
Feminine sounds/feelings are very low.
Pronunciation is easiest.

KURT

Cheerfulness	xxx
Activity	xxxxxx
Toughness	xxxxxxxxxx
Unpleasantness	xxxxxxxxx
Sadness	x
Passivity	xxx
Gentleness	x
Pleasantness	x

Masculine sounds/feelings are very high.
Feminine sounds/feelings are very low.
Pronunciation is easiest.

KYLE

Cheerfulness	xxxxx
Activity	x
Toughness	xxxx
Unpleasantness	xxxxx
Sadness	xxxxx
Passivity	xxxxx
Gentleness	xxxxxxxxxx
Pleasantness	xxxxxxxxxxxxxxxxx

Masculine sounds/feelings are medium.
Feminine sounds/feelings are very high.
Pronunciation is easiest.

LANCE

Cheerfulness	x
Activity	x
Toughness	x
Unpleasantness	x
Sadness	xxxxxxxxx
Passivity	xxxxxxx
Gentleness	xxxx
Pleasantness	xxxxxx

Masculine sounds/feelings are very low.
Feminine sounds/feelings are medium high.
Pronunciation is easier.

LARRY

Cheerfulness	xxx
Activity	xxx
Toughness	xxxx
Unpleasantness	xxxxx
Sadness	xxxxx
Passivity	xxxxx
Gentleness	xxxxxxx
Pleasantness	xxxxxxxxxxx

Masculine sounds/feelings are medium.
Feminine sounds/feelings are high.
Pronunciation is easier.

LAWRENCE

Cheerfulness	xxx
Activity	xxx
Toughness	xxxx
Unpleasantness	xxxxx

Sadness	xxxxxxxx
Passivity	xxxxxxxx
Gentleness	xxxxxxxxxx
Pleasantness	xxxxxx

Masculine sounds/feelings are low.
Feminine sounds/feelings are very high.
Pronunciation is more difficult.

LEE

Cheerfulness	xxx
Activity	x
Toughness	x
Unpleasantness	x

Sadness	xxxxx
Passivity	xxx
Gentleness	xxxxxxx
Pleasantness	xxxxxxxxxxx

Masculine sounds/feelings are low.
Feminine sounds/feelings are medium high.
Pronunciation is easiest.

LEO

Cheerfulness	xxx
Activity	x
Toughness	x
Unpleasantness	xxxxx

Sadness	xxxxxxxx
Passivity	xxxxx
Gentleness	xxxxxxx
Pleasantness	xxxxxxxxxxx

Masculine sounds/feelings are medium low.
Feminine sounds/feelings are very high.
Pronunciation is easiest.

LEON

Cheerfulness	xxx
Activity	x
Toughness	x
Unpleasantness	x

Sadness	xxxxxxxxx
Passivity	xxxxx
Gentleness	xxxxxxx
Pleasantness	xxxxxxxxxxxx

Masculine sounds/feelings are low.
Feminine sounds/feelings are very high.
Pronunciation is easier.

LEONARD

Cheerfulness	xxxxxxxx
Activity	xxxxxxxx
Toughness	xxxxxxx
Unpleasantness	xxxxxxxxx

Sadness	xxxxxxxxxxxx
Passivity	xxxxxxx
Gentleness	xxxxxxx
Pleasantness	xxxxxxxxxxx

Masculine sounds/feelings are very high.
Feminine sounds/feelings are very high.
Pronunciation is more difficult.

LEROY

Cheerfulness	xxxxx
Activity	xxxxx
Toughness	xxxxxxx
Unpleasantness	xxxxx

Sadness	xxxxx
Passivity	xxxxx
Gentleness	xxxxxxx
Pleasantness	xxxxx

Masculine sounds/feelings are very high.
Feminine sounds/feelings are medium.
Pronunciation is more difficult.

LESLIE

Cheerfulness	xxxxxx
Activity	x
Toughness	x
Unpleasantness	x
Sadness	xxxxxxxxx
Passivity	xxxxxxx
Gentleness	xxxxxxxxxxxxxx
Pleasantness	xxxxxxxxxxxxxxxxx

Masculine sounds/feelings are very low.
Feminine sounds/feelings are very high.
Pronunciation is average.

LESTER

Cheerfulness	xxxxxx
Activity	xxxxxx
Toughness	xxxxxxx
Unpleasantness	xxxxx
Sadness	xxxxx
Passivity	xxxxx
Gentleness	xxxxxxx
Pleasantness	xxxxxx

Masculine sounds/feelings are medium.
Feminine sounds/feelings are medium.
Pronunciation is more difficult.

LEWIS

Cheerfulness	xxx
Activity	xxxxxx
Toughness	xxxxxxx
Unpleasantness	x
Sadness	xxxxx
Passivity	xxx
Gentleness	xxxx
Pleasantness	xxxxxx

Masculine sounds/feelings are medium high.
Feminine sounds/feelings are medium low.
Pronunciation is easier.

LLOYD

Cheerfulness	xxx
Activity	xxx
Toughness	xxxxxxx
Unpleasantness	xxxxx
Sadness	xxxxxxxxx
Passivity	xxxxx
Gentleness	xxxx
Pleasantness	xxxxx

Masculine sounds/feelings are medium high.
Feminine sounds/feelings are medium.
Pronunciation is easier.

LONNIE

Cheerfulness	xxx
Activity	x
Toughness	x
Unpleasantness	x
Sadness	xxxxxxxxxxxx
Passivity	xxxxxxxxx
Gentleness	xxxxxxx
Pleasantness	xxxxxxxxxxx

Masculine sounds/feelings are very low.
Feminine sounds/feelings are very high.
Pronunciation is easier.

LOUIS

Cheerfulness	xxx
Activity	xxx
Toughness	xxxx
Unpleasantness	xxxxx
Sadness	xxxxxxxxx
Passivity	xxxxxxx
Gentleness	xxxxxxx
Pleasantness	xxxxxxxxxxx

Masculine sounds/feelings are medium.
Feminine sounds/feelings are very high.
Pronunciation is easier.

LUIS

Cheerfulness	xxx
Activity	xxxxxx
Toughness	xxxxxxx
Unpleasantness	x
Sadness	xxxxx
Passivity	xxxxx
Gentleness	xxxxxxx
Pleasantness	xxxxxxxxxxx

Masculine sounds/feelings are medium high.
Feminine sounds/feelings are high.
Pronunciation is easier.

LUTHER

Cheerfulness	xxx
Activity	xxx
Toughness	xxxx
Unpleasantness	x
Sadness	xxxxx
Passivity	xxxxxxx
Gentleness	xxxxxxx
Pleasantness	xxxxxxxxxxx

Masculine sounds/feelings are medium.
Feminine sounds/feelings are high.
Pronunciation is average.

MANUEL

Cheerfulness	xxx
Activity	xxx
Toughness	xxxx
Unpleasantness	x
Sadness	xxxxxxxx
Passivity	xxxxxxxxxx
Gentleness	xxxxxxxxxx
Pleasantness	xxxxxx

Masculine sounds/feelings are very low.
Feminine sounds/feelings are very high.
Pronunciation is more difficult.

MARC

Cheerfulness	xxx
Activity	xxxxxx
Toughness	xxxxxxx
Unpleasantness	xxxxxxxxx
Sadness	x
Passivity	xxxxx
Gentleness	xxxx
Pleasantness	x

Masculine sounds/feelings are very high.
Feminine sounds/feelings are very low.
Pronunciation is easiest.

MARCUS

Cheerfulness	xxx
Activity	xxxxxx
Toughness	xxxxxxx
Unpleasantness	xxxxxxxxx
Sadness	x
Passivity	xxxxxxx
Gentleness	xxxx
Pleasantness	x

Masculine sounds/feelings are medium high.
Feminine sounds/feelings are very low.
Pronunciation is average.

MARIO

Cheerfulness	xxxxxx
Activity	xxxxxx
Toughness	xxxxxxx
Unpleasantness	xxxxxxxxx
Sadness	xxxxx
Passivity	xxxxxxx
Gentleness	xxxxxxx
Pleasantness	x

Masculine sounds/feelings are high.
Feminine sounds/feelings are medium.
Pronunciation is easier.

MARION

Cheerfulness	xxxxxx
Activity	xxxxxx
Toughness	xxxxxxx
Unpleasantness	xxxxx
Sadness	xxxxx
Passivity	xxxxxxx
Gentleness	xxxxxxx
Pleasantness	x

Masculine sounds/feelings are medium.
Feminine sounds/feelings are medium.
Pronunciation is more difficult.

MARK

Cheerfulness	xxx
Activity	xxxxxx
Toughness	xxxxxxx
Unpleasantness	xxxxxxxxx
Sadness	x
Passivity	xxxxx
Gentleness	xxxx
Pleasantness	x

Masculine sounds/feelings are very high.
Feminine sounds/feelings are very low.
Pronunciation is easiest.

MARSHALL

Cheerfulness	xxx
Activity	xxxxxxxxx
Toughness	xxxxxxx
Unpleasantness	xxxxx
Sadness	xxxxx
Passivity	xxxxxxx
Gentleness	xxxxxxxxxxx
Pleasantness	xxxxxx

Masculine sounds/feelings are medium.
Feminine sounds/feelings are high.
Pronunciation is more difficult.

MARTIN

Cheerfulness	xxxxxx
Activity	xxxxxxxxxxx
Toughness	xxxxxxxxxx
Unpleasantness	xxxxxxxxx
Sadness	xxxxx
Passivity	xxxxx
Gentleness	xxxx
Pleasantness	x

Masculine sounds/feelings are very high.
Feminine sounds/feelings are low.
Pronunciation is average.

MARVIN

Cheerfulness	xxxxxxxxx
Activity	xxxxxxxxx
Toughness	xxxxxxx
Unpleasantness	xxxxx
Sadness	xxxxx
Passivity	xxxxx
Gentleness	xxxxxxx
Pleasantness	xxxxxx

Masculine sounds/feelings are high.
Feminine sounds/feelings are medium.
Pronunciation is more difficult.

MATHEW

Cheerfulness	xxxxxx
Activity	x
Toughness	x
Unpleasantness	x
Sadness	x
Passivity	xxxxx
Gentleness	xxxxxxx
Pleasantness	xxxxxxxxxxx

Masculine sounds/feelings are low.
Feminine sounds/feelings are medium.
Pronunciation is easier.

MATTHEW

Cheerfulness	xxxxx
Activity	xxx
Toughness	xxxx
Unpleasantness	xxxxx
Sadness	x
Passivity	xxxxx
Gentleness	xxxxxx
Pleasantness	xxxxxxxxxx

Masculine sounds/feelings are medium.
Feminine sounds/feelings are medium.
Pronunciation is average.

MAURICE

Cheerfulness	xxx
Activity	xxxxxx
Toughness	xxxxxxx
Unpleasantness	xxxxx
Sadness	x
Passivity	xxxxx
Gentleness	xxxxxxx
Pleasantness	x

Masculine sounds/feelings are medium.
Feminine sounds/feelings are low.
Pronunciation is easier.

MAX

Cheerfulness	x
Activity	x
Toughness	xxxx
Unpleasantness	xxxxx
Sadness	x
Passivity	xxxxxxx
Gentleness	xxxx
Pleasantness	x

Masculine sounds/feelings are medium low.
Feminine sounds/feelings are very low.
Pronunciation is easiest.

MELVIN

Cheerfulness	xxxxxxxxx
Activity	xxx
Toughness	xxxx
Unpleasantness	x
Sadness	xxxxxxxxx
Passivity	xxxxxxxxx
Gentleness	xxxxxxxxxxxxx
Pleasantness	xxxxxxxxxxx

Masculine sounds/feelings are medium low.
Feminine sounds/feelings are very high.
Pronunciation is more difficult.

MICHAEL

Cheerfulness	xxxxxxxxx
Activity	xxxxxx
Toughness	xxxx
Unpleasantness	x
Sadness	xxxxx
Passivity	xxxxxxxxx
Gentleness	xxxxxxxxxxx
Pleasantness	xxxxx

Masculine sounds/feelings are medium.
Feminine sounds/feelings are high.
Pronunciation is more difficult.

MICHEAL

Cheerfulness	xxxxxxxxx
Activity	xxxxxx
Toughness	xxxx
Unpleasantness	x
Sadness	xxxxx
Passivity	xxxxx
Gentleness	xxxxxxxxxx
Pleasantness	xxxxxxxxxxx

Masculine sounds/feelings are medium.
Feminine sounds/feelings are very high.
Pronunciation is easier.

MIGUEL

Cheerfulness	xxxxx
Activity	xxxxx
Toughness	xxxxxx
Unpleasantness	x
Sadness	xxxxx
Passivity	xxxxxx
Gentleness	xxxxxxxxxx
Pleasantness	xxxxx

Masculine sounds/feelings are medium.
Feminine sounds/feelings are high.
Pronunciation is easier.

MIKE

Cheerfulness	xxx
Activity	x
Toughness	xxxx
Unpleasantness	xxxxx
Sadness	x
Passivity	xxxxx
Gentleness	xxxxxx
Pleasantness	xxxxxx

Masculine sounds/feelings are medium.
Feminine sounds/feelings are medium.
Pronunciation is easiest.

MILTON

Cheerfulness	xxx
Activity	xxxxxx
Toughness	xxxxxxx
Unpleasantness	xxxxx
Sadness	xxxxxxxxx
Passivity	xxxxxxx
Gentleness	xxxxxxx
Pleasantness	xxxxxx

Masculine sounds/feelings are medium.
Feminine sounds/feelings are high.
Pronunciation is more difficult.

MITCHELL

Cheerfulness	xxxxxxxxx
Activity	xxxxxxxx
Toughness	xxxxxxx
Unpleasantness	xxxxx
Sadness	xxxxx
Passivity	xxxxxxx
Gentleness	xxxxxxxxxx
Pleasantness	xxxxx

Masculine sounds/feelings are high.
Feminine sounds/feelings are high.
Pronunciation is more difficult.

MORRIS

Cheerfulness	xxx
Activity	xxxxxxxxx
Toughness	xxxxxxxxxx
Unpleasantness	xxxxxxxxx
Sadness	x
Passivity	xxxxx
Gentleness	xxxxxxx
Pleasantness	x

Masculine sounds/feelings are very high.
Feminine sounds/feelings are low.
Pronunciation is more difficult.

NATHAN

Cheerfulness	xxx
Activity	x
Toughness	x
Unpleasantness	x
Sadness	xxxxxxxxx
Passivity	xxxxxxxxx
Gentleness	xxxx
Pleasantness	xxxxxx

Masculine sounds/feelings are very low.
Feminine sounds/feelings are medium high.
Pronunciation is easier.

NATHANIEL

Cheerfulness	xxxxxxxx
Activity	x
Toughness	x
Unpleasantness	x
Sadness	xxxxxxxxxxxx
Passivity	xxxxxxxxxx
Gentleness	xxxxxxxxxxxx
Pleasantness	xxxxxxxxxxxxxxxx

Masculine sounds/feelings are very low.
Feminine sounds/feelings are very high.
Pronunciation is most difficult.

NEIL

Cheerfulness	xxx
Activity	x
Toughness	x
Unpleasantness	x
Sadness	xxxxxxxx
Passivity	xxxxx
Gentleness	xxxxxxx
Pleasantness	xxxxxxxxxxx

Masculine sounds/feelings are low.
Feminine sounds/feelings are very high.
Pronunciation is easiest.

NELSON

Cheerfulness	xxx
Activity	x
Toughness	x
Unpleasantness	x
Sadness	xxxxxxxxxxxx
Passivity	xxxxxxxxx
Gentleness	xxxxxxx
Pleasantness	xxxxxx

Masculine sounds/feelings are very low.
Feminine sounds/feelings are very high.
Pronunciation is more difficult.

NICHOLAS

Cheerfulness	xxxxxxxx
Activity	xxxxxxxx
Toughness	xxxx
Unpleasantness	x
Sadness	xxxxxxxx
Passivity	xxxxxxx
Gentleness	xxxx
Pleasantness	xxxxx

Masculine sounds/feelings are medium.
Feminine sounds/feelings are medium high.
Pronunciation is more difficult.

NICK

Cheerfulness	xxx
Activity	xxx
Toughness	xxxxxxx
Unpleasantness	xxxxx
Sadness	xxxxx
Passivity	xxxxx
Gentleness	x
Pleasantness	x

Masculine sounds/feelings are medium high.
Feminine sounds/feelings are very low.
Pronunciation is easiest.

NORMAN

Cheerfulness	x
Activity	xxx
Toughness	xxxx
Unpleasantness	xxxxx
Sadness	xxxxxxxx
Passivity	xxxxxxxxxx
Gentleness	xxxxxxx
Pleasantness	x

Masculine sounds/feelings are low.
Feminine sounds/feelings are medium high.
Pronunciation is easier.

Men's And Boys' Names

OSCAR

Cheerfulness	xxxxxx
Activity	xxxxxx
Toughness	xxxxxxx
Unpleasantness	xxxxx
Sadness	x
Passivity	xxx
Gentleness	x
Pleasantness	x

Masculine sounds/feelings are very high.
Feminine sounds/feelings are very low.
Pronunciation is easiest.

PATRICK

Cheerfulness	xxx
Activity	xxxxxxxxxxx
Toughness	xxxxxxxxxxxxxxx
Unpleasantness	xxxxxxxxxxxx
Sadness	x
Passivity	xxxxx
Gentleness	x
Pleasantness	x

Masculine sounds/feelings are very high.
Feminine sounds/feelings are very low.
Pronunciation is average.

PAUL

Cheerfulness	x
Activity	xxx
Toughness	xxxx
Unpleasantness	x
Sadness	xxxxx
Passivity	xxxxx
Gentleness	xxxxxxx
Pleasantness	xxxxxx

Masculine sounds/feelings are medium low.
Feminine sounds/feelings are medium.
Pronunciation is easiest.

PEDRO

Cheerfulness	xxx
Activity	xxxxxx
Toughness	xxxxxxxxx
Unpleasantness	xxxxxxxxxxxxx
Sadness	xxxxxxxxx
Passivity	xxxxxxx
Gentleness	xxxx
Pleasantness	x

Masculine sounds/feelings are very high.
Feminine sounds/feelings are medium.
Pronunciation is average.

PERRY

Cheerfulness	xxxxxx
Activity	xxxxxxxxx
Toughness	xxxxxxxxxx
Unpleasantness	xxxxx
Sadness	x
Passivity	x
Gentleness	xxxx
Pleasantness	xxxxxx

Masculine sounds/feelings are very high.
Feminine sounds/feelings are very low.
Pronunciation is easier.

PETER

Cheerfulness	xxxxxx
Activity	xxxxxxxxx
Toughness	xxxxxxxxxx
Unpleasantness	xxxxx
Sadness	x
Passivity	x
Gentleness	xxxx
Pleasantness	xxxxxx

Masculine sounds/feelings are very high.
Feminine sounds/feelings are very low.
Pronunciation is easiest.

PHILIP

Cheerfulness	xxxxxxxx
Activity	xxxxxxxx
Toughness	xxxxxxx
Unpleasantness	x
Sadness	xxxxx
Passivity	xxx
Gentleness	xxxxxx
Pleasantness	xxxxxxxxxxx

Masculine sounds/feelings are medium high.
Feminine sounds/feelings are medium high.
Pronunciation is easier.

PHILLIP

Cheerfulness	xxxxxxxx
Activity	xxxxxxxxxxxx
Toughness	xxxxxxxxxx
Unpleasantness	x
Sadness	xxxxx
Passivity	xxx
Gentleness	xxxx
Pleasantness	xxxxxx

Masculine sounds/feelings are very high.
Feminine sounds/feelings are medium low.
Pronunciation is easier.

RAFAEL

Cheerfulness	xxxxxx
Activity	xxxxxx
Toughness	xxxx
Unpleasantness	xxxxx
Sadness	xxxxx
Passivity	xxxxxxxxx
Gentleness	xxxxxxx
Pleasantness	xxxxxx

Masculine sounds/feelings are medium.
Feminine sounds/feelings are medium high.
Pronunciation is more difficult.

RALPH

Cheerfulness	xxx
Activity	xxxxxx
Toughness	xxxx
Unpleasantness	xxxxx
Sadness	xxxxx
Passivity	xxxxx
Gentleness	xxxxxxx
Pleasantness	xxxxx

Masculine sounds/feelings are medium high.
Feminine sounds/feelings are medium.
Pronunciation is easier.

RAMON

Cheerfulness	x
Activity	xxx
Toughness	xxxx
Unpleasantness	xxxxx
Sadness	xxxxx
Passivity	xxxxxxx
Gentleness	xxxx
Pleasantness	x

Masculine sounds/feelings are low.
Feminine sounds/feelings are medium low.
Pronunciation is average.

RANDALL

Cheerfulness	x
Activity	xxx
Toughness	xxxxxxx
Unpleasantness	xxxxxxxx
Sadness	xxxxxxxxxxxx
Passivity	xxxxxxxxxx
Gentleness	xxxxxxx
Pleasantness	xxxxx

Masculine sounds/feelings are medium.
Feminine sounds/feelings are very high.
Pronunciation is more difficult.

RANDY

Cheerfulness	xxx
Activity	xxx
Toughness	xxxxxxx
Unpleasantness	xxxxxxxxx
Sadness	xxxxxxxxx
Passivity	xxxxxxx
Gentleness	xxxx
Pleasantness	xxxxxx

Masculine sounds/feelings are medium.
Feminine sounds/feelings are medium high.
Pronunciation is easier.

RAUL

Cheerfulness	x
Activity	xxx
Toughness	xxxx
Unpleasantness	xxxxx
Sadness	xxxxx
Passivity	xxxxx
Gentleness	xxxxxxx
Pleasantness	xxxxxx

Masculine sounds/feelings are medium.
Feminine sounds/feelings are medium.
Pronunciation is easier.

RAY

Cheerfulness	x
Activity	xxx
Toughness	xxxx
Unpleasantness	xxxxx
Sadness	x
Passivity	x
Gentleness	x
Pleasantness	x

Masculine sounds/feelings are medium.
Feminine sounds/feelings are very low.
Pronunciation is easiest.

RAYMOND

Cheerfulness	xxx
Activity	xxxxx
Toughness	xxxxxx
Unpleasantness	xxxxxxxxx
Sadness	xxxxxxxxx
Passivity	xxxxxxx
Gentleness	xxxx
Pleasantness	x

Masculine sounds/feelings are medium high.
Feminine sounds/feelings are medium.
Pronunciation is average.

REGINALD

Cheerfulness	xxxxxxxxx
Activity	xxxxxxxxx
Toughness	xxxxxxxxxx
Unpleasantness	xxxxxxxxx
Sadness	xxxxxxxxxxxx
Passivity	xxxxxxxxx
Gentleness	xxxxxxxxxxx
Pleasantness	xxxxxxxxxxx

Masculine sounds/feelings are very high.
Feminine sounds/feelings are very high.
Pronunciation is most difficult.

RENE

Cheerfulness	xxx
Activity	xxx
Toughness	xxxx
Unpleasantness	xxxxx
Sadness	xxxxx
Passivity	xxx
Gentleness	xxxx
Pleasantness	xxxxxx

Masculine sounds/feelings are medium.
Feminine sounds/feelings are medium low.
Pronunciation is easiest.

RICARDO

Cheerfulness	xxxxx
Activity	xxxxxxxxxxx
Toughness	xxxxxxxxxxxxxxx
Unpleasantness	xxxxxxxxxxxxxxxxxxx
Sadness	xxxxxxxx
Passivity	xxxxxx
Gentleness	x
Pleasantness	x

Masculine sounds/feelings are very high.
Feminine sounds/feelings are medium low.
Pronunciation is most difficult.

RICHARD

Cheerfulness	xxxxxxxxx
Activity	xxxxxxxxxxxxxxx
Toughness	xxxxxxxxxxxxx
Unpleasantness	xxxxxxxxxxxx
Sadness	xxxxx
Passivity	xxx
Gentleness	x
Pleasantness	x

Masculine sounds/feelings are very high.
Feminine sounds/feelings are very low.
Pronunciation is most difficult.

RICK

Cheerfulness	xxx
Activity	xxxxxx
Toughness	xxxxxxxxxx
Unpleasantness	xxxxxxxx
Sadness	x
Passivity	xxx
Gentleness	x
Pleasantness	x

Masculine sounds/feelings are very high.
Feminine sounds/feelings are very low.
Pronunciation is easiest.

RICKY

Cheerfulness	xxxxx
Activity	xxxxx
Toughness	xxxxxxxxx
Unpleasantness	xxxxxxxx
Sadness	x
Passivity	xxx
Gentleness	xxxx
Pleasantness	xxxxx

Masculine sounds/feelings are very high.
Feminine sounds/feelings are low.
Pronunciation is easiest.

ROBERT

Cheerfulness	xxx
Activity	xxxxxxxxx
Toughness	xxxxxxxxx
Unpleasantness	xxxxxxxxxxxxxxxxx
Sadness	xxxxxxxxx
Passivity	xxx
Gentleness	x
Pleasantness	x

Masculine sounds/feelings are very high.
Feminine sounds/feelings are very low.
Pronunciation is average.

ROBERTO

Cheerfulness	xxx
Activity	xxxxxxxxxxx
Toughness	xxxxxxxxxxxx
Unpleasantness	xxxxxxxxxxxxxxxxx
Sadness	xxxxxxxxx
Passivity	xxx
Gentleness	x
Pleasantness	x

Masculine sounds/feelings are very high.
Feminine sounds/feelings are very low.
Pronunciation is more difficult.

RODNEY

Cheerfulness	xxxxxx
Activity	xxxxxx
Toughness	xxxxxxx
Unpleasantness	xxxxxxxx
Sadness	xxxxxxxxx
Passivity	xxxxx
Gentleness	xxxx
Pleasantness	xxxxxx

Masculine sounds/feelings are high.
Feminine sounds/feelings are medium.
Pronunciation is easier.

ROGER

Cheerfulness	xxxxxx
Activity	xxxxxxxxx
Toughness	xxxxxxx
Unpleasantness	xxxxxxxxx
Sadness	xxxxx
Passivity	xxx
Gentleness	x
Pleasantness	x

Masculine sounds/feelings are very high.
Feminine sounds/feelings are very low.
Pronunciation is more difficult.

ROLAND

Cheerfulness	xxx
Activity	xxxxxx
Toughness	xxxxxxx
Unpleasantness	xxxxxxxxx
Sadness	xxxxxxxxxxxx
Passivity	xxxxxxxxx
Gentleness	xxxx
Pleasantness	xxxxxx

Masculine sounds/feelings are medium high.
Feminine sounds/feelings are very high.
Pronunciation is more difficult.

RON

Cheerfulness	x
Activity	xxx
Toughness	xxxx
Unpleasantness	xxxxx
Sadness	xxxxx
Passivity	xxxxx
Gentleness	x
Pleasantness	x

Masculine sounds/feelings are medium.
Feminine sounds/feelings are very low.
Pronunciation is easiest.

RONALD

Cheerfulness	x
Activity	xxx
Toughness	xxxxxxx
Unpleasantness	xxxxxxxxx
Sadness	xxxxxxxxxxxxx
Passivity	xxxxxxxxxxx
Gentleness	xxxxxxx
Pleasantness	xxxxxx

Masculine sounds/feelings are medium.
Feminine sounds/feelings are very high.
Pronunciation is more difficult.

RONNIE

Cheerfulness	xxx
Activity	xxx
Toughness	xxxx
Unpleasantness	xxxxx
Sadness	xxxxxxxxx
Passivity	xxxxxxx
Gentleness	xxxx
Pleasantness	xxxxxx

Masculine sounds/feelings are low.
Feminine sounds/feelings are medium high.
Pronunciation is easier.

ROSS

Cheerfulness	x
Activity	xxx
Toughness	xxxx
Unpleasantness	xxxxx
Sadness	x
Passivity	xxx
Gentleness	xxxx
Pleasantness	x

Masculine sounds/feelings are medium.
Feminine sounds/feelings are very low.
Pronunciation is easiest.

ROY

Cheerfulness	xxx
Activity	xxxxxx
Toughness	xxxxxxx
Unpleasantness	xxxxx
Sadness	x
Passivity	x
Gentleness	x
Pleasantness	x

Masculine sounds/feelings are high.
Feminine sounds/feelings are very low.
Pronunciation is easier.

RUBEN

Cheerfulness	xxx
Activity	xxxxxx
Toughness	xxxxxxx
Unpleasantness	xxxxxxxx
Sadness	xxxxxxxx
Passivity	xxxxx
Gentleness	xxxx
Pleasantness	x

Masculine sounds/feelings are medium high.
Feminine sounds/feelings are medium.
Pronunciation is easier.

RUSSELL

Cheerfulness	xxx
Activity	xxx
Toughness	xxxx
Unpleasantness	xxxxx
Sadness	xxxxx
Passivity	xxxxxx
Gentleness	xxxxxx
Pleasantness	xxxxx

Masculine sounds/feelings are low.
Feminine sounds/feelings are medium.
Pronunciation is more difficult.

RYAN

Cheerfulness	xxx
Activity	xxx
Toughness	xxxx
Unpleasantness	xxxxx
Sadness	xxxxx
Passivity	xxxxx
Gentleness	xxxx
Pleasantness	xxxxxx

Masculine sounds/feelings are medium.
Feminine sounds/feelings are medium.
Pronunciation is easiest.

SALVADOR

Cheerfulness	xxxxxx
Activity	xxx
Toughness	xxxxxxx
Unpleasantness	xxxxx
Sadness	xxxxxxxx
Passivity	xxxxxxxx
Gentleness	xxxxxxxxxx
Pleasantness	xxxxxxxxxxx

Masculine sounds/feelings are medium.
Feminine sounds/feelings are very high.
Pronunciation is most difficult.

Men's And Boys' Names

SAM

Cheerfulness	x
Activity	x
Toughness	x
Unpleasantness	x
Sadness	x
Passivity	xxxxx
Gentleness	xxxx
Pleasantness	x

Masculine sounds/feelings are very low.
Feminine sounds/feelings are very low.
Pronunciation is easiest.

SAMUEL

Cheerfulness	xxx
Activity	xxx
Toughness	xxxx
Unpleasantness	x
Sadness	xxxxx
Passivity	xxxxxxxxx
Gentleness	xxxxxxxxxxx
Pleasantness	xxxxxx

Masculine sounds/feelings are very low.
Feminine sounds/feelings are high.
Pronunciation is more difficult.

SCOTT

Cheerfulness	xxx
Activity	xxxxxxxxx
Toughness	xxxxxxxxxx
Unpleasantness	xxxxxxxxxxxx
Sadness	x
Passivity	xxx
Gentleness	x
Pleasantness	x

Masculine sounds/feelings are very high.
Feminine sounds/feelings are very low.
Pronunciation is easier.

SEAN

Cheerfulness	xxx
Activity	x
Toughness	x
Unpleasantness	x
Sadness	xxxxx
Passivity	xxx
Gentleness	xxxx
Pleasantness	xxxxxx

Masculine sounds/feelings are low.
Feminine sounds/feelings are medium low.
Pronunciation is easiest.

SERGIO

Cheerfulness	xxxxxxxxx
Activity	xxxxxxxxx
Toughness	xxxxxxx
Unpleasantness	xxxxx
Sadness	xxxxx
Passivity	xxx
Gentleness	x
Pleasantness	x

Masculine sounds/feelings are high.
Feminine sounds/feelings are very low.
Pronunciation is more difficult.

SETH

Cheerfulness	xxxxxx
Activity	x
Toughness	x
Unpleasantness	x
Sadness	x
Passivity	xxx
Gentleness	xxxxxxx
Pleasantness	xxxxxx

Masculine sounds/feelings are low.
Feminine sounds/feelings are medium low.
Pronunciation is easier.

SHANE

Cheerfulness	x
Activity	xxx
Toughness	xxxx
Unpleasantness	x
Sadness	xxxxx
Passivity	xxx
Gentleness	x
Pleasantness	x

Masculine sounds/feelings are medium low.
Feminine sounds/feelings are very low.
Pronunciation is easiest.

SHAWN

Cheerfulness	x
Activity	xxx
Toughness	xxxx
Unpleasantness	x
Sadness	xxxxx
Passivity	xxxxx
Gentleness	xxxx
Pleasantness	x

Masculine sounds/feelings are medium low.
Feminine sounds/feelings are low.
Pronunciation is easiest.

SIDNEY

Cheerfulness	xxxxx
Activity	xxx
Toughness	xxxxxxx
Unpleasantness	xxxxx
Sadness	xxxxxxxx
Passivity	xxxxx
Gentleness	xxxx
Pleasantness	xxxxxx

Masculine sounds/feelings are medium.
Feminine sounds/feelings are medium.
Pronunciation is easier.

STANLEY

Cheerfulness	xxx
Activity	xxx
Toughness	xxxx
Unpleasantness	xxxxx
Sadness	xxxxxxxx
Passivity	xxxxxx
Gentleness	xxxxxxx
Pleasantness	xxxxxxxxxxx

Masculine sounds/feelings are low.
Feminine sounds/feelings are very high.
Pronunciation is more difficult.

STEPHEN

Cheerfulness	xxxxxxxx
Activity	xxxxxx
Toughness	xxxx
Unpleasantness	xxxxx
Sadness	xxxxx
Passivity	xxxxxxx
Gentleness	xxxxxxx
Pleasantness	x

Masculine sounds/feelings are medium.
Feminine sounds/feelings are medium.
Pronunciation is average.

STEVE

Cheerfulness	xxxxxx
Activity	xxx
Toughness	xxxx
Unpleasantness	xxxxx
Sadness	x
Passivity	x
Gentleness	xxxxxxx
Pleasantness	xxxxxxxxxxx

Masculine sounds/feelings are medium high.
Feminine sounds/feelings are medium.
Pronunciation is easier.

Men's And Boys' Names

STEVEN

Cheerfulness	xxxxxxxx
Activity	xxx
Toughness	xxxx
Unpleasantness	xxxxx
Sadness	xxxxx
Passivity	xxxxx
Gentleness	xxxxxxxxxxx
Pleasantness	xxxxxxxxxxx

Masculine sounds/feelings are medium.
Feminine sounds/feelings are very high.
Pronunciation is average.

STUART

Cheerfulness	xxxxxx
Activity	xxxxxxxxxxxxxxx
Toughness	xxxxxxxxxx
Unpleasantness	xxxxxxxxx
Sadness	x
Passivity	x
Gentleness	x
Pleasantness	x

Masculine sounds/feelings are very high.
Feminine sounds/feelings are very low.
Pronunciation is more difficult.

TED

Cheerfulness	xxx
Activity	xxx
Toughness	xxxxxxx
Unpleasantness	xxxxxxxxx
Sadness	xxxxx
Passivity	xxxxx
Gentleness	xxxx
Pleasantness	x

Masculine sounds/feelings are high.
Feminine sounds/feelings are low.
Pronunciation is easiest.

TERRANCE

Cheerfulness	xxx
Activity	xxxxxxxx
Toughness	xxxxxxxxxx
Unpleasantness	xxxxxxxxx
Sadness	xxxxx
Passivity	xxxxx
Gentleness	x
Pleasantness	x

Masculine sounds/feelings are very high.
Feminine sounds/feelings are very low.
Pronunciation is more difficult.

TERRENCE

Cheerfulness	xxxxxx
Activity	xxxxxxxxx
Toughness	xxxxxxxxxx
Unpleasantness	xxxxxxxxx
Sadness	xxxxx
Passivity	xxxxx
Gentleness	xxxx
Pleasantness	x

Masculine sounds/feelings are very high.
Feminine sounds/feelings are low.
Pronunciation is more difficult.

TERRY

Cheerfulness	xxxxxx
Activity	xxxxxxxx
Toughness	xxxxxxxxxx
Unpleasantness	xxxxxxxxx
Sadness	x
Passivity	x
Gentleness	xxxx
Pleasantness	xxxxxx

Masculine sounds/feelings are very high.
Feminine sounds/feelings are very low.
Pronunciation is easier.

THEODORE

Cheerfulness	xxxxxxxx
Activity	xxxxxx
Toughness	xxxxxxx
Unpleasantness	xxxxxxxx
Sadness	xxxxx
Passivity	xxxxx
Gentleness	xxxxxxxxxx
Pleasantness	xxxxxxxxxxx

Masculine sounds/feelings are very high.
Feminine sounds/feelings are very high.
Pronunciation is more difficult.

THOMAS

Cheerfulness	xxxxxx
Activity	xxx
Toughness	x
Unpleasantness	x
Sadness	x
Passivity	xxxxx
Gentleness	xxxxxxx
Pleasantness	xxxxxx

Masculine sounds/feelings are very low.
Feminine sounds/feelings are medium.
Pronunciation is easier.

TIM

Cheerfulness	xxx
Activity	xxxxxx
Toughness	xxxxxxx
Unpleasantness	xxxxx
Sadness	x
Passivity	xxx
Gentleness	xxxx
Pleasantness	x

Masculine sounds/feelings are high.
Feminine sounds/feelings are very low.
Pronunciation is easiest.

TIMOTHY

Cheerfulness	xxxxxxxxxxxx
Activity	xxxxxxxxx
Toughness	xxxxxxx
Unpleasantness	xxxxx
Sadness	x
Passivity	xxx
Gentleness	xxxxxxxxxx
Pleasantness	xxxxxxxxxxxx

Masculine sounds/feelings are very high.
Feminine sounds/feelings are medium high.
Pronunciation is average.

TODD

Cheerfulness	xxx
Activity	xxxxxx
Toughness	xxxxxxxxxx
Unpleasantness	xxxxxxxxxxxxx
Sadness	xxxxxxxxx
Passivity	xxxxx
Gentleness	x
Pleasantness	x

Masculine sounds/feelings are very high.
Feminine sounds/feelings are low.
Pronunciation is easier.

TOM

Cheerfulness	xxx
Activity	xxxxxx
Toughness	xxxx
Unpleasantness	xxxxx
Sadness	x
Passivity	xxx
Gentleness	xxxx
Pleasantness	x

Masculine sounds/feelings are medium high.
Feminine sounds/feelings are very low.
Pronunciation is easiest.

Men's And Boys' Names

TOMMY

Cheerfulness	xxxxxx
Activity	xxxxxx
Toughness	xxxx
Unpleasantness	xxxxx
Sadness	x
Passivity	xxxxx
Gentleness	xxxxxxxxxx
Pleasantness	xxxxxx

Masculine sounds/feelings are medium.
Feminine sounds/feelings are medium.
Pronunciation is easiest.

TONY

Cheerfulness	xxx
Activity	xxx
Toughness	xxxx
Unpleasantness	xxxxx
Sadness	xxxxx
Passivity	xxxxx
Gentleness	xxxx
Pleasantness	xxxxxx

Masculine sounds/feelings are medium.
Feminine sounds/feelings are medium.
Pronunciation is easiest.

TRACY

Cheerfulness	xxx
Activity	xxxxxx
Toughness	xxxxxxx
Unpleasantness	xxxxxxxxx
Sadness	x
Passivity	x
Gentleness	xxxx
Pleasantness	xxxxxx

Masculine sounds/feelings are medium high.
Feminine sounds/feelings are very low.
Pronunciation is average.

TRAVIS

Cheerfulness	xxxxxx
Activity	xxxxxxxxx
Toughness	xxxxxxxxxx
Unpleasantness	xxxxxxxxx
Sadness	x
Passivity	xxx
Gentleness	xxxx
Pleasantness	xxxxxx

Masculine sounds/feelings are very high.
Feminine sounds/feelings are low.
Pronunciation is more difficult.

TROY

Cheerfulness	xxx
Activity	xxxxxxxx
Toughness	xxxxxxxxxx
Unpleasantness	xxxxxxxxx
Sadness	x
Passivity	x
Gentleness	x
Pleasantness	x

Masculine sounds/feelings are very high.
Feminine sounds/feelings are very low.
Pronunciation is easier.

TYLER

Cheerfulness	xxxxxx
Activity	xxxxxx
Toughness	xxxxxxx
Unpleasantness	xxxxx
Sadness	xxxxx
Passivity	xxx
Gentleness	xxxxxxx
Pleasantness	xxxxxxxxxxxx

Masculine sounds/feelings are very high.
Feminine sounds/feelings are medium high.
Pronunciation is easier.

TYRONE

Cheerfulness	xxx
Activity	xxxxxx
Toughness	xxxxxxx
Unpleasantness	xxxxxxxxxxxx
Sadness	xxxxxxxxx
Passivity	xxxxx
Gentleness	xxxx
Pleasantness	xxxxxx

Masculine sounds/feelings are high.
Feminine sounds/feelings are medium.
Pronunciation is easier.

VERNON

Cheerfulness	xxxxxx
Activity	xxx
Toughness	xxxx
Unpleasantness	x
Sadness	xxxxxxxxx
Passivity	xxxxx
Gentleness	xxxx
Pleasantness	xxxxxx

Masculine sounds/feelings are low.
Feminine sounds/feelings are medium.
Pronunciation is more difficult.

VICTOR

Cheerfulness	xxxxxxxxx
Activity	xxxxxxxxx
Toughness	xxxxxxxxxxxxx
Unpleasantness	xxxxxxxxx
Sadness	x
Passivity	xxx
Gentleness	xxxx
Pleasantness	xxxxxx

Masculine sounds/feelings are very high.
Feminine sounds/feelings are low.
Pronunciation is average.

VINCENT

Cheerfulness	xxxxxxxxx
Activity	xxxxxx
Toughness	xxxxxxx
Unpleasantness	xxxxx
Sadness	xxxxxxxxx
Passivity	xxxxxx
Gentleness	xxxxxxx
Pleasantness	xxxxx

Masculine sounds/feelings are medium high.
Feminine sounds/feelings are high.
Pronunciation is more difficult.

VIRGIL

Cheerfulness	xxxxxxxxxxxx
Activity	xxxxxxxxx
Toughness	xxxxxxx
Unpleasantness	x
Sadness	xxxxx
Passivity	xxx
Gentleness	xxxxxxx
Pleasantness	xxxxxxxxxxxx

Masculine sounds/feelings are high.
Feminine sounds/feelings are medium high.
Pronunciation is most difficult.

WADE

Cheerfulness	xxx
Activity	x
Toughness	xxxx
Unpleasantness	xxxxx
Sadness	xxxxx
Passivity	xxx
Gentleness	x
Pleasantness	xxxxxx

Masculine sounds/feelings are medium.
Feminine sounds/feelings are low.
Pronunciation is easiest.

Men's And Boys' Names

WALLACE

Cheerfulness	xxx
Activity	x
Toughness	x
Unpleasantness	x
Sadness	xxxxx
Passivity	xxxxx
Gentleness	xxxxxxx
Pleasantness	xxxxxxxxxxx

Masculine sounds/feelings are very low.
Feminine sounds/feelings are high.
Pronunciation is average.

WALTER

Cheerfulness	xxxxxx
Activity	xxxxxx
Toughness	xxxxxxx
Unpleasantness	xxxxx
Sadness	xxxxx
Passivity	xxxxx
Gentleness	xxxxxxx
Pleasantness	xxxxxxxxxxxx

Masculine sounds/feelings are medium.
Feminine sounds/feelings are high.
Pronunciation is average.

WARREN

Cheerfulness	xxxxxx
Activity	xxxxxx
Toughness	xxxxxxx
Unpleasantness	xxxxxxxx
Sadness	xxxxx
Passivity	xxxxxxx
Gentleness	xxxxxxx
Pleasantness	xxxxxx

Masculine sounds/feelings are high.
Feminine sounds/feelings are medium.
Pronunciation is more difficult.

WAYNE

Cheerfulness	xxx
Activity	x
Toughness	x
Unpleasantness	x
Sadness	xxxxx
Passivity	xxx
Gentleness	x
Pleasantness	xxxxx

Masculine sounds/feelings are low.
Feminine sounds/feelings are low.
Pronunciation is easiest.

WESLEY

Cheerfulness	xxxxxxxxx
Activity	x
Toughness	x
Unpleasantness	x
Sadness	xxxxx
Passivity	xxxxx
Gentleness	xxxxxxxxxx
Pleasantness	xxxxxxxxxxxxxxxx

Masculine sounds/feelings are very low.
Feminine sounds/feelings are very high.
Pronunciation is more difficult.

WILLARD

Cheerfulness	xxxxxxxxx
Activity	xxxxxxxxx
Toughness	xxxxxxxxxx
Unpleasantness	xxxxxxxx
Sadness	xxxxxxxxx
Passivity	xxxxx
Gentleness	xxxx
Pleasantness	xxxxxxxxxxxx

Masculine sounds/feelings are very high.
Feminine sounds/feelings are high.
Pronunciation is more difficult.

WILLIAM

Cheerfulness	xxxxxxxx
Activity	xxxxx
Toughness	xxxxxx
Unpleasantness	x

Sadness	xxxx
Passivity	xxxxxx
Gentleness	xxxxxx
Pleasantness	xxxxxxxxxx

Masculine sounds/feelings are medium.
Feminine sounds/feelings are high.
Pronunciation is average.

WILLIE

Cheerfulness	xxxxxxxx
Activity	xxx
Toughness	xxxx
Unpleasantness	x

Sadness	xxxxx
Passivity	xxx
Gentleness	xxxxxxx
Pleasantness	xxxxxxxxxxxxxxxx

Masculine sounds/feelings are medium.
Feminine sounds/feelings are very high.
Pronunciation is easiest.

ZACHARY

Cheerfulness	xxxxxxxx
Activity	xxxxxxxx
Toughness	xxxx
Unpleasantness	xxxxx

Sadness	x
Passivity	xxxxx
Gentleness	xxxxxxx
Pleasantness	xxxxxxxxxxx

Masculine sounds/feelings are medium high.
Feminine sounds/feelings are medium.
Pronunciation is more difficult.

WOMEN'S AND GIRLS' NAMES

ABBY

Cheerfulness	xxx
Activity	x
Toughness	x
Unpleasantness	xxxxxxxx
Sadness	xxxxxxxx
Passivity	xxx
Gentleness	xxxx
Pleasantness	xxxxxx

Masculine sounds/feelings are medium.
Feminine sounds/feelings are medium.
Pronunciation is easiest.

ABIGAIL

Cheerfulness	xxx
Activity	xxxxxx
Toughness	xxxxxxx
Unpleasantness	xxxxx
Sadness	xxxxxxxxx
Passivity	xxxxx
Gentleness	xxxx
Pleasantness	xxxxxx

Masculine sounds/feelings are medium.
Feminine sounds/feelings are medium.
Pronunciation is easier.

ADA

Cheerfulness	x
Activity	x
Toughness	xxxx
Unpleasantness	xxxxx
Sadness	xxxxx
Passivity	xxxxx
Gentleness	x
Pleasantness	x

Masculine sounds/feelings are medium low.
Feminine sounds/feelings are very low.
Pronunciation is easier.

ADDIE

Cheerfulness	xxx
Activity	x
Toughness	xxxxxx
Unpleasantness	xxxxxxxx
Sadness	xxxxxxxx
Passivity	xxxxxx
Gentleness	xxxx
Pleasantness	xxxxx

Masculine sounds/feelings are medium high.
Feminine sounds/feelings are medium high.
Pronunciation is easiest.

ADELA

Cheerfulness	xxx
Activity	x
Toughness	xxxx
Unpleasantness	xxxxx
Sadness	xxxxxxxx
Passivity	xxxxxxxx
Gentleness	xxxxxx
Pleasantness	xxxxx

Masculine sounds/feelings are low.
Feminine sounds/feelings are very high.
Pronunciation is more difficult.

ADELE

Cheerfulness	xxx
Activity	x
Toughness	xxxx
Unpleasantness	xxxxx
Sadness	xxxxxxxx
Passivity	xxxxxxx
Gentleness	xxxxxxx
Pleasantness	xxxxxxxxxxx

Masculine sounds/feelings are medium.
Feminine sounds/feelings are very high.
Pronunciation is easiest.

ADELINE

Cheerfulness	xxxxxx
Activity	xxx
Toughness	xxxxxxx
Unpleasantness	xxxxx

Sadness	xxxxxxxxxxxx
Passivity	xxxxxxxxxxx
Gentleness	xxxxxxx
Pleasantness	xxxxxx

Masculine sounds/feelings are medium.
Feminine sounds/feelings are very high.
Pronunciation is more difficult.

ADRIANA

Cheerfulness	xxx
Activity	xxxxxx
Toughness	xxxxxxxxxx
Unpleasantness	xxxxxxxxx

Sadness	xxxxxxxxx
Passivity	xxxxxxxxx
Gentleness	x
Pleasantness	x

Masculine sounds/feelings are high.
Feminine sounds/feelings are medium.
Pronunciation is most difficult.

ADRIENNE

Cheerfulness	xxxxxx
Activity	xxx
Toughness	xxxxxxx
Unpleasantness	xxxxxxxxx

Sadness	xxxxxxxxxxxx
Passivity	xxxxxxxxxxx
Gentleness	xxxxxxx
Pleasantness	xxxxxx

Masculine sounds/feelings are medium high.
Feminine sounds/feelings are very high.
Pronunciation is more difficult.

AGNES

Cheerfulness	x
Activity	xxx
Toughness	xxxx
Unpleasantness	x

Sadness	xxxxx
Passivity	xxxxxxx
Gentleness	xxxx
Pleasantness	xxxxx

Masculine sounds/feelings are medium low.
Feminine sounds/feelings are medium.
Pronunciation is easiest.

AIDA

Cheerfulness	x
Activity	x
Toughness	xxxx
Unpleasantness	xxxxx

Sadness	xxxxx
Passivity	xxx
Gentleness	x
Pleasantness	x

Masculine sounds/feelings are medium low.
Feminine sounds/feelings are very low.
Pronunciation is easier.

AILEEN

Cheerfulness	xxx
Activity	x
Toughness	x
Unpleasantness	x

Sadness	xxxxxxxxx
Passivity	xxxxx
Gentleness	xxxxxxx
Pleasantness	xxxxxxxxxxx

Masculine sounds/feelings are low.
Feminine sounds/feelings are very high.
Pronunciation is easiest.

AIMEE

Cheerfulness	xxx
Activity	x
Toughness	x
Unpleasantness	x
Sadness	x
Passivity	xxx
Gentleness	xxxxxx
Pleasantness	xxxxxx

Masculine sounds/feelings are low.
Feminine sounds/feelings are medium low.
Pronunciation is easiest.

ALANA

Cheerfulness	x
Activity	x
Toughness	x
Unpleasantness	x
Sadness	xxxxxxxx
Passivity	xxxxxxx
Gentleness	xxxx
Pleasantness	xxxxxx

Masculine sounds/feelings are very low.
Feminine sounds/feelings are medium high.
Pronunciation is more difficult.

ALBERTA

Cheerfulness	xxx
Activity	xxxxxx
Toughness	xxxxxxx
Unpleasantness	xxxxxxxx
Sadness	xxxxxxxx
Passivity	xxxxx
Gentleness	xxxxxxx
Pleasantness	xxxxxx

Masculine sounds/feelings are medium high.
Feminine sounds/feelings are medium high.
Pronunciation is more difficult.

ALEJANDRA

Cheerfulness	xxxxx
Activity	xxxxxx
Toughness	xxxxxx
Unpleasantness	xxxxxxxx
Sadness	xxxxxxxxxxx
Passivity	xxxxxxxxxx
Gentleness	xxxxxxx
Pleasantness	xxxxx

Masculine sounds/feelings are high.
Feminine sounds/feelings are very high.
Pronunciation is most difficult.

ALEXANDRA

Cheerfulness	xxx
Activity	xxx
Toughness	xxxxxxxxx
Unpleasantness	xxxxxxxxxxxx
Sadness	xxxxxxxxxxxx
Passivity	xxxxxxxxxxxxx
Gentleness	xxxxxxx
Pleasantness	xxxxx

Masculine sounds/feelings are high.
Feminine sounds/feelings are very high.
Pronunciation is most difficult.

ALEXANDRIA

Cheerfulness	xxxxx
Activity	xxxxxx
Toughness	xxxxxxxxxxxx
Unpleasantness	xxxxxxxxxxxx
Sadness	xxxxxxxxxxxx
Passivity	xxxxxxxxxxxxx
Gentleness	xxxxxxx
Pleasantness	xxxxx

Masculine sounds/feelings are very high.
Feminine sounds/feelings are very high.
Pronunciation is most difficult.

ALEXIS

Cheerfulness	xxxxx
Activity	xxx
Toughness	xxxxxxx
Unpleasantness	xxxxx
Sadness	xxxxx
Passivity	xxxxxxx
Gentleness	xxxxxxx
Pleasantness	xxxxxx

Masculine sounds/feelings are medium.
Feminine sounds/feelings are medium.
Pronunciation is most difficult.

ALICE

Cheerfulness	xxx
Activity	xxx
Toughness	xxxx
Unpleasantness	x
Sadness	xxxxx
Passivity	xxx
Gentleness	xxxx
Pleasantness	xxxxxx

Masculine sounds/feelings are medium.
Feminine sounds/feelings are medium low.
Pronunciation is average.

ALICIA

Cheerfulness	xxx
Activity	xxxxxx
Toughness	xxxxxxx
Unpleasantness	x
Sadness	xxxxx
Passivity	xxx
Gentleness	xxxx
Pleasantness	xxxxxx

Masculine sounds/feelings are medium low.
Feminine sounds/feelings are medium low.
Pronunciation is most difficult.

ALINE

Cheerfulness	xxx
Activity	xxx
Toughness	xxxx
Unpleasantness	x
Sadness	xxxxxxxxx
Passivity	xxxxx
Gentleness	xxxx
Pleasantness	xxxxxx

Masculine sounds/feelings are medium.
Feminine sounds/feelings are medium.
Pronunciation is easier.

ALISA

Cheerfulness	xxx
Activity	xxx
Toughness	xxxx
Unpleasantness	x
Sadness	xxxxx
Passivity	xxxxx
Gentleness	xxxxxxx
Pleasantness	xxxxxxxxxxxx

Masculine sounds/feelings are very low.
Feminine sounds/feelings are high.
Pronunciation is most difficult.

ALISHA

Cheerfulness	xxx
Activity	xxxxxx
Toughness	xxxxxxx
Unpleasantness	x
Sadness	xxxxx
Passivity	xxx
Gentleness	xxxx
Pleasantness	xxxxxx

Masculine sounds/feelings are medium low.
Feminine sounds/feelings are medium low.
Pronunciation is most difficult.

ALISON

Cheerfulness	xxx
Activity	xxx
Toughness	xxxx
Unpleasantness	x
Sadness	xxxxxxxx
Passivity	xxxxxx
Gentleness	xxxxxx
Pleasantness	xxxxxxxxxx

Masculine sounds/feelings are very low.
Feminine sounds/feelings are very high.
Pronunciation is most difficult.

ALISSA

Cheerfulness	xxx
Activity	xxx
Toughness	xxxx
Unpleasantness	x
Sadness	xxxxx
Passivity	xxx
Gentleness	xxxx
Pleasantness	xxxxxx

Masculine sounds/feelings are very low.
Feminine sounds/feelings are medium low.
Pronunciation is most difficult.

ALLIE

Cheerfulness	xxx
Activity	x
Toughness	x
Unpleasantness	x
Sadness	xxxxx
Passivity	xxxxx
Gentleness	xxxxxxxxxx
Pleasantness	xxxxxxxxxxx

Masculine sounds/feelings are low.
Feminine sounds/feelings are very high.
Pronunciation is easiest.

ALLISON

Cheerfulness	xxx
Activity	xxx
Toughness	xxxx
Unpleasantness	x
Sadness	xxxxxxxx
Passivity	xxxxxxxxx
Gentleness	xxxxxxxxxxx
Pleasantness	xxxxxxxxxxx

Masculine sounds/feelings are very low.
Feminine sounds/feelings are very high.
Pronunciation is more difficult.

ALLYSON

Cheerfulness	xxx
Activity	xxx
Toughness	xxxx
Unpleasantness	x
Sadness	xxxxxxxxx
Passivity	xxxxxxx
Gentleness	xxxxxxx
Pleasantness	xxxxxx

Masculine sounds/feelings are very low.
Feminine sounds/feelings are high.
Pronunciation is more difficult.

ALMA

Cheerfulness	x
Activity	x
Toughness	x
Unpleasantness	x
Sadness	xxxxx
Passivity	xxxxxxx
Gentleness	xxxxxxxxxx
Pleasantness	xxxxx

Masculine sounds/feelings are very low.
Feminine sounds/feelings are high.
Pronunciation is average.

ALTA

Cheerfulness	x
Activity	xxx
Toughness	xxxx
Unpleasantness	xxxxx
Sadness	xxxxx
Passivity	xxxxx
Gentleness	xxxxxxx
Pleasantness	xxxxxx

Masculine sounds/feelings are medium.
Feminine sounds/feelings are medium.
Pronunciation is average.

ALTHEA

Cheerfulness	xxxxxx
Activity	x
Toughness	x
Unpleasantness	x
Sadness	xxxxx
Passivity	xxxxx
Gentleness	xxxxxxxxxxxx
Pleasantness	xxxxxxxxxxxxxxxx

Masculine sounds/feelings are very low.
Feminine sounds/feelings are very high.
Pronunciation is more difficult.

ALYCE

Cheerfulness	xxx
Activity	xxx
Toughness	xxxx
Unpleasantness	x
Sadness	xxxxx
Passivity	xxxxx
Gentleness	xxxx
Pleasantness	xxxxxx

Masculine sounds/feelings are medium.
Feminine sounds/feelings are medium.
Pronunciation is easier.

ALYSSA

Cheerfulness	xxx
Activity	xxx
Toughness	xxxx
Unpleasantness	x
Sadness	xxxxx
Passivity	xxxxx
Gentleness	xxxx
Pleasantness	xxxxxx

Masculine sounds/feelings are very low.
Feminine sounds/feelings are medium.
Pronunciation is more difficult.

AMALIA

Cheerfulness	xxx
Activity	xxx
Toughness	xxxx
Unpleasantness	x
Sadness	xxxxx
Passivity	xxxxxxx
Gentleness	xxxxxxx
Pleasantness	xxxxxx

Masculine sounds/feelings are very low.
Feminine sounds/feelings are medium.
Pronunciation is more difficult.

AMANDA

Cheerfulness	x
Activity	x
Toughness	xxxx
Unpleasantness	xxxxx
Sadness	xxxxxxxxx
Passivity	xxxxxxxxxxx
Gentleness	xxxx
Pleasantness	x

Masculine sounds/feelings are very low.
Feminine sounds/feelings are medium.
Pronunciation is average.

AMBER

Cheerfulness	xxx
Activity	xxx
Toughness	xxxx
Unpleasantness	xxxxx
Sadness	xxxxx
Passivity	xxxxx
Gentleness	xxxx
Pleasantness	x

Masculine sounds/feelings are medium.
Feminine sounds/feelings are low.
Pronunciation is easiest.

AMELIA

Cheerfulness	xxxxxx
Activity	xxx
Toughness	xxxx
Unpleasantness	x
Sadness	xxxxx
Passivity	xxxxxxxx
Gentleness	xxxxxxxxxx
Pleasantness	xxxxxx

Masculine sounds/feelings are low.
Feminine sounds/feelings are high.
Pronunciation is more difficult.

AMIE

Cheerfulness	xxx
Activity	x
Toughness	x
Unpleasantness	x
Sadness	x
Passivity	xxx
Gentleness	xxxxxxx
Pleasantness	xxxxxx

Masculine sounds/feelings are low.
Feminine sounds/feelings are medium low.
Pronunciation is easiest.

AMY

Cheerfulness	xxx
Activity	x
Toughness	x
Unpleasantness	x
Sadness	x
Passivity	xxx
Gentleness	xxxxxx
Pleasantness	xxxxx

Masculine sounds/feelings are low.
Feminine sounds/feelings are medium low.
Pronunciation is easiest.

ANA

Cheerfulness	x
Activity	x
Toughness	x
Unpleasantness	x
Sadness	xxxxx
Passivity	xxxxx
Gentleness	x
Pleasantness	x

Masculine sounds/feelings are very low.
Feminine sounds/feelings are very low.
Pronunciation is easiest.

ANASTASIA

Cheerfulness	xxx
Activity	xxxxxx
Toughness	xxxxxxx
Unpleasantness	xxxxx
Sadness	xxxxx
Passivity	xxxxxxx
Gentleness	x
Pleasantness	x

Masculine sounds/feelings are medium.
Feminine sounds/feelings are very low.
Pronunciation is most difficult.

ANDREA

Cheerfulness	xxx
Activity	xxx
Toughness	xxxxxx
Unpleasantness	xxxxxxxx
Sadness	xxxxxxxx
Passivity	xxxxxx
Gentleness	xxxx
Pleasantness	xxxxx

Masculine sounds/feelings are medium.
Feminine sounds/feelings are medium high.
Pronunciation is more difficult.

ANGEL

Cheerfulness	xxxxxx
Activity	xxx
Toughness	x
Unpleasantness	x
Sadness	xxxxxxxxx
Passivity	xxxxxx
Gentleness	xxxxxx
Pleasantness	xxxxx

Masculine sounds/feelings are very low.
Feminine sounds/feelings are high.
Pronunciation is more difficult.

ANGELA

Cheerfulness	xxxxxx
Activity	xxx
Toughness	x
Unpleasantness	x
Sadness	xxxxxxxxx
Passivity	xxxxxx
Gentleness	xxxxxx
Pleasantness	xxxxxx

Masculine sounds/feelings are very low.
Feminine sounds/feelings are high.
Pronunciation is most difficult.

ANGELIA

Cheerfulness	xxxxxxxx
Activity	xxxxxx
Toughness	xxxx
Unpleasantness	x
Sadness	xxxxxxxx
Passivity	xxxxxx
Gentleness	xxxxxx
Pleasantness	xxxxx

Masculine sounds/feelings are medium.
Feminine sounds/feelings are high.
Pronunciation is most difficult.

ANGELICA

Cheerfulness	xxxxxxxxx
Activity	xxxxxx
Toughness	xxxxxx
Unpleasantness	xxxxx
Sadness	xxxxxxxx
Passivity	xxxxxxxxx
Gentleness	xxxxxx
Pleasantness	xxxxx

Masculine sounds/feelings are medium high.
Feminine sounds/feelings are very high.
Pronunciation is most difficult.

ANGELINA

Cheerfulness	xxxxxxxxx
Activity	xxxxxx
Toughness	xxxx
Unpleasantness	x
Sadness	xxxxxxxxxxxx
Passivity	xxxxxxxxx
Gentleness	xxxxxxx
Pleasantness	xxxxxx

Masculine sounds/feelings are medium.
Feminine sounds/feelings are very high.
Pronunciation is most difficult.

ANGELINE

Cheerfulness	xxxxxxxx
Activity	xxxxxx
Toughness	xxxx
Unpleasantness	x
Sadness	xxxxxxxxxxxx
Passivity	xxxxxxxx
Gentleness	xxxxxx
Pleasantness	xxxxxx

Masculine sounds/feelings are medium.
Feminine sounds/feelings are very high.
Pronunciation is most difficult.

ANGIE

Cheerfulness	xxxxxx
Activity	xxx
Toughness	x
Unpleasantness	x
Sadness	xxxxx
Passivity	xxx
Gentleness	xxxx
Pleasantness	xxxxxx

Masculine sounds/feelings are medium.
Feminine sounds/feelings are medium low.
Pronunciation is easier.

ANITA

Cheerfulness	xxx
Activity	xxxxxx
Toughness	xxxxxxx
Unpleasantness	xxxxx
Sadness	xxxxx
Passivity	xxxxx
Gentleness	x
Pleasantness	x

Masculine sounds/feelings are medium.
Feminine sounds/feelings are very low.
Pronunciation is average.

ANN

Cheerfulness	x
Activity	x
Toughness	x
Unpleasantness	x
Sadness	xxxxxxxx
Passivity	xxxxxx
Gentleness	x
Pleasantness	x

Masculine sounds/feelings are very low.
Feminine sounds/feelings are medium low.
Pronunciation is easiest.

ANNA

Cheerfulness	x
Activity	x
Toughness	x
Unpleasantness	x
Sadness	xxxxxxxx
Passivity	xxxxxx
Gentleness	x
Pleasantness	x

Masculine sounds/feelings are very low.
Feminine sounds/feelings are medium low.
Pronunciation is easier.

ANNABELLE

Cheerfulness	xxx
Activity	x
Toughness	x
Unpleasantness	xxxxx
Sadness	xxxxxxxxxxxxxxxx
Passivity	xxxxxxxxxxxxx
Gentleness	xxxxxxx
Pleasantness	xxxxx

Masculine sounds/feelings are very low.
Feminine sounds/feelings are very high.
Pronunciation is average.

Women's And Girls' Names

ANNE

Cheerfulness	x
Activity	x
Toughness	x
Unpleasantness	x
Sadness	xxxxxxxx
Passivity	xxxxxxx
Gentleness	x
Pleasantness	x

Masculine sounds/feelings are very low.
Feminine sounds/feelings are medium low.
Pronunciation is easiest.

ANNETTE

Cheerfulness	xxx
Activity	xxxxxx
Toughness	xxxxxxx
Unpleasantness	xxxxxxxxx
Sadness	xxxxxxxxx
Passivity	xxxxxxxxx
Gentleness	xxxx
Pleasantness	x

Masculine sounds/feelings are medium high.
Feminine sounds/feelings are medium.
Pronunciation is average.

ANNIE

Cheerfulness	xxx
Activity	x
Toughness	x
Unpleasantness	x
Sadness	xxxxxxxxx
Passivity	xxxxxxx
Gentleness	xxxx
Pleasantness	xxxxxx

Masculine sounds/feelings are low.
Feminine sounds/feelings are medium high.
Pronunciation is easiest.

ANTOINETTE

Cheerfulness	xxxxx
Activity	xxxxxxxxxxx
Toughness	xxxxxxxxxxx
Unpleasantness	xxxxxxxxxxx
Sadness	xxxxxxxxx
Passivity	xxxxxxxxx
Gentleness	xxxx
Pleasantness	x

Masculine sounds/feelings are very high.
Feminine sounds/feelings are medium.
Pronunciation is most difficult.

ANTONIA

Cheerfulness	xxx
Activity	xxxxxx
Toughness	xxxxxxx
Unpleasantness	xxxxxxxxx
Sadness	xxxxxxxxxxxxx
Passivity	xxxxxxxxx
Gentleness	x
Pleasantness	x

Masculine sounds/feelings are medium high.
Feminine sounds/feelings are medium.
Pronunciation is more difficult.

APRIL

Cheerfulness	xxx
Activity	xxxxxxxxx
Toughness	xxxxxxxxxx
Unpleasantness	xxxxx
Sadness	xxxxx
Passivity	xxxxx
Gentleness	xxxx
Pleasantness	xxxxxx

Masculine sounds/feelings are medium high.
Feminine sounds/feelings are medium.
Pronunciation is average.

ARACELI

Cheerfulness	xxxxxxxx
Activity	xxxxx
Toughness	xxxxxxx
Unpleasantness	xxxxx
Sadness	xxxxx
Passivity	xxxxxxxx
Gentleness	xxxxxxxxxx
Pleasantness	xxxxxx

Masculine sounds/feelings are medium high.
Feminine sounds/feelings are high.
Pronunciation is most difficult.

ARLENE

Cheerfulness	xxxxxx
Activity	xxxxxx
Toughness	xxxx
Unpleasantness	xxxxx
Sadness	xxxxxxxxx
Passivity	xxxxx
Gentleness	xxxxxxx
Pleasantness	xxxxxxxxxxx

Masculine sounds/feelings are medium.
Feminine sounds/feelings are very high.
Pronunciation is more difficult.

ARLINE

Cheerfulness	xxxxxx
Activity	xxxxxxxxx
Toughness	xxxxxxx
Unpleasantness	xxxxx
Sadness	xxxxxxxxx
Passivity	xxxxx
Gentleness	xxxx
Pleasantness	xxxxxx

Masculine sounds/feelings are medium high.
Feminine sounds/feelings are medium.
Pronunciation is average.

ASHLEE

Cheerfulness	xxx
Activity	xxx
Toughness	xxxx
Unpleasantness	x
Sadness	xxxxx
Passivity	xxxxx
Gentleness	xxxxxxx
Pleasantness	xxxxxxxxxxx

Masculine sounds/feelings are very low.
Feminine sounds/feelings are high.
Pronunciation is average.

ASHLEY

Cheerfulness	xxx
Activity	xxx
Toughness	xxxx
Unpleasantness	x
Sadness	xxxxx
Passivity	xxxxx
Gentleness	xxxxxxx
Pleasantness	xxxxxxxxxxx

Masculine sounds/feelings are very low.
Feminine sounds/feelings are high.
Pronunciation is average.

AUDRA

Cheerfulness	x
Activity	xxx
Toughness	xxxxxxx
Unpleasantness	xxxxxxxx
Sadness	xxxxx
Passivity	xxxxx
Gentleness	xxxx
Pleasantness	x

Masculine sounds/feelings are medium high.
Feminine sounds/feelings are low.
Pronunciation is average.

Women's And Girls' Names

AUDREY

Cheerfulness	xxx
Activity	xxx
Toughness	xxxxxx
Unpleasantness	xxxxxxxxx
Sadness	xxxxx
Passivity	xxxxx
Gentleness	xxxxxxx
Pleasantness	xxxxxx

Masculine sounds/feelings are high.
Feminine sounds/feelings are medium.
Pronunciation is easier.

AUGUSTA

Cheerfulness	x
Activity	xxxxxx
Toughness	xxxxxxx
Unpleasantness	xxxxx
Sadness	x
Passivity	xxxxx
Gentleness	xxxx
Pleasantness	x

Masculine sounds/feelings are medium.
Feminine sounds/feelings are very low.
Pronunciation is more difficult.

AURELIA

Cheerfulness	xxxxx
Activity	xxxxxx
Toughness	xxxxxxx
Unpleasantness	xxxxx
Sadness	xxxxx
Passivity	xxxxxxx
Gentleness	xxxxxxxxxxx
Pleasantness	xxxxxx

Masculine sounds/feelings are medium.
Feminine sounds/feelings are high.
Pronunciation is most difficult.

AURORA

Cheerfulness	x
Activity	xxxxxx
Toughness	xxxxxxx
Unpleasantness	xxxxxxxxx
Sadness	x
Passivity	xxxxx
Gentleness	xxxxxxx
Pleasantness	x

Masculine sounds/feelings are medium.
Feminine sounds/feelings are low.
Pronunciation is more difficult.

AUTUMN

Cheerfulness	x
Activity	xxx
Toughness	xxxx
Unpleasantness	xxxxx
Sadness	xxxxx
Passivity	xxxxxxxxx
Gentleness	xxxxxxx
Pleasantness	x

Masculine sounds/feelings are low.
Feminine sounds/feelings are medium.
Pronunciation is easier.

AVA

Cheerfulness	xxx
Activity	x
Toughness	x
Unpleasantness	x
Sadness	x
Passivity	xxx
Gentleness	xxxx
Pleasantness	xxxxxx

Masculine sounds/feelings are low.
Feminine sounds/feelings are low.
Pronunciation is easier.

AVIS

Cheerfulness	xxxxxx
Activity	xxx
Toughness	xxxx
Unpleasantness	x
Sadness	x
Passivity	xxx
Gentleness	xxxx
Pleasantness	xxxxxx

Masculine sounds/feelings are medium.
Feminine sounds/feelings are low.
Pronunciation is easier.

BARBARA

Cheerfulness	xxxxxx
Activity	xxxxxxxxx
Toughness	xxxxxxx
Unpleasantness	xxxxxxxxxxxxxxxxx
Sadness	xxxxxxxxx
Passivity	xxx
Gentleness	xxxx
Pleasantness	x

Masculine sounds/feelings are very high.
Feminine sounds/feelings are low.
Pronunciation is most difficult.

BARBRA

Cheerfulness	xxx
Activity	xxxxxxxxx
Toughness	xxxxxxx
Unpleasantness	xxxxxxxxxxxxxxxxxx
Sadness	xxxxxxxxx
Passivity	x
Gentleness	x
Pleasantness	x

Masculine sounds/feelings are very high.
Feminine sounds/feelings are very low.
Pronunciation is more difficult.

BEATRICE

Cheerfulness	xxxxxx
Activity	xxxxxxxxx
Toughness	xxxxxxxxxx
Unpleasantness	xxxxxxxxxxxxx
Sadness	xxxxx
Passivity	x
Gentleness	xxxx
Pleasantness	xxxxxx

Masculine sounds/feelings are very high.
Feminine sounds/feelings are low.
Pronunciation is average.

BEATRIZ

Cheerfulness	xxxxxx
Activity	xxxxxxxxx
Toughness	xxxxxxxxxx
Unpleasantness	xxxxxxxxxxxx
Sadness	xxxxx
Passivity	xxx
Gentleness	xxxxxxx
Pleasantness	xxxxxxxxxxxx

Masculine sounds/feelings are very high.
Feminine sounds/feelings are medium high.
Pronunciation is average.

BECKY

Cheerfulness	xxxxxx
Activity	x
Toughness	xxxx
Unpleasantness	xxxxxxxxx
Sadness	xxxxx
Passivity	xxxxx
Gentleness	xxxxxxx
Pleasantness	xxxxxx

Masculine sounds/feelings are medium high.
Feminine sounds/feelings are medium.
Pronunciation is easiest.

Women's And Girls' Names

BELINDA

Cheerfulness	xxxxxx
Activity	xxx
Toughness	xxxxxxx
Unpleasantness	xxxxxxxxx
Sadness	xxxxxxxxxxxxxxxx
Passivity	xxxxxxx
Gentleness	xxxxxxx
Pleasantness	xxxxxxxxxxx

Masculine sounds/feelings are medium high.
Feminine sounds/feelings are very high.
Pronunciation is more difficult.

BENITA

Cheerfulness	xxxxxx
Activity	xxxxxxxxx
Toughness	xxxxxxxxxx
Unpleasantness	xxxxxxxxx
Sadness	xxxxxxxxx
Passivity	xxx
Gentleness	x
Pleasantness	x

Masculine sounds/feelings are very high.
Feminine sounds/feelings are very low.
Pronunciation is average.

BERNADETTE

Cheerfulness	xxxxxx
Activity	xxxxxxxxx
Toughness	xxxxxxxxxxxxx
Unpleasantness	xxxxxxxxxxxxxxxxxx
Sadness	xxxxxxxxxxxx
Passivity	xxxxxxxxx
Gentleness	xxxx
Pleasantness	x

Masculine sounds/feelings are very high.
Feminine sounds/feelings are medium high.
Pronunciation is most difficult.

BERNADINE

Cheerfulness	xxxxxx
Activity	xxxxxx
Toughness	xxxxxxxxxx
Unpleasantness	xxxxxxxxx
Sadness	xxxxxxxxxxxxxxxx
Passivity	xxxxxxxxx
Gentleness	x
Pleasantness	x

Masculine sounds/feelings are very high.
Feminine sounds/feelings are medium high.
Pronunciation is average.

BERNICE

Cheerfulness	xxxxxx
Activity	xxxxxx
Toughness	xxxxxxx
Unpleasantness	xxxxx
Sadness	xxxxxxxxx
Passivity	xxx
Gentleness	x
Pleasantness	x

Masculine sounds/feelings are medium.
Feminine sounds/feelings are very low.
Pronunciation is easier.

BERTA

Cheerfulness	xxx
Activity	xxxxxx
Toughness	xxxxxxx
Unpleasantness	xxxxxxxxx
Sadness	xxxxx
Passivity	x
Gentleness	x
Pleasantness	x

Masculine sounds/feelings are very high.
Feminine sounds/feelings are very low.
Pronunciation is easier.

BERTHA

Cheerfulness	xxxxxx
Activity	xxx
Toughness	xxxx
Unpleasantness	xxxxx
Sadness	xxxxx
Passivity	x
Gentleness	xxxx
Pleasantness	xxxxxx

Masculine sounds/feelings are medium high.
Feminine sounds/feelings are low.
Pronunciation is more difficult.

BESSIE

Cheerfulness	xxxxxx
Activity	x
Toughness	x
Unpleasantness	xxxxx
Sadness	xxxxx
Passivity	xxx
Gentleness	xxxxxxx
Pleasantness	xxxxxx

Masculine sounds/feelings are medium.
Feminine sounds/feelings are medium.
Pronunciation is easiest.

BETH

Cheerfulness	xxxxxx
Activity	x
Toughness	x
Unpleasantness	xxxxx
Sadness	xxxxx
Passivity	xxx
Gentleness	xxxxxxx
Pleasantness	xxxxxx

Masculine sounds/feelings are medium.
Feminine sounds/feelings are medium.
Pronunciation is easiest.

BETHANY

Cheerfulness	xxxxxxxxx
Activity	x
Toughness	x
Unpleasantness	xxxxx
Sadness	xxxxxxxxx
Passivity	xxxxxx
Gentleness	xxxxxxxxxx
Pleasantness	xxxxxxxxxxx

Masculine sounds/feelings are low.
Feminine sounds/feelings are very high.
Pronunciation is average.

BETSY

Cheerfulness	xxxxx
Activity	xxx
Toughness	xxxx
Unpleasantness	xxxxxxxx
Sadness	xxxxx
Passivity	xxx
Gentleness	xxxxxxx
Pleasantness	xxxxxx

Masculine sounds/feelings are medium.
Feminine sounds/feelings are medium.
Pronunciation is easier.

BETTE

Cheerfulness	xxx
Activity	xxxxxx
Toughness	xxxxxxx
Unpleasantness	xxxxxxxxxxxx
Sadness	xxxxx
Passivity	xxx
Gentleness	xxxx
Pleasantness	x

Masculine sounds/feelings are very high.
Feminine sounds/feelings are very low.
Pronunciation is easier.

BETTIE

Cheerfulness	xxxxxx
Activity	xxxxxx
Toughness	xxxxxxx
Unpleasantness	xxxxxxxxxxxx

Sadness	xxxxx
Passivity	xxx
Gentleness	xxxxxxx
Pleasantness	xxxxxx

Masculine sounds/feelings are very high.
Feminine sounds/feelings are medium.
Pronunciation is easier.

BETTY

Cheerfulness	xxxxxx
Activity	xxxxxx
Toughness	xxxxxxx
Unpleasantness	xxxxxxxxxxxx

Sadness	xxxxx
Passivity	xxx
Gentleness	xxxxxxx
Pleasantness	xxxxxx

Masculine sounds/feelings are very high.
Feminine sounds/feelings are medium.
Pronunciation is easier.

BETTYE

Cheerfulness	xxxxxx
Activity	xxxxxxxxx
Toughness	xxxxxxxxxx
Unpleasantness	xxxxxxxxxxxx

Sadness	xxxxx
Passivity	xxx
Gentleness	xxxx
Pleasantness	x

Masculine sounds/feelings are very high.
Feminine sounds/feelings are very low.
Pronunciation is easier.

BEULAH

Cheerfulness	x
Activity	xxx
Toughness	xxxx
Unpleasantness	xxxxx

Sadness	xxxxxxxxx
Passivity	xxxxx
Gentleness	xxxx
Pleasantness	xxxxxx

Masculine sounds/feelings are low.
Feminine sounds/feelings are medium.
Pronunciation is easier.

BEVERLY

Cheerfulness	xxxxxxxxxxxx
Activity	xxxxxx
Toughness	xxxxxxx
Unpleasantness	xxxxx

Sadness	xxxxxxxxx
Passivity	xxx
Gentleness	xxxxxxxxxxx
Pleasantness	xxxxxxxxxxxxxxxxx

Masculine sounds/feelings are high.
Feminine sounds/feelings are very high.
Pronunciation is more difficult.

BIANCA

Cheerfulness	xxx
Activity	xxx
Toughness	xxxxxxx
Unpleasantness	xxxxxxxxx

Sadness	xxxxxxxxx
Passivity	xxxxxxx
Gentleness	x
Pleasantness	x

Masculine sounds/feelings are medium.
Feminine sounds/feelings are medium low.
Pronunciation is easier.

BILLIE

Cheerfulness	xxxxx
Activity	xxx
Toughness	xxxx
Unpleasantness	xxxxx
Sadness	xxxxxxxx
Passivity	xxx
Gentleness	xxxxxx
Pleasantness	xxxxxxxxxxx

Masculine sounds/feelings are medium high.
Feminine sounds/feelings are high.
Pronunciation is easiest.

BLANCA

Cheerfulness	x
Activity	x
Toughness	xxxx
Unpleasantness	xxxxxxxxx
Sadness	xxxxxxxxxxxx
Passivity	xxxxxxxxx
Gentleness	xxxx
Pleasantness	xxxxxx

Masculine sounds/feelings are low.
Feminine sounds/feelings are very high.
Pronunciation is average.

BLANCHE

Cheerfulness	xxx
Activity	xxx
Toughness	x
Unpleasantness	xxxxx
Sadness	xxxxxxxxxxxx
Passivity	xxxxxxx
Gentleness	xxxx
Pleasantness	xxxxxx

Masculine sounds/feelings are low.
Feminine sounds/feelings are high.
Pronunciation is easier.

BOBBI

Cheerfulness	xxxxx
Activity	xxxxxx
Toughness	xxxx
Unpleasantness	xxxxxxxxxxxx
Sadness	xxxxxxxxxxxx
Passivity	x
Gentleness	x
Pleasantness	x

Masculine sounds/feelings are high.
Feminine sounds/feelings are low.
Pronunciation is easiest.

BOBBIE

Cheerfulness	xxxxx
Activity	xxx
Toughness	x
Unpleasantness	xxxxxxxxxxxx
Sadness	xxxxxxxxxxxx
Passivity	x
Gentleness	xxxx
Pleasantness	xxxxxx

Masculine sounds/feelings are medium.
Feminine sounds/feelings are medium.
Pronunciation is easiest.

BONITA

Cheerfulness	xxx
Activity	xxxxx
Toughness	xxxxxxx
Unpleasantness	xxxxxxxxx
Sadness	xxxxxxxxx
Passivity	xxxxx
Gentleness	x
Pleasantness	x

Masculine sounds/feelings are medium high.
Feminine sounds/feelings are low.
Pronunciation is average.

BONNIE

Cheerfulness	xxx
Activity	x
Toughness	x
Unpleasantness	xxxxx
Sadness	xxxxxxxxxxxx
Passivity	xxxxxxx
Gentleness	xxxx
Pleasantness	xxxxxx

Masculine sounds/feelings are very low.
Feminine sounds/feelings are high.
Pronunciation is easiest.

BRANDI

Cheerfulness	xxx
Activity	xxxxxx
Toughness	xxxxxxxxxx
Unpleasantness	xxxxxxxxxxxx
Sadness	xxxxxxxxxxxx
Passivity	xxxxxxx
Gentleness	x
Pleasantness	x

Masculine sounds/feelings are very high.
Feminine sounds/feelings are medium.
Pronunciation is average.

BRANDY

Cheerfulness	xxx
Activity	xxx
Toughness	xxxxxxx
Unpleasantness	xxxxxxxxxxxx
Sadness	xxxxxxxxxxxx
Passivity	xxxxxxx
Gentleness	xxxx
Pleasantness	xxxxxx

Masculine sounds/feelings are medium high.
Feminine sounds/feelings are high.
Pronunciation is easier.

BRENDA

Cheerfulness	xxx
Activity	xxx
Toughness	xxxxxx
Unpleasantness	xxxxxxxxxxxx
Sadness	xxxxxxxxxxxx
Passivity	xxxxxxx
Gentleness	xxxx
Pleasantness	x

Masculine sounds/feelings are medium high.
Feminine sounds/feelings are medium.
Pronunciation is more difficult.

BRIANA

Cheerfulness	xxx
Activity	xxxxxx
Toughness	xxxxxxx
Unpleasantness	xxxxxxxxx
Sadness	xxxxxxxxx
Passivity	xxxxx
Gentleness	x
Pleasantness	x

Masculine sounds/feelings are medium high.
Feminine sounds/feelings are low.
Pronunciation is more difficult.

BRIANNA

Cheerfulness	xxx
Activity	xxxxxx
Toughness	xxxxxxx
Unpleasantness	xxxxxxxxx
Sadness	xxxxxxxxxxxx
Passivity	xxxxxxx
Gentleness	x
Pleasantness	x

Masculine sounds/feelings are medium high.
Feminine sounds/feelings are medium.
Pronunciation is more difficult.

BRIDGET

Cheerfulness	xxxxx
Activity	xxxxxxxxxxx
Toughness	xxxxxxxxxxxxxxx
Unpleasantness	xxxxxxxxxxxxxxxxx
Sadness	xxxxxxxx
Passivity	xxxxx
Gentleness	xxxx
Pleasantness	x

Masculine sounds/feelings are very high.
Feminine sounds/feelings are medium.
Pronunciation is more difficult.

BRIDGETTE

Cheerfulness	xxxxxx
Activity	xxxxxxxxxxxxxx
Toughness	xxxxxxxxxxxxxxxxx
Unpleasantness	xxxxxxxxxxxxxxxxxx
Sadness	xxxxxxxx
Passivity	xxxxx
Gentleness	xxxx
Pleasantness	x

Masculine sounds/feelings are very high.
Feminine sounds/feelings are medium.
Pronunciation is most difficult.

BRITTANY

Cheerfulness	xxxxxx
Activity	xxxxxxxxxxx
Toughness	xxxxxxxxxxx
Unpleasantness	xxxxxxxxxxxxxxxx
Sadness	xxxxxxxx
Passivity	xxxxx
Gentleness	xxxx
Pleasantness	xxxxx

Masculine sounds/feelings are very high.
Feminine sounds/feelings are medium.
Pronunciation is more difficult.

BRITTNEY

Cheerfulness	xxxxx
Activity	xxxxxxxxxxx
Toughness	xxxxxxxxxxxx
Unpleasantness	xxxxxxxxxxxxxxxxx
Sadness	xxxxxxxx
Passivity	xxx
Gentleness	xxxx
Pleasantness	xxxxx

Masculine sounds/feelings are very high.
Feminine sounds/feelings are medium.
Pronunciation is more difficult.

BROOKE

Cheerfulness	xxx
Activity	xxx
Toughness	xxxxxx
Unpleasantness	xxxxxxxxxxxx
Sadness	xxxxx
Passivity	xxx
Gentleness	x
Pleasantness	xxxxx

Masculine sounds/feelings are very high.
Feminine sounds/feelings are low.
Pronunciation is easiest.

CAITLIN

Cheerfulness	xxx
Activity	xxxxx
Toughness	xxxxxxxxx
Unpleasantness	xxxxxxxx
Sadness	xxxxxxxx
Passivity	xxxxxx
Gentleness	xxxx
Pleasantness	xxxxx

Masculine sounds/feelings are high.
Feminine sounds/feelings are medium high.
Pronunciation is average.

CALLIE

Cheerfulness	xxx
Activity	x
Toughness	xxxx
Unpleasantness	xxxxx
Sadness	xxxxx
Passivity	xxxxxxx
Gentleness	xxxxxxxxxx
Pleasantness	xxxxxxxxxxx

Masculine sounds/feelings are medium.
Feminine sounds/feelings are very high.
Pronunciation is easiest.

CAMILLE

Cheerfulness	xxx
Activity	xxx
Toughness	xxxxxxx
Unpleasantness	xxxxx
Sadness	xxxxx
Passivity	xxxxxxxxx
Gentleness	xxxxxxx
Pleasantness	xxxxxx

Masculine sounds/feelings are medium.
Feminine sounds/feelings are medium high.
Pronunciation is easier.

CANDACE

Cheerfulness	x
Activity	x
Toughness	xxxxxxx
Unpleasantness	xxxxxxxxx
Sadness	xxxxxxxxx
Passivity	xxxxxxxxx
Gentleness	x
Pleasantness	x

Masculine sounds/feelings are medium low.
Feminine sounds/feelings are medium.
Pronunciation is easier.

CANDICE

Cheerfulness	xxx
Activity	xxx
Toughness	xxxxxxxxx
Unpleasantness	xxxxxxxxx
Sadness	xxxxxxxxx
Passivity	xxxxxxxxx
Gentleness	x
Pleasantness	x

Masculine sounds/feelings are medium high.
Feminine sounds/feelings are medium.
Pronunciation is easier.

CANDY

Cheerfulness	xxx
Activity	x
Toughness	xxxxxxx
Unpleasantness	xxxxxxxxx
Sadness	xxxxxxxxx
Passivity	xxxxxxxxx
Gentleness	xxxx
Pleasantness	xxxxxx

Masculine sounds/feelings are medium.
Feminine sounds/feelings are medium high.
Pronunciation is easiest.

CARA

Cheerfulness	xxx
Activity	xxx
Toughness	xxxxxxx
Unpleasantness	xxxxxxxxx
Sadness	x
Passivity	xxxxx
Gentleness	xxxx
Pleasantness	x

Masculine sounds/feelings are high.
Feminine sounds/feelings are very low.
Pronunciation is average.

CARLA

Cheerfulness	xxx
Activity	xxxxxx
Toughness	xxxxxxx
Unpleasantness	xxxxxxxxx
Sadness	xxxxx
Passivity	xxxxx
Gentleness	xxxx
Pleasantness	xxxxxx

Masculine sounds/feelings are medium high.
Feminine sounds/feelings are medium.
Pronunciation is more difficult.

CARLENE

Cheerfulness	xxxxxx
Activity	xxxxxx
Toughness	xxxxxxx
Unpleasantness	xxxxxxxxx
Sadness	xxxxxxxxx
Passivity	xxxxxxx
Gentleness	xxxxxxx
Pleasantness	xxxxxxxxxxx

Masculine sounds/feelings are high.
Feminine sounds/feelings are very high.
Pronunciation is most difficult.

CARLY

Cheerfulness	xxxxxx
Activity	xxxxxx
Toughness	xxxxxxx
Unpleasantness	xxxxxxxxx
Sadness	xxxxx
Passivity	xxxxx
Gentleness	xxxxxxx
Pleasantness	xxxxxxxxxxx

Masculine sounds/feelings are high.
Feminine sounds/feelings are high.
Pronunciation is easier.

CARMELA

Cheerfulness	xxxxx
Activity	xxxxx
Toughness	xxxxxx
Unpleasantness	xxxxxxxxx
Sadness	xxxxx
Passivity	xxxxxxxxx
Gentleness	xxxxxxxxxx
Pleasantness	xxxxx

Masculine sounds/feelings are high.
Feminine sounds/feelings are high.
Pronunciation is most difficult.

CARMELLA

Cheerfulness	xxxxx
Activity	xxxxx
Toughness	xxxxxx
Unpleasantness	xxxxxxxxx
Sadness	xxxxx
Passivity	xxxxxxxxx
Gentleness	xxxxxxxxxx
Pleasantness	xxxxx

Masculine sounds/feelings are high.
Feminine sounds/feelings are high.
Pronunciation is most difficult.

CARMEN

Cheerfulness	xxxxx
Activity	xxxxx
Toughness	xxxxxx
Unpleasantness	xxxxxxxxx
Sadness	xxxxx
Passivity	xxxxxxxxx
Gentleness	xxxxxxx
Pleasantness	x

Masculine sounds/feelings are high.
Feminine sounds/feelings are medium.
Pronunciation is average.

CAROL

Cheerfulness	xxxxx
Activity	xxxxx
Toughness	xxxxxx
Unpleasantness	xxxxxxxxx
Sadness	xxxxx
Passivity	xxxxxxx
Gentleness	xxxxxxx
Pleasantness	xxxxx

Masculine sounds/feelings are high.
Feminine sounds/feelings are medium.
Pronunciation is average.

CAROLE

Cheerfulness	xxx
Activity	xxx
Toughness	xxxxxx
Unpleasantness	xxxxxxxxxxxx
Sadness	xxxxxxxxx
Passivity	xxxxxxxxx
Gentleness	xxxxxxx
Pleasantness	xxxxx

Masculine sounds/feelings are medium high.
Feminine sounds/feelings are very high.
Pronunciation is average.

CAROLINA

Cheerfulness	xxxxxxxxx
Activity	xxxxxxxxx
Toughness	xxxxxxxxxx
Unpleasantness	xxxxxxxxx
Sadness	xxxxxxxxx
Passivity	xxxxxxxxx
Gentleness	xxxxxxx
Pleasantness	xxxxx

Masculine sounds/feelings are very high.
Feminine sounds/feelings are very high.
Pronunciation is most difficult.

CAROLINE

Cheerfulness	xxxxxxxxx
Activity	xxxxxxxxx
Toughness	xxxxxxxxxx
Unpleasantness	xxxxxxxxx
Sadness	xxxxxxxxx
Passivity	xxxxxxxxx
Gentleness	xxxxxxx
Pleasantness	xxxxx

Masculine sounds/feelings are very high.
Feminine sounds/feelings are very high.
Pronunciation is more difficult.

CAROLYN

Cheerfulness	xxxxxxxxx
Activity	xxxxxxxxx
Toughness	xxxxxxxxxx
Unpleasantness	xxxxxxxxx
Sadness	xxxxxxxxx
Passivity	xxxxxxxxx
Gentleness	xxxxxxx
Pleasantness	xxxxx

Masculine sounds/feelings are very high.
Feminine sounds/feelings are very high.
Pronunciation is more difficult.

CARRIE

Cheerfulness	xxx
Activity	xxx
Toughness	xxxxxxx
Unpleasantness	xxxxxxxxx
Sadness	x
Passivity	xxxxx
Gentleness	xxxx
Pleasantness	xxxxx

Masculine sounds/feelings are high.
Feminine sounds/feelings are low.
Pronunciation is easiest.

CASEY

Cheerfulness	xxx
Activity	x
Toughness	xxxx
Unpleasantness	xxxxx
Sadness	x
Passivity	xxx
Gentleness	xxxx
Pleasantness	xxxxxx

Masculine sounds/feelings are medium.
Feminine sounds/feelings are low.
Pronunciation is easiest.

CASSANDRA

Cheerfulness	x
Activity	xxx
Toughness	xxxxxxxxx
Unpleasantness	xxxxxxxxxxxx
Sadness	xxxxxxxxx
Passivity	xxxxxxxxxxx
Gentleness	x
Pleasantness	x

Masculine sounds/feelings are medium high.
Feminine sounds/feelings are medium.
Pronunciation is most difficult.

CASSIE

Cheerfulness	xxx
Activity	x
Toughness	xxxx
Unpleasantness	xxxxx
Sadness	x
Passivity	xxxxx
Gentleness	xxxx
Pleasantness	xxxxxx

Masculine sounds/feelings are medium.
Feminine sounds/feelings are low.
Pronunciation is easiest.

CATALINA

Cheerfulness	xxx
Activity	xxxxxx
Toughness	xxxxxxxxxx
Unpleasantness	xxxxxxxxx
Sadness	xxxxxxxxx
Passivity	xxxxxxxxxxx
Gentleness	xxxx
Pleasantness	xxxxx

Masculine sounds/feelings are high.
Feminine sounds/feelings are high.
Pronunciation is most difficult.

CATHERINE

Cheerfulness	xxxxx
Activity	xxxxxx
Toughness	xxxxxxxxxx
Unpleasantness	xxxxx
Sadness	xxxxx
Passivity	xxxxxxxxx
Gentleness	xxxx
Pleasantness	xxxxx

Masculine sounds/feelings are medium high.
Feminine sounds/feelings are medium.
Pronunciation is more difficult.

CATHLEEN

Cheerfulness	xxxxx
Activity	x
Toughness	xxxx
Unpleasantness	xxxxx
Sadness	xxxxxxxxx
Passivity	xxxxxxxxx
Gentleness	xxxxxxxxxx
Pleasantness	xxxxxxxxxxxxxxx

Masculine sounds/feelings are low.
Feminine sounds/feelings are very high.
Pronunciation is most difficult.

CATHY

Cheerfulness	xxxxxx
Activity	x
Toughness	xxxx
Unpleasantness	xxxxx
Sadness	x
Passivity	xxxxx
Gentleness	xxxxxxx
Pleasantness	xxxxxxxxxxx

Masculine sounds/feelings are medium.
Feminine sounds/feelings are medium.
Pronunciation is easiest.

CECELIA

Cheerfulness	xxxxxxxxx
Activity	xxx
Toughness	xxxx
Unpleasantness	x
Sadness	xxxxx
Passivity	xxxxx
Gentleness	xxxxxxxxxxx
Pleasantness	xxxxxxxxxxx

Masculine sounds/feelings are medium low.
Feminine sounds/feelings are very high.
Pronunciation is most difficult.

CECILE

Cheerfulness	xxxxxx
Activity	xxx
Toughness	xxxx
Unpleasantness	x
Sadness	xxxxx
Passivity	xxxxx
Gentleness	xxxxxxx
Pleasantness	xxxxxx

Masculine sounds/feelings are low.
Feminine sounds/feelings are medium.
Pronunciation is average.

CECILIA

Cheerfulness	xxxxxxxxx
Activity	xxxxx
Toughness	xxxxxx
Unpleasantness	x
Sadness	xxxxx
Passivity	xxxxx
Gentleness	xxxxxxx
Pleasantness	xxxxxx

Masculine sounds/feelings are medium.
Feminine sounds/feelings are medium.
Pronunciation is most difficult.

CELESTE

Cheerfulness	xxxxxx
Activity	xxx
Toughness	xxxx
Unpleasantness	xxxxx
Sadness	xxxxx
Passivity	xxxxx
Gentleness	xxxxxxxxxxx
Pleasantness	xxxxxxxxxxx

Masculine sounds/feelings are medium.
Feminine sounds/feelings are very high.
Pronunciation is more difficult.

CELIA

Cheerfulness	xxxxxx
Activity	xxx
Toughness	xxxx
Unpleasantness	x
Sadness	xxxxx
Passivity	xxxxx
Gentleness	xxxxxxx
Pleasantness	xxxxxx

Masculine sounds/feelings are low.
Feminine sounds/feelings are medium.
Pronunciation is more difficult.

CHANDRA

Cheerfulness	xxx
Activity	xxxxx
Toughness	xxxxxx
Unpleasantness	xxxxxxxxx
Sadness	xxxxxxxxx
Passivity	xxxxxx
Gentleness	x
Pleasantness	x

Masculine sounds/feelings are medium high.
Feminine sounds/feelings are medium low.
Pronunciation is most difficult.

CHARITY

Cheerfulness	xxxxxxxxxxx
Activity	xxxxxxxxxxx
Toughness	xxxxxxxxxx
Unpleasantness	xxxxxxxx
Sadness	x
Passivity	xxx
Gentleness	xxxxxxx
Pleasantness	xxxxx

Masculine sounds/feelings are very high.
Feminine sounds/feelings are medium low.
Pronunciation is more difficult.

CHARLENE

Cheerfulness	xxxxxxxx
Activity	xxxxxxxx
Toughness	xxxx
Unpleasantness	xxxxx
Sadness	xxxxxxxxx
Passivity	xxxxx
Gentleness	xxxxxxx
Pleasantness	xxxxxxxxxxx

Masculine sounds/feelings are medium high.
Feminine sounds/feelings are very high.
Pronunciation is most difficult.

CHARLOTTE

Cheerfulness	xxxxxxxx
Activity	xxxxxxxxxxxxxxxx
Toughness	xxxxxxxxx
Unpleasantness	xxxxxxxxxxxx
Sadness	xxxxx
Passivity	xxx
Gentleness	xxxx
Pleasantness	xxxxx

Masculine sounds/feelings are very high.
Feminine sounds/feelings are medium low.
Pronunciation is most difficult.

CHARMAINE

Cheerfulness	xxxxx
Activity	xxxxxxxx
Toughness	xxxx
Unpleasantness	xxxxx
Sadness	xxxxx
Passivity	xxxxx
Gentleness	xxxx
Pleasantness	x

Masculine sounds/feelings are medium.
Feminine sounds/feelings are low.
Pronunciation is more difficult.

CHASITY

Cheerfulness	xxxxxxxxx
Activity	xxxxxxxxx
Toughness	xxxxxx
Unpleasantness	xxxxx
Sadness	x
Passivity	x
Gentleness	xxxx
Pleasantness	xxxxxx

Masculine sounds/feelings are high.
Feminine sounds/feelings are very low.
Pronunciation is average.

CHELSEA

Cheerfulness	xxxxxxxx
Activity	xxx
Toughness	x
Unpleasantness	x
Sadness	xxxxx
Passivity	xxxxx
Gentleness	xxxxxxxxxx
Pleasantness	xxxxxxxxxxx

Masculine sounds/feelings are low.
Feminine sounds/feelings are very high.
Pronunciation is most difficult.

CHERI

Cheerfulness	xxxxxxxx
Activity	xxxxxxxx
Toughness	xxxxxxx
Unpleasantness	xxxxx
Sadness	x
Passivity	xxx
Gentleness	xxxx
Pleasantness	x

Masculine sounds/feelings are very high.
Feminine sounds/feelings are very low.
Pronunciation is average.

CHERIE

Cheerfulness	xxxxxxxx
Activity	xxxxxx
Toughness	xxxx
Unpleasantness	xxxxx
Sadness	x
Passivity	x
Gentleness	xxxxxxx
Pleasantness	xxxxxxxxxxx

Masculine sounds/feelings are very high.
Feminine sounds/feelings are medium.
Pronunciation is easier.

CHERYL

Cheerfulness	xxxxxxxx
Activity	xxxxxxxx
Toughness	xxxxxxx
Unpleasantness	x
Sadness	xxxxx
Passivity	xxx
Gentleness	xxxx
Pleasantness	xxxxxx

Masculine sounds/feelings are very high.
Feminine sounds/feelings are medium low.
Pronunciation is average.

CHRIS

Cheerfulness	xxx
Activity	xxxxxx
Toughness	xxxxxxxxxx
Unpleasantness	xxxxxxxxx
Sadness	x
Passivity	xxxxx
Gentleness	xxxx
Pleasantness	xxxxxx

Masculine sounds/feelings are very high.
Feminine sounds/feelings are low.
Pronunciation is easier.

CHRISTA

Cheerfulness	xxx
Activity	xxxxxxxx
Toughness	xxxxxxxxxxxx
Unpleasantness	xxxxxxxxxxxx
Sadness	x
Passivity	xxx
Gentleness	x
Pleasantness	x

Masculine sounds/feelings are very high.
Feminine sounds/feelings are very low.
Pronunciation is more difficult.

CHRISTI

Cheerfulness	xxxxxx
Activity	xxxxxxxxxxx
Toughness	xxxxxxxxxxxxxxx
Unpleasantness	xxxxxxxxxxxx
Sadness	x
Passivity	xxx
Gentleness	x
Pleasantness	x

Masculine sounds/feelings are very high.
Feminine sounds/feelings are very low.
Pronunciation is average.

CHRISTIAN

Cheerfulness	xxxxxx
Activity	xxxxxxxxx
Toughness	xxxxxxxxxx
Unpleasantness	xxxxxxxxx
Sadness	xxxxx
Passivity	xxxxxxx
Gentleness	x
Pleasantness	x

Masculine sounds/feelings are very high.
Feminine sounds/feelings are very low.
Pronunciation is more difficult.

CHRISTIE

Cheerfulness	xxxxxx
Activity	xxxxxxxxx
Toughness	xxxxxxxxxxxx
Unpleasantness	xxxxxxxxxxxx
Sadness	x
Passivity	xxx
Gentleness	xxxx
Pleasantness	xxxxxx

Masculine sounds/feelings are very high.
Feminine sounds/feelings are low.
Pronunciation is average.

CHRISTINA

Cheerfulness	xxxxx
Activity	xxxxxxxxxxx
Toughness	xxxxxxxxxxxxxx
Unpleasantness	xxxxxxxxxxxx
Sadness	xxxxx
Passivity	xxxxx
Gentleness	x
Pleasantness	x

Masculine sounds/feelings are very high.
Feminine sounds/feelings are very low.
Pronunciation is most difficult.

CHRISTINE

Cheerfulness	xxxxx
Activity	xxxxxxxxxxx
Toughness	xxxxxxxxxxxxxxx
Unpleasantness	xxxxxxxxxxxx
Sadness	xxxxx
Passivity	xxxxx
Gentleness	x
Pleasantness	x

Masculine sounds/feelings are very high.
Feminine sounds/feelings are very low.
Pronunciation is more difficult.

CHRISTY

Cheerfulness	xxxxx
Activity	xxxxxxxxx
Toughness	xxxxxxxxxxxx
Unpleasantness	xxxxxxxxxxxx
Sadness	x
Passivity	xxx
Gentleness	xxxx
Pleasantness	xxxxx

Masculine sounds/feelings are very high.
Feminine sounds/feelings are low.
Pronunciation is average.

CHRYSTAL

Cheerfulness	xxx
Activity	xxxxxxxx
Toughness	xxxxxxxxxxxx
Unpleasantness	xxxxxxxxxxxx
Sadness	xxxxx
Passivity	xxxxxxx
Gentleness	xxxx
Pleasantness	xxxxxx

Masculine sounds/feelings are very high.
Feminine sounds/feelings are medium.
Pronunciation is more difficult.

CINDY

Cheerfulness	xxxxxx
Activity	x
Toughness	xxxx
Unpleasantness	xxxxx
Sadness	xxxxxxxxx
Passivity	xxxxx
Gentleness	xxxxxxx
Pleasantness	xxxxxxxxxxxx

Masculine sounds/feelings are low.
Feminine sounds/feelings are very high.
Pronunciation is easier.

CLAIRE

Cheerfulness	xxx
Activity	xxx
Toughness	xxxxxxx
Unpleasantness	xxxxxxxxx
Sadness	xxxxx
Passivity	xxxxxxx
Gentleness	xxxxxxx
Pleasantness	xxxxx

Masculine sounds/feelings are high.
Feminine sounds/feelings are medium.
Pronunciation is easier.

CLARA

Cheerfulness	xxx
Activity	xxx
Toughness	xxxxxxx
Unpleasantness	xxxxxxxxx
Sadness	xxxxx
Passivity	xxxxxxx
Gentleness	xxxxxxx
Pleasantness	xxxxxx

Masculine sounds/feelings are medium.
Feminine sounds/feelings are medium.
Pronunciation is more difficult.

CLARE

Cheerfulness	xxx
Activity	xxx
Toughness	xxxxxxx
Unpleasantness	xxxxxxxxx
Sadness	xxxxx
Passivity	xxxxxxx
Gentleness	xxxxxxx
Pleasantness	xxxxxx

Masculine sounds/feelings are high.
Feminine sounds/feelings are medium.
Pronunciation is easier.

CLARICE

Cheerfulness	xxxxxx
Activity	xxxxxx
Toughness	xxxxxxxxxx
Unpleasantness	xxxxxxxxx
Sadness	xxxxx
Passivity	xxxxxxx
Gentleness	xxxxxxx
Pleasantness	xxxxxx

Masculine sounds/feelings are very high.
Feminine sounds/feelings are medium.
Pronunciation is more difficult.

CLARISSA

Cheerfulness	xxxxx
Activity	xxxxxx
Toughness	xxxxxxxxx
Unpleasantness	xxxxxxxxx
Sadness	xxxxx
Passivity	xxxxxxx
Gentleness	xxxxxxx
Pleasantness	xxxxx

Masculine sounds/feelings are very high.
Feminine sounds/feelings are medium.
Pronunciation is most difficult.

CLAUDETTE

Cheerfulness	xxx
Activity	xxxxxx
Toughness	xxxxxxxxxxxx
Unpleasantness	xxxxxxxxxxxxxxxxxx
Sadness	xxxxxxxxx
Passivity	xxxxxxxxxxx
Gentleness	xxxxxxxxxxx
Pleasantness	xxxxxx

Masculine sounds/feelings are very high.
Feminine sounds/feelings are very high.
Pronunciation is most difficult.

CLAUDIA

Cheerfulness	xxx
Activity	xxx
Toughness	xxxxxxxxx
Unpleasantness	xxxxxxxxx
Sadness	xxxxxxxxx
Passivity	xxxxxxxxx
Gentleness	xxxxxxx
Pleasantness	xxxxx

Masculine sounds/feelings are medium high.
Feminine sounds/feelings are very high.
Pronunciation is more difficult.

CLAUDINE

Cheerfulness	xxx
Activity	xxx
Toughness	xxxxxxxxx
Unpleasantness	xxxxxxxxx
Sadness	xxxxxxxxxxxx
Passivity	xxxxxxxxxxx
Gentleness	xxxxxx
Pleasantness	xxxxx

Masculine sounds/feelings are medium high.
Feminine sounds/feelings are very high.
Pronunciation is average.

CLEO

Cheerfulness	xxx
Activity	x
Toughness	xxxx
Unpleasantness	xxxxxxxxx
Sadness	xxxxxxxxx
Passivity	xxxxxxx
Gentleness	xxxxxx
Pleasantness	xxxxxxxxxxx

Masculine sounds/feelings are medium.
Feminine sounds/feelings are very high.
Pronunciation is easiest.

COLETTE

Cheerfulness	xxx
Activity	xxxxx
Toughness	xxxxxxxxx
Unpleasantness	xxxxxxxxxxxxxxxxx
Sadness	xxxxxxxxx
Passivity	xxxxxxxxx
Gentleness	xxxxxx
Pleasantness	xxxxx

Masculine sounds/feelings are very high.
Feminine sounds/feelings are very high.
Pronunciation is more difficult.

COLLEEN

Cheerfulness	xxxxxx
Activity	xxx
Toughness	xxxx
Unpleasantness	xxxxx
Sadness	xxxxxxxxx
Passivity	xxxxxxx
Gentleness	xxxxxxx
Pleasantness	xxxxxxxxxxx

Masculine sounds/feelings are medium.
Feminine sounds/feelings are very high.
Pronunciation is easiest.

CONCEPCION

Cheerfulness	xxxxxx
Activity	xxxxxxxxx
Toughness	xxxxxxxxxx
Unpleasantness	xxxxx
Sadness	xxxxxxxx
Passivity	xxxxxxxxx
Gentleness	xxxx
Pleasantness	x

Masculine sounds/feelings are high.
Feminine sounds/feelings are medium.
Pronunciation is most difficult.

CONNIE

Cheerfulness	xxxxxx
Activity	xxx
Toughness	xxxx
Unpleasantness	xxxxx
Sadness	xxxxxxxxx
Passivity	xxxxxxx
Gentleness	xxxx
Pleasantness	xxxxxx

Masculine sounds/feelings are medium.
Feminine sounds/feelings are medium high.
Pronunciation is easiest.

CONSTANCE

Cheerfulness	xxx
Activity	xxxxxx
Toughness	xxxxxxx
Unpleasantness	xxxxxxxxx
Sadness	xxxxxxxxx
Passivity	xxxxxxxxx
Gentleness	x
Pleasantness	x

Masculine sounds/feelings are medium high.
Feminine sounds/feelings are medium.
Pronunciation is more difficult.

CONSUELO

Cheerfulness	xxxxxx
Activity	xxxxxx
Toughness	xxxxxxx
Unpleasantness	xxxxxxxxx
Sadness	xxxxxxxxxxxxx
Passivity	xxxxxxxxxxx
Gentleness	xxxxxxx
Pleasantness	xxxxxx

Masculine sounds/feelings are high.
Feminine sounds/feelings are very high.
Pronunciation is more difficult.

CORA

Cheerfulness	x
Activity	xxx
Toughness	xxxxxxx
Unpleasantness	xxxxxxxxx
Sadness	x
Passivity	xxxxx
Gentleness	xxxx
Pleasantness	x

Masculine sounds/feelings are medium high.
Feminine sounds/feelings are very low.
Pronunciation is average.

CORINA

Cheerfulness	xxx
Activity	xxxxxx
Toughness	xxxxxxxxxx
Unpleasantness	xxxxxxxxx
Sadness	xxxxx
Passivity	xxxxxxx
Gentleness	xxxx
Pleasantness	x

Masculine sounds/feelings are high.
Feminine sounds/feelings are medium low.
Pronunciation is more difficult.

CORNELIA

Cheerfulness	xxxxx
Activity	xxxxxx
Toughness	xxxxxxxxxx
Unpleasantness	xxxxxxxxx
Sadness	xxxxxxxxx
Passivity	xxxxxxxxxxx
Gentleness	xxxxxxxxxxx
Pleasantness	xxxxx

Masculine sounds/feelings are very high.
Feminine sounds/feelings are very high.
Pronunciation is most difficult.

CORINE

Cheerfulness	xxx
Activity	xxxxxx
Toughness	xxxxxxxxxx
Unpleasantness	xxxxxxxxx
Sadness	xxxxx
Passivity	xxxxxxx
Gentleness	xxxx
Pleasantness	x

Masculine sounds/feelings are high.
Feminine sounds/feelings are medium low.
Pronunciation is easier.

CORRINE

Cheerfulness	xxx
Activity	xxxxxxxxx
Toughness	xxxxxxxxxxxx
Unpleasantness	xxxxxxxxxxxx
Sadness	xxxxx
Passivity	xxxxxxx
Gentleness	xxxx
Pleasantness	x

Masculine sounds/feelings are very high.
Feminine sounds/feelings are medium low.
Pronunciation is more difficult.

CORINNE

Cheerfulness	xxx
Activity	xxxxxx
Toughness	xxxxxxxxxx
Unpleasantness	xxxxxxxxx
Sadness	xxxxxxxxx
Passivity	xxxxxxxxx
Gentleness	xxxx
Pleasantness	x

Masculine sounds/feelings are high.
Feminine sounds/feelings are medium.
Pronunciation is average.

COURTNEY

Cheerfulness	xxx
Activity	xxxxx
Toughness	xxxxxxxxxx
Unpleasantness	xxxxxxxxxxxx
Sadness	xxxxx
Passivity	xxxxxxx
Gentleness	xxxxxxx
Pleasantness	xxxxx

Masculine sounds/feelings are very high.
Feminine sounds/feelings are medium.
Pronunciation is easier.

CRISTINA

Cheerfulness xxxxx
Activity xxxxxxxxxxx
Toughness xxxxxxxxxxxxxxx
Unpleasantness xxxxxxxxxxxx

Sadness xxxxx
Passivity xxxxx
Gentleness x
Pleasantness x

Masculine sounds/feelings are very high.
Feminine sounds/feelings are very low.
Pronunciation is most difficult.

CRYSTAL

Cheerfulness xxx
Activity xxxxxxxxx
Toughness xxxxxxxxxxxx
Unpleasantness xxxxxxxxxxxx

Sadness xxxxx
Passivity xxxxxxx
Gentleness xxxx
Pleasantness xxxxxx

Masculine sounds/feelings are very high.
Feminine sounds/feelings are medium.
Pronunciation is more difficult.

CYNTHIA

Cheerfulness xxxxxxxxx
Activity xxxxxx
Toughness xxxxxxx
Unpleasantness x

Sadness xxxxx
Passivity xxx
Gentleness xxxx
Pleasantness xxxxxx

Masculine sounds/feelings are medium.
Feminine sounds/feelings are medium low.
Pronunciation is most difficult.

DAISY

Cheerfulness xxx
Activity x
Toughness xxxx
Unpleasantness xxxxx

Sadness xxxxx
Passivity xxx
Gentleness xxxx
Pleasantness xxxxxx

Masculine sounds/feelings are medium.
Feminine sounds/feelings are medium low.
Pronunciation is easiest.

DALE

Cheerfulness x
Activity x
Toughness xxxx
Unpleasantness xxxxx

Sadness xxxxxxxxx
Passivity xxxxx
Gentleness xxxx
Pleasantness xxxxxx

Masculine sounds/feelings are medium low.
Feminine sounds/feelings are medium.
Pronunciation is easier.

DANA

Cheerfulness x
Activity x
Toughness xxxx
Unpleasantness xxxxx

Sadness xxxxxxxxx
Passivity xxxxxxx
Gentleness x
Pleasantness x

Masculine sounds/feelings are medium low.
Feminine sounds/feelings are medium low.
Pronunciation is easier.

DANIELLE

Cheerfulness	xxxxx
Activity	x
Toughness	xxxx
Unpleasantness	xxxxx
Sadness	xxxxxxxxxxx
Passivity	xxxxxxxx
Gentleness	xxxxxxxxxx
Pleasantness	xxxxxxxxxxx

Masculine sounds/feelings are low.
Feminine sounds/feelings are very high.
Pronunciation is average.

DAPHNE

Cheerfulness	xxx
Activity	xxx
Toughness	xxxx
Unpleasantness	xxxxx
Sadness	xxxxxxxx
Passivity	xxxxxx
Gentleness	x
Pleasantness	x

Masculine sounds/feelings are medium.
Feminine sounds/feelings are medium low.
Pronunciation is easiest.

DARCY

Cheerfulness	xxxxxx
Activity	xxxxxx
Toughness	xxxxxxx
Unpleasantness	xxxxxxxxx
Sadness	xxxxx
Passivity	xxx
Gentleness	xxxx
Pleasantness	xxxxxx

Masculine sounds/feelings are high.
Feminine sounds/feelings are medium low.
Pronunciation is easier.

DARLA

Cheerfulness	xxx
Activity	xxxxxx
Toughness	xxxxxxx
Unpleasantness	xxxxxxxx
Sadness	xxxxxxxx
Passivity	xxxxx
Gentleness	xxxx
Pleasantness	xxxxx

Masculine sounds/feelings are medium high.
Feminine sounds/feelings are medium.
Pronunciation is more difficult.

DARLENE

Cheerfulness	xxxxx
Activity	xxxxxx
Toughness	xxxxxx
Unpleasantness	xxxxxxxx
Sadness	xxxxxxxxxxxx
Passivity	xxxxxxx
Gentleness	xxxxxxx
Pleasantness	xxxxxxxxxxx

Masculine sounds/feelings are high.
Feminine sounds/feelings are very high.
Pronunciation is most difficult.

DAWN

Cheerfulness	x
Activity	x
Toughness	xxxx
Unpleasantness	xxxxx
Sadness	xxxxxxxx
Passivity	xxxxxx
Gentleness	xxxx
Pleasantness	x

Masculine sounds/feelings are medium low.
Feminine sounds/feelings are medium.
Pronunciation is easiest.

DEANA

Cheerfulness	xxx
Activity	x
Toughness	xxxx
Unpleasantness	xxxxx
Sadness	xxxxxxxxx
Passivity	xxxxx
Gentleness	xxxx
Pleasantness	xxxxxx

Masculine sounds/feelings are medium.
Feminine sounds/feelings are medium.
Pronunciation is easier.

DEANNA

Cheerfulness	xxx
Activity	x
Toughness	xxxx
Unpleasantness	xxxxx
Sadness	xxxxxxxxxxxx
Passivity	xxxxxxx
Gentleness	xxxx
Pleasantness	xxxxxx

Masculine sounds/feelings are low.
Feminine sounds/feelings are high.
Pronunciation is easier.

DEANNE

Cheerfulness	xxx
Activity	x
Toughness	xxxx
Unpleasantness	xxxxx
Sadness	xxxxxxxxxxxx
Passivity	xxxxxxx
Gentleness	xxxx
Pleasantness	xxxxxx

Masculine sounds/feelings are medium.
Feminine sounds/feelings are high.
Pronunciation is easiest.

DEBBIE

Cheerfulness	xxxxxx
Activity	x
Toughness	xxxx
Unpleasantness	xxxxxxxxxxxx
Sadness	xxxxxxxxxxxx
Passivity	xxxxx
Gentleness	xxxxxxx
Pleasantness	xxxxxx

Masculine sounds/feelings are medium.
Feminine sounds/feelings are very high.
Pronunciation is easiest.

DEBORA

Cheerfulness	xxx
Activity	xxxxxx
Toughness	xxxxxxxxxx
Unpleasantness	xxxxxxxxxxxx
Sadness	xxxxxxxxx
Passivity	xxxxx
Gentleness	xxxx
Pleasantness	x

Masculine sounds/feelings are very high.
Feminine sounds/feelings are medium.
Pronunciation is more difficult.

DEBORAH

Cheerfulness	xxx
Activity	xxxxxx
Toughness	xxxxxxxxxx
Unpleasantness	xxxxxxxxxxxx
Sadness	xxxxxxxxx
Passivity	xxxxxxx
Gentleness	xxxx
Pleasantness	x

Masculine sounds/feelings are very high.
Feminine sounds/feelings are medium.
Pronunciation is average.

DEBRA

Cheerfulness	xxx
Activity	xxx
Toughness	xxxxxx
Unpleasantness	xxxxxxxxxxxx
Sadness	xxxxxxxx
Passivity	xxxxx
Gentleness	xxxx
Pleasantness	x

Masculine sounds/feelings are medium high.
Feminine sounds/feelings are medium.
Pronunciation is more difficult.

DEE

Cheerfulness	xxx
Activity	x
Toughness	xxxx
Unpleasantness	xxxxx
Sadness	xxxxx
Passivity	xxx
Gentleness	xxxx
Pleasantness	xxxxxx

Masculine sounds/feelings are medium.
Feminine sounds/feelings are medium low.
Pronunciation is easiest.

DEENA

Cheerfulness	xxx
Activity	x
Toughness	xxxx
Unpleasantness	xxxxx
Sadness	xxxxxxxx
Passivity	xxxxx
Gentleness	xxxx
Pleasantness	xxxxxx

Masculine sounds/feelings are medium.
Feminine sounds/feelings are medium.
Pronunciation is easier.

DEIDRE

Cheerfulness	xxx
Activity	xxx
Toughness	xxxxxxxxx
Unpleasantness	xxxxxxxxxxxx
Sadness	xxxxxxxx
Passivity	xxxxx
Gentleness	xxxx
Pleasantness	xxxxx

Masculine sounds/feelings are very high.
Feminine sounds/feelings are medium.
Pronunciation is easier.

DEIRDRE

Cheerfulness	xxx
Activity	xxxxxx
Toughness	xxxxxxxxxxxx
Unpleasantness	xxxxxxxxxxxxxxxxxx
Sadness	xxxxxxxx
Passivity	xxxxx
Gentleness	xxxx
Pleasantness	xxxxx

Masculine sounds/feelings are very high.
Feminine sounds/feelings are medium.
Pronunciation is more difficult.

DELIA

Cheerfulness	xxxxx
Activity	xxxxx
Toughness	xxxxxxxxx
Unpleasantness	xxxxx
Sadness	xxxxxxxx
Passivity	xxxxx
Gentleness	xxxx
Pleasantness	xxxxx

Masculine sounds/feelings are medium high.
Feminine sounds/feelings are medium.
Pronunciation is more difficult.

Women's And Girls' Names

DELLA

Cheerfulness	xxx
Activity	x
Toughness	xxxx
Unpleasantness	xxxxx
Sadness	xxxxxxxx
Passivity	xxxxxx
Gentleness	xxxxxx
Pleasantness	xxxxx

Masculine sounds/feelings are medium.
Feminine sounds/feelings are high.
Pronunciation is more difficult.

DELORES

Cheerfulness	xxx
Activity	xxxxxx
Toughness	xxxxxxxxx
Unpleasantness	xxxxxxxxx
Sadness	xxxxxxxx
Passivity	xxxxxxxxx
Gentleness	xxxxxxxxxx
Pleasantness	xxxxxxxxxxx

Masculine sounds/feelings are high.
Feminine sounds/feelings are very high.
Pronunciation is more difficult.

DELORIS

Cheerfulness	xxxxx
Activity	xxxxxxxxx
Toughness	xxxxxxxxxxxx
Unpleasantness	xxxxxxxxx
Sadness	xxxxxxxxx
Passivity	xxxxxx
Gentleness	xxxxxx
Pleasantness	xxxxxx

Masculine sounds/feelings are very high.
Feminine sounds/feelings are high.
Pronunciation is most difficult.

DENA

Cheerfulness	xxx
Activity	xxx
Toughness	xxxxxxx
Unpleasantness	xxxxx
Sadness	xxxxxxxxx
Passivity	xxxxx
Gentleness	x
Pleasantness	x

Masculine sounds/feelings are medium high.
Feminine sounds/feelings are low.
Pronunciation is easier.

DENISE

Cheerfulness	xxxxxx
Activity	xxx
Toughness	xxxxxxx
Unpleasantness	xxxxx
Sadness	xxxxxxxxx
Passivity	xxxxxxx
Gentleness	xxxxxxx
Pleasantness	xxxxxxxxxxx

Masculine sounds/feelings are medium.
Feminine sounds/feelings are very high.
Pronunciation is easier.

DESIREE

Cheerfulness	xxxxxxxxx
Activity	xxxxxxxxx
Toughness	xxxxxxxxxxxx
Unpleasantness	xxxxxxxxx
Sadness	xxxxx
Passivity	xxxxx
Gentleness	xxxxxxx
Pleasantness	xxxxxxxxxxx

Masculine sounds/feelings are very high.
Feminine sounds/feelings are high.
Pronunciation is average.

DIANA

Cheerfulness	xxx
Activity	xxx
Toughness	xxxxxxx
Unpleasantness	xxxxx
Sadness	xxxxxxxx
Passivity	xxxxxxx
Gentleness	x
Pleasantness	x

Masculine sounds/feelings are medium.
Feminine sounds/feelings are medium low.
Pronunciation is average.

DIANE

Cheerfulness	xxx
Activity	xxx
Toughness	xxxxxxx
Unpleasantness	xxxxx
Sadness	xxxxxxxx
Passivity	xxxxx
Gentleness	x
Pleasantness	x

Masculine sounds/feelings are medium high.
Feminine sounds/feelings are low.
Pronunciation is easier.

DIANNA

Cheerfulness	xxx
Activity	xxx
Toughness	xxxxxxx
Unpleasantness	xxxxx
Sadness	xxxxxxxxxxx
Passivity	xxxxxxxxx
Gentleness	x
Pleasantness	x

Masculine sounds/feelings are medium.
Feminine sounds/feelings are medium.
Pronunciation is more difficult.

DIANNE

Cheerfulness	xxx
Activity	xxx
Toughness	xxxxxxx
Unpleasantness	xxxxx
Sadness	xxxxxxxxxxxx
Passivity	xxxxxxxxx
Gentleness	x
Pleasantness	x

Masculine sounds/feelings are medium.
Feminine sounds/feelings are medium.
Pronunciation is easier.

DINA

Cheerfulness	xxx
Activity	xxx
Toughness	xxxxxxx
Unpleasantness	xxxxx
Sadness	xxxxxxxxx
Passivity	xxxxx
Gentleness	x
Pleasantness	x

Masculine sounds/feelings are medium high.
Feminine sounds/feelings are low.
Pronunciation is easier.

DIXIE

Cheerfulness	xxxxxx
Activity	xxx
Toughness	xxxxxxxxxx
Unpleasantness	xxxxxxxxx
Sadness	xxxxx
Passivity	xxxxx
Gentleness	xxxx
Pleasantness	xxxxx

Masculine sounds/feelings are high.
Feminine sounds/feelings are medium.
Pronunciation is easier.

DOLLIE

Cheerfulness	xxxxxx
Activity	xxx
Toughness	xxxx
Unpleasantness	xxxxx
Sadness	xxxxxxxxx
Passivity	xxxxx
Gentleness	xxxxxx
Pleasantness	xxxxxxxxxxxx

Masculine sounds/feelings are medium high.
Feminine sounds/feelings are very high.
Pronunciation is easier.

DOLLY

Cheerfulness	xxxxxx
Activity	xxx
Toughness	xxxx
Unpleasantness	xxxxx
Sadness	xxxxxxxxx
Passivity	xxxxx
Gentleness	xxxxxxx
Pleasantness	xxxxxxxxxxxx

Masculine sounds/feelings are medium high.
Feminine sounds/feelings are very high.
Pronunciation is easier.

DOLORES

Cheerfulness	xxx
Activity	xxxxxx
Toughness	xxxxxxx
Unpleasantness	xxxxxxxxx
Sadness	xxxxxxxxx
Passivity	xxxxxxxxx
Gentleness	xxxxxxxxxxx
Pleasantness	xxxxxxxxxxxx

Masculine sounds/feelings are medium high.
Feminine sounds/feelings are very high.
Pronunciation is more difficult.

DOMINIQUE

Cheerfulness	xxxxxxxxx
Activity	xxxxxx
Toughness	xxxxxxxxxx
Unpleasantness	xxxxxxxxx
Sadness	xxxxxxxxx
Passivity	xxxxxxxxx
Gentleness	xxxxxxx
Pleasantness	xxxxx

Masculine sounds/feelings are very high.
Feminine sounds/feelings are very high.
Pronunciation is easier.

DONA

Cheerfulness	x
Activity	x
Toughness	xxxx
Unpleasantness	xxxxx
Sadness	xxxxxxxxx
Passivity	xxxxxxx
Gentleness	x
Pleasantness	x

Masculine sounds/feelings are medium low.
Feminine sounds/feelings are medium low.
Pronunciation is easier.

DONNA

Cheerfulness	x
Activity	x
Toughness	xxxx
Unpleasantness	xxxxx
Sadness	xxxxxxxxxxxx
Passivity	xxxxxxxxx
Gentleness	x
Pleasantness	x

Masculine sounds/feelings are very low.
Feminine sounds/feelings are medium.
Pronunciation is average.

DORA

Cheerfulness	x
Activity	xxx
Toughness	xxxxxxx
Unpleasantness	xxxxxxxx
Sadness	xxxxx
Passivity	xxxxx
Gentleness	xxxx
Pleasantness	x

Masculine sounds/feelings are medium high.
Feminine sounds/feelings are low.
Pronunciation is average.

DOREEN

Cheerfulness	xxx
Activity	xxx
Toughness	xxxxxxx
Unpleasantness	xxxxxxxx
Sadness	xxxxxxxx
Passivity	xxxxxxx
Gentleness	xxxxxxx
Pleasantness	xxxxxx

Masculine sounds/feelings are medium.
Feminine sounds/feelings are high.
Pronunciation is easier.

DORIS

Cheerfulness	xxx
Activity	xxxxxx
Toughness	xxxxxxxxx
Unpleasantness	xxxxxxxx
Sadness	xxxxx
Passivity	xxxxx
Gentleness	xxxx
Pleasantness	x

Masculine sounds/feelings are high.
Feminine sounds/feelings are low.
Pronunciation is average.

DOROTHEA

Cheerfulness	xxxxxxxx
Activity	xxxxx
Toughness	xxxxxx
Unpleasantness	xxxxxxxx
Sadness	xxxxx
Passivity	xxxxx
Gentleness	xxxxxxxxxx
Pleasantness	xxxxxxxxxxx

Masculine sounds/feelings are very high.
Feminine sounds/feelings are very high.
Pronunciation is most difficult.

DOROTHY

Cheerfulness	xxxxxxxx
Activity	xxxxx
Toughness	xxxxxx
Unpleasantness	xxxxxxxx
Sadness	xxxxx
Passivity	xxxxx
Gentleness	xxxxxxxxxx
Pleasantness	xxxxxxxxxxx

Masculine sounds/feelings are very high.
Feminine sounds/feelings are very high.
Pronunciation is more difficult.

DORTHY

Cheerfulness	xxxxxx
Activity	xxx
Toughness	xxxxxx
Unpleasantness	xxxxxxxx
Sadness	xxxxx
Passivity	xxxxx
Gentleness	xxxxxxxxxx
Pleasantness	xxxxxxxxxxx

Masculine sounds/feelings are medium high.
Feminine sounds/feelings are very high.
Pronunciation is more difficult.

Women's And Girls' Names

EARLENE

Cheerfulness	xxxxx
Activity	xxx
Toughness	xxxx
Unpleasantness	x

Sadness	xxxxxxxx
Passivity	xxxxx
Gentleness	xxxxxxx
Pleasantness	xxxxxxxxxxx

Masculine sounds/feelings are low.
Feminine sounds/feelings are very high.
Pronunciation is average.

EARLINE

Cheerfulness	xxxxx
Activity	xxxxxx
Toughness	xxxxxxx
Unpleasantness	x

Sadness	xxxxxxxxx
Passivity	xxxxx
Gentleness	xxxx
Pleasantness	xxxxxx

Masculine sounds/feelings are medium high.
Feminine sounds/feelings are medium.
Pronunciation is easier.

EARNESTINE

Cheerfulness	xxxxxxxxx
Activity	xxxxxxxxx
Toughness	xxxxxxxxxx
Unpleasantness	xxxxx

Sadness	xxxxxxxxx
Passivity	xxxxxxx
Gentleness	xxxx
Pleasantness	x

Masculine sounds/feelings are very high.
Feminine sounds/feelings are medium.
Pronunciation is more difficult.

EBONY

Cheerfulness	xxxxxx
Activity	x
Toughness	x
Unpleasantness	xxxxx

Sadness	xxxxxxxxx
Passivity	xxxxx
Gentleness	xxxxxxx
Pleasantness	xxxxxx

Masculine sounds/feelings are low.
Feminine sounds/feelings are medium high.
Pronunciation is easier.

EDDIE

Cheerfulness	xxxxxx
Activity	x
Toughness	xxxxxxx
Unpleasantness	xxxxxxxxx

Sadness	xxxxxxxxx
Passivity	xxxxxxx
Gentleness	xxxxxxx
Pleasantness	xxxxxx

Masculine sounds/feelings are high.
Feminine sounds/feelings are high.
Pronunciation is easier.

EDITH

Cheerfulness	xxxxxxxxx
Activity	xxx
Toughness	xxxxxxx
Unpleasantness	xxxxx

Sadness	xxxxx
Passivity	xxxxx
Gentleness	xxxxxxx
Pleasantness	xxxxxx

Masculine sounds/feelings are very high.
Feminine sounds/feelings are medium.
Pronunciation is average.

EDNA

Cheerfulness	xxx
Activity	x
Toughness	xxxx
Unpleasantness	xxxxx
Sadness	xxxxxxxx
Passivity	xxxxxx
Gentleness	xxxx
Pleasantness	x

Masculine sounds/feelings are medium.
Feminine sounds/feelings are medium.
Pronunciation is average.

EDWINA

Cheerfulness	xxxxxxxxx
Activity	xxx
Toughness	xxxxxxx
Unpleasantness	xxxxx
Sadness	xxxxxxxxx
Passivity	xxxxxxx
Gentleness	xxxx
Pleasantness	xxxxx

Masculine sounds/feelings are medium.
Feminine sounds/feelings are medium high.
Pronunciation is more difficult.

EFFIE

Cheerfulness	xxxxxxxxxxx
Activity	xxxxxx
Toughness	x
Unpleasantness	x
Sadness	x
Passivity	xxx
Gentleness	xxxxxxx
Pleasantness	xxxxxx

Masculine sounds/feelings are medium high.
Feminine sounds/feelings are medium low.
Pronunciation is easiest.

EILEEN

Cheerfulness	xxxxxx
Activity	x
Toughness	x
Unpleasantness	x
Sadness	xxxxxxxxx
Passivity	xxxxx
Gentleness	xxxxxxxxxx
Pleasantness	xxxxxxxxxxxxxxxxx

Masculine sounds/feelings are low.
Feminine sounds/feelings are very high.
Pronunciation is easiest.

ELAINE

Cheerfulness	xxx
Activity	x
Toughness	x
Unpleasantness	x
Sadness	xxxxxxxxx
Passivity	xxxxxxx
Gentleness	xxxxxxx
Pleasantness	xxxxx

Masculine sounds/feelings are low.
Feminine sounds/feelings are high.
Pronunciation is easier.

ELEANOR

Cheerfulness	xxxxxxxxx
Activity	xxx
Toughness	xxxx
Unpleasantness	x
Sadness	xxxxxxxxx
Passivity	xxxxx
Gentleness	xxxxxxxxxx
Pleasantness	xxxxxxxxxxxxxxxx

Masculine sounds/feelings are medium low.
Feminine sounds/feelings are very high.
Pronunciation is easier.

Women's And Girls' Names

ELENA

Cheerfulness	xxxxxx
Activity	x
Toughness	x
Unpleasantness	x
Sadness	xxxxxxxx
Passivity	xxxxxxx
Gentleness	xxxxxxxxxxx
Pleasantness	xxxxxxxxxxx

Masculine sounds/feelings are very low.
Feminine sounds/feelings are very high.
Pronunciation is average.

ELINOR

Cheerfulness	xxxxxxxxx
Activity	xxxxxx
Toughness	xxxxxxx
Unpleasantness	x
Sadness	xxxxxxxxx
Passivity	xxxxxxx
Gentleness	xxxxxxx
Pleasantness	xxxxxx

Masculine sounds/feelings are medium.
Feminine sounds/feelings are high.
Pronunciation is average.

ELISA

Cheerfulness	xxxxxx
Activity	xxx
Toughness	xxxx
Unpleasantness	x
Sadness	xxxxx
Passivity	xxxxxxx
Gentleness	xxxxxxxxxxx
Pleasantness	xxxxxxxxxxx

Masculine sounds/feelings are low.
Feminine sounds/feelings are very high.
Pronunciation is more difficult.

ELISABETH

Cheerfulness	xxxxxxxxxxx
Activity	xxx
Toughness	xxxx
Unpleasantness	xxxxx
Sadness	xxxxxxxxx
Passivity	xxxxxxxxx
Gentleness	xxxxxxxxxxxxxxxx
Pleasantness	xxxxxxxxxxxxxxx

Masculine sounds/feelings are medium.
Feminine sounds/feelings are very high.
Pronunciation is most difficult.

ELISE

Cheerfulness	xxxxxx
Activity	x
Toughness	x
Unpleasantness	x
Sadness	xxxxx
Passivity	xxxxxxx
Gentleness	xxxxxxxxxxxxx
Pleasantness	xxxxxxxxxxxxxxxx

Masculine sounds/feelings are low.
Feminine sounds/feelings are very high.
Pronunciation is easier.

ELIZA

Cheerfulness	xxxxxx
Activity	xxx
Toughness	xxxx
Unpleasantness	x
Sadness	xxxxx
Passivity	xxxxxxx
Gentleness	xxxxxxxxxxx
Pleasantness	xxxxxxxxxxx

Masculine sounds/feelings are low.
Feminine sounds/feelings are very high.
Pronunciation is more difficult.

ELIZABETH

Cheerfulness	xxxxxxxxxxx
Activity	xxx
Toughness	xxxx
Unpleasantness	xxxxx

Sadness	xxxxxxxx
Passivity	xxxxxxxx
Gentleness	xxxxxxxxxxxxxxxx
Pleasantness	xxxxxxxxxxxxxxxx

Masculine sounds/feelings are medium.
Feminine sounds/feelings are very high.
Pronunciation is most difficult.

ELLA

Cheerfulness	xxx
Activity	x
Toughness	x
Unpleasantness	x

Sadness	xxxxx
Passivity	xxxxx
Gentleness	xxxxxxx
Pleasantness	xxxxxx

Masculine sounds/feelings are low.
Feminine sounds/feelings are medium.
Pronunciation is easier.

ELLEN

Cheerfulness	xxxxxx
Activity	x
Toughness	x
Unpleasantness	x

Sadness	xxxxxxxx
Passivity	xxxxxxxx
Gentleness	xxxxxxxxxx
Pleasantness	xxxxxx

Masculine sounds/feelings are low.
Feminine sounds/feelings are very high.
Pronunciation is easier.

ELMA

Cheerfulness	xxx
Activity	x
Toughness	x
Unpleasantness	x

Sadness	xxxxx
Passivity	xxxxxx
Gentleness	xxxxxxxxxx
Pleasantness	xxxxx

Masculine sounds/feelings are low.
Feminine sounds/feelings are high.
Pronunciation is average.

ELNORA

Cheerfulness	xxx
Activity	xxx
Toughness	xxxx
Unpleasantness	xxxxx

Sadness	xxxxxxxxx
Passivity	xxxxxxxxx
Gentleness	xxxxxxxxxxx
Pleasantness	xxxxxx

Masculine sounds/feelings are low.
Feminine sounds/feelings are very high.
Pronunciation is most difficult.

ELOISE

Cheerfulness	xxxxxx
Activity	xxx
Toughness	xxxx
Unpleasantness	x

Sadness	xxxxx
Passivity	xxxxxx
Gentleness	xxxxxxxxxx
Pleasantness	xxxxxxxxxxx

Masculine sounds/feelings are medium.
Feminine sounds/feelings are very high.
Pronunciation is average.

Women's And Girls' Names

ELSA

Cheerfulness	xxx
Activity	x
Toughness	x
Unpleasantness	x
Sadness	xxxxx
Passivity	xxxxx
Gentleness	xxxxxxx
Pleasantness	xxxxxx

Masculine sounds/feelings are low.
Feminine sounds/feelings are medium.
Pronunciation is average.

ELSIE

Cheerfulness	xxxxxx
Activity	x
Toughness	x
Unpleasantness	x
Sadness	xxxxx
Passivity	xxxxx
Gentleness	xxxxxxxxxx
Pleasantness	xxxxxxxxxx

Masculine sounds/feelings are low.
Feminine sounds/feelings are very high.
Pronunciation is easier.

ELVA

Cheerfulness	xxxxxx
Activity	x
Toughness	x
Unpleasantness	x
Sadness	xxxxx
Passivity	xxxxx
Gentleness	xxxxxxxxxx
Pleasantness	xxxxxxxxxx

Masculine sounds/feelings are low.
Feminine sounds/feelings are very high.
Pronunciation is more difficult.

ELVIA

Cheerfulness	xxxxxxxx
Activity	xxx
Toughness	xxxx
Unpleasantness	x
Sadness	xxxxx
Passivity	xxxxx
Gentleness	xxxxxxxxxx
Pleasantness	xxxxxxxxxxx

Masculine sounds/feelings are medium low.
Feminine sounds/feelings are very high.
Pronunciation is more difficult.

ELVIRA

Cheerfulness	xxxxxxxxx
Activity	xxx
Toughness	xxxx
Unpleasantness	xxxxx
Sadness	xxxxx
Passivity	xxxxx
Gentleness	xxxxxxxxxxxxx
Pleasantness	xxxxxxxxxxxxxxx

Masculine sounds/feelings are medium.
Feminine sounds/feelings are very high.
Pronunciation is most difficult.

EMILIA

Cheerfulness	xxxxxxxxx
Activity	xxxxxx
Toughness	xxxxxxx
Unpleasantness	x
Sadness	xxxxx
Passivity	xxxxxxx
Gentleness	xxxxxxxxxx
Pleasantness	xxxxxx

Masculine sounds/feelings are medium.
Feminine sounds/feelings are high.
Pronunciation is more difficult.

EMILY

Cheerfulness	xxxxxxxx
Activity	xxx
Toughness	xxxx
Unpleasantness	x
Sadness	xxxxx
Passivity	xxxxxxx
Gentleness	xxxxxxxxxxxxx
Pleasantness	xxxxxxxxxxx

Masculine sounds/feelings are medium low.
Feminine sounds/feelings are very high.
Pronunciation is easier.

EMMA

Cheerfulness	xxx
Activity	x
Toughness	x
Unpleasantness	x
Sadness	x
Passivity	xxxxxxx
Gentleness	xxxxxxxxxx
Pleasantness	x

Masculine sounds/feelings are low.
Feminine sounds/feelings are medium.
Pronunciation is easier.

ERICA

Cheerfulness	xxxxx
Activity	xxxxxx
Toughness	xxxxxxxxxx
Unpleasantness	xxxxxxxxx
Sadness	x
Passivity	xxxxx
Gentleness	xxxx
Pleasantness	x

Masculine sounds/feelings are very high.
Feminine sounds/feelings are very low.
Pronunciation is more difficult.

ERICKA

Cheerfulness	xxxxx
Activity	xxxxxx
Toughness	xxxxxxxxx
Unpleasantness	xxxxxxxxx
Sadness	x
Passivity	xxxxx
Gentleness	xxxx
Pleasantness	x

Masculine sounds/feelings are very high.
Feminine sounds/feelings are very low.
Pronunciation is more difficult.

ERIKA

Cheerfulness	xxxxx
Activity	xxxxxx
Toughness	xxxxxxxxxx
Unpleasantness	xxxxxxxxx
Sadness	x
Passivity	xxxxx
Gentleness	xxxx
Pleasantness	x

Masculine sounds/feelings are very high.
Feminine sounds/feelings are very low.
Pronunciation is more difficult.

ERIN

Cheerfulness	xxxxx
Activity	xxxxxx
Toughness	xxxxxxx
Unpleasantness	xxxxx
Sadness	xxxxx
Passivity	xxxxx
Gentleness	xxxx
Pleasantness	x

Masculine sounds/feelings are very high.
Feminine sounds/feelings are low.
Pronunciation is easier.

Women's And Girls' Names

ERMA

Cheerfulness	xxx
Activity	xxx
Toughness	xxxx
Unpleasantness	x
Sadness	x
Passivity	xxx
Gentleness	xxxx
Pleasantness	x

Masculine sounds/feelings are medium.
Feminine sounds/feelings are very low.
Pronunciation is easier.

ERNESTINE

Cheerfulness	xxxxxxxxx
Activity	xxxxxxxxx
Toughness	xxxxxxxxxx
Unpleasantness	xxxxx
Sadness	xxxxxxxxx
Passivity	xxxxxxx
Gentleness	xxxx
Pleasantness	x

Masculine sounds/feelings are very high.
Feminine sounds/feelings are medium.
Pronunciation is more difficult.

ESMERALDA

Cheerfulness	xxxxxx
Activity	xxx
Toughness	xxxxxxx
Unpleasantness	xxxxx
Sadness	xxxxxxxxx
Passivity	xxxxxxxxxxxxx
Gentleness	xxxxxxxxxxxxxxxx
Pleasantness	xxxxxxxxxxx

Masculine sounds/feelings are medium.
Feminine sounds/feelings are very high.
Pronunciation is most difficult.

ESPERANZA

Cheerfulness	xxxxxx
Activity	xxxxxx
Toughness	xxxxxxx
Unpleasantness	x
Sadness	xxxxx
Passivity	xxxxxxxxx
Gentleness	xxxxxxx
Pleasantness	xxxxx

Masculine sounds/feelings are medium.
Feminine sounds/feelings are medium high.
Pronunciation is most difficult.

ESSIE

Cheerfulness	xxxxxx
Activity	x
Toughness	x
Unpleasantness	x
Sadness	x
Passivity	xxx
Gentleness	xxxxxxx
Pleasantness	xxxxxx

Masculine sounds/feelings are low.
Feminine sounds/feelings are medium low.
Pronunciation is easiest.

ESTELA

Cheerfulness	xxxxxx
Activity	xxx
Toughness	xxxx
Unpleasantness	xxxxx
Sadness	xxxxx
Passivity	xxxxxxx
Gentleness	xxxxxxxxxxx
Pleasantness	xxxxxx

Masculine sounds/feelings are medium.
Feminine sounds/feelings are high.
Pronunciation is most difficult.

ESTELLA

Cheerfulness	xxxxx
Activity	xxx
Toughness	xxxx
Unpleasantness	xxxxx
Sadness	xxxxx
Passivity	xxxxxxx
Gentleness	xxxxxxxxxx
Pleasantness	xxxxxx

Masculine sounds/feelings are medium.
Feminine sounds/feelings are high.
Pronunciation is most difficult.

ESTELLE

Cheerfulness	xxxxxx
Activity	xxx
Toughness	xxxx
Unpleasantness	xxxxx
Sadness	xxxxx
Passivity	xxxxxxx
Gentleness	xxxxxxxxxxx
Pleasantness	xxxxxx

Masculine sounds/feelings are medium.
Feminine sounds/feelings are high.
Pronunciation is more difficult.

ESTER

Cheerfulness	xxxxxx
Activity	xxxxxx
Toughness	xxxxxxx
Unpleasantness	xxxxx
Sadness	x
Passivity	xxx
Gentleness	xxxx
Pleasantness	x

Masculine sounds/feelings are very high.
Feminine sounds/feelings are very low.
Pronunciation is easier.

ESTHER

Cheerfulness	xxxxxx
Activity	xxx
Toughness	xxxx
Unpleasantness	x
Sadness	x
Passivity	xxxxx
Gentleness	xxxxxxx
Pleasantness	xxxxxx

Masculine sounds/feelings are medium.
Feminine sounds/feelings are medium.
Pronunciation is average.

ETHEL

Cheerfulness	xxxxxxxxx
Activity	x
Toughness	x
Unpleasantness	x
Sadness	xxxxx
Passivity	xxxxxxx
Gentleness	xxxxxxxxxxxxx
Pleasantness	xxxxxxxxxxx

Masculine sounds/feelings are medium.
Feminine sounds/feelings are very high.
Pronunciation is more difficult.

ETTA

Cheerfulness	xxx
Activity	xxxxxx
Toughness	xxxxxxx
Unpleasantness	xxxxxxxx
Sadness	x
Passivity	xxx
Gentleness	xxxx
Pleasantness	x

Masculine sounds/feelings are very high.
Feminine sounds/feelings are very low.
Pronunciation is average.

Women's And Girls' Names

EUGENIA

Cheerfulness	xxxxxxxx
Activity	xxxxxxxx
Toughness	xxxxxxx
Unpleasantness	x
Sadness	xxxxx
Passivity	xxxxx
Gentleness	xxxx
Pleasantness	x

Masculine sounds/feelings are medium high.
Feminine sounds/feelings are low.
Pronunciation is most difficult.

EULA

Cheerfulness	x
Activity	xxx
Toughness	xxxx
Unpleasantness	x
Sadness	xxxxx
Passivity	xxx
Gentleness	xxxx
Pleasantness	xxxxxx

Masculine sounds/feelings are medium low.
Feminine sounds/feelings are medium low.
Pronunciation is average.

EUNICE

Cheerfulness	xxx
Activity	xxxxxx
Toughness	xxxxxxx
Unpleasantness	x
Sadness	xxxxx
Passivity	xxx
Gentleness	x
Pleasantness	x

Masculine sounds/feelings are medium low.
Feminine sounds/feelings are very low.
Pronunciation is easier.

EVA

Cheerfulness	xxxxxx
Activity	x
Toughness	x
Unpleasantness	x
Sadness	x
Passivity	xxx
Gentleness	xxxxxxx
Pleasantness	xxxxxx

Masculine sounds/feelings are low.
Feminine sounds/feelings are medium low.
Pronunciation is easier.

EVANGELINE

Cheerfulness	xxxxxxxxxxxxxxx
Activity	xxxxxx
Toughness	xxxx
Unpleasantness	x
Sadness	xxxxxxxxxxxx
Passivity	xxxxxxxxxx
Gentleness	xxxxxxxxxxxxxx
Pleasantness	xxxxxxxxxxx

Masculine sounds/feelings are medium high.
Feminine sounds/feelings are very high.
Pronunciation is most difficult.

EVE

Cheerfulness	xxxxxx
Activity	x
Toughness	x
Unpleasantness	x
Sadness	x
Passivity	x
Gentleness	xxxxxxx
Pleasantness	xxxxxxxxxxx

Masculine sounds/feelings are low.
Feminine sounds/feelings are medium.
Pronunciation is easiest.

EVELYN

Cheerfulness	xxxxxxxxxxx
Activity	xxx
Toughness	xxxx
Unpleasantness	x
Sadness	xxxxxxxx
Passivity	xxxxxx
Gentleness	xxxxxxxxxxxxx
Pleasantness	xxxxxxxxxxxxxxxxx

Masculine sounds/feelings are medium.
Feminine sounds/feelings are very high.
Pronunciation is more difficult.

FAITH

Cheerfulness	xxxxxx
Activity	xxx
Toughness	x
Unpleasantness	x
Sadness	x
Passivity	x
Gentleness	xxxx
Pleasantness	xxxxxx

Masculine sounds/feelings are medium.
Feminine sounds/feelings are very low.
Pronunciation is easier.

FANNIE

Cheerfulness	xxxxxx
Activity	xxx
Toughness	x
Unpleasantness	x
Sadness	xxxxxxxxx
Passivity	xxxxxxx
Gentleness	xxxx
Pleasantness	xxxxxx

Masculine sounds/feelings are very low.
Feminine sounds/feelings are medium high.
Pronunciation is easiest.

FAY

Cheerfulness	xxx
Activity	xxx
Toughness	x
Unpleasantness	x
Sadness	x
Passivity	x
Gentleness	x
Pleasantness	x

Masculine sounds/feelings are low.
Feminine sounds/feelings are very low.
Pronunciation is easiest.

FAYE

Cheerfulness	xxxxxx
Activity	xxxxxx
Toughness	xxxx
Unpleasantness	x
Sadness	x
Passivity	x
Gentleness	x
Pleasantness	x

Masculine sounds/feelings are medium.
Feminine sounds/feelings are very low.
Pronunciation is easiest.

FELICIA

Cheerfulness	xxxxxxxxx
Activity	xxxxxxxxx
Toughness	xxxxxxx
Unpleasantness	x
Sadness	xxxxx
Passivity	xxxxx
Gentleness	xxxxxxx
Pleasantness	xxxxx

Masculine sounds/feelings are medium high.
Feminine sounds/feelings are medium.
Pronunciation is most difficult.

Women's And Girls' Names

FERN

Cheerfulness	xxxxxx
Activity	xxxxxx
Toughness	xxxx
Unpleasantness	x
Sadness	xxxxx
Passivity	xxx
Gentleness	x
Pleasantness	x

Masculine sounds/feelings are medium.
Feminine sounds/feelings are very low.
Pronunciation is easiest.

FLORA

Cheerfulness	xxx
Activity	xxxxxx
Toughness	xxxx
Unpleasantness	xxxxx
Sadness	xxxxx
Passivity	xxxxx
Gentleness	xxxxxxx
Pleasantness	xxxxxx

Masculine sounds/feelings are medium.
Feminine sounds/feelings are medium.
Pronunciation is more difficult.

FLORENCE

Cheerfulness	xxxxxx
Activity	xxxxxx
Toughness	xxxx
Unpleasantness	xxxxx
Sadness	xxxxxxxxx
Passivity	xxxxxxxxx
Gentleness	xxxxxxxxxxx
Pleasantness	xxxxxx

Masculine sounds/feelings are medium.
Feminine sounds/feelings are very high.
Pronunciation is most difficult.

FLOSSIE

Cheerfulness	xxxxxxxxx
Activity	xxxxxx
Toughness	x
Unpleasantness	x
Sadness	xxxxx
Passivity	xxx
Gentleness	xxxxxxx
Pleasantness	xxxxxxxxxxx

Masculine sounds/feelings are medium low.
Feminine sounds/feelings are medium high.
Pronunciation is easier.

FRAN

Cheerfulness	xxx
Activity	xxxxxx
Toughness	xxxx
Unpleasantness	xxxxx
Sadness	xxxxx
Passivity	xxxxx
Gentleness	x
Pleasantness	x

Masculine sounds/feelings are medium high.
Feminine sounds/feelings are very low.
Pronunciation is easier.

FRANCES

Cheerfulness	xxxxxx
Activity	xxxxxxxxx
Toughness	xxxxxxx
Unpleasantness	xxxxx
Sadness	xxxxx
Passivity	xxxxxxx
Gentleness	xxxx
Pleasantness	xxxxxx

Masculine sounds/feelings are medium high.
Feminine sounds/feelings are medium.
Pronunciation is more difficult.

FRANCINE

Cheerfulness	xxxxx
Activity	xxxxxxxx
Toughness	xxxxxx
Unpleasantness	xxxxx
Sadness	xxxxxxxx
Passivity	xxxxxxx
Gentleness	x
Pleasantness	x

Masculine sounds/feelings are medium high.
Feminine sounds/feelings are medium low.
Pronunciation is more difficult.

FRANCIS

Cheerfulness	xxxxx
Activity	xxxxxxxx
Toughness	xxxxxxx
Unpleasantness	xxxxx
Sadness	xxxxx
Passivity	xxxxx
Gentleness	x
Pleasantness	x

Masculine sounds/feelings are medium high.
Feminine sounds/feelings are very low.
Pronunciation is more difficult.

FRANCISCA

Cheerfulness	xxxxx
Activity	xxxxxxxx
Toughness	xxxxxxxxx
Unpleasantness	xxxxxxxx
Sadness	xxxxx
Passivity	xxxxxxx
Gentleness	x
Pleasantness	x

Masculine sounds/feelings are very high.
Feminine sounds/feelings are very low.
Pronunciation is most difficult.

FRANKIE

Cheerfulness	xxxxxxxxx
Activity	xxxxxxxx
Toughness	xxxxxxxxx
Unpleasantness	xxxxxxxx
Sadness	x
Passivity	xxxxx
Gentleness	xxxx
Pleasantness	xxxxxx

Masculine sounds/feelings are very high.
Feminine sounds/feelings are low.
Pronunciation is average.

FREDA

Cheerfulness	xxxxx
Activity	xxxxx
Toughness	xxxxxxx
Unpleasantness	xxxxxxxx
Sadness	xxxxx
Passivity	xxxxx
Gentleness	xxxx
Pleasantness	x

Masculine sounds/feelings are high.
Feminine sounds/feelings are low.
Pronunciation is more difficult.

FRIEDA

Cheerfulness	xxxxxxxxx
Activity	xxxxx
Toughness	xxxxxx
Unpleasantness	xxxxxxxx
Sadness	xxxxx
Passivity	xxxxx
Gentleness	xxxxxxx
Pleasantness	xxxxxx

Masculine sounds/feelings are very high.
Feminine sounds/feelings are medium.
Pronunciation is most difficult.

GABRIELA

Cheerfulness	xxxxxx
Activity	xxxxxx
Toughness	xxxxxxx
Unpleasantness	xxxxxxxxx
Sadness	xxxxxxxxx
Passivity	xxxxxxx
Gentleness	xxxxxxxxxxx
Pleasantness	xxxxxxxxxxxx

Masculine sounds/feelings are high.
Feminine sounds/feelings are very high.
Pronunciation is most difficult.

GABRIELLE

Cheerfulness	xxxxxx
Activity	xxxxxx
Toughness	xxxxxxx
Unpleasantness	xxxxxxxxx
Sadness	xxxxxxxxx
Passivity	xxxxxxx
Gentleness	xxxxxxxxxxx
Pleasantness	xxxxxxxxxxxx

Masculine sounds/feelings are high.
Feminine sounds/feelings are very high.
Pronunciation is more difficult.

GAIL

Cheerfulness	x
Activity	xxx
Toughness	xxxx
Unpleasantness	x
Sadness	xxxxx
Passivity	xxx
Gentleness	xxxx
Pleasantness	xxxxxx

Masculine sounds/feelings are medium low.
Feminine sounds/feelings are medium low.
Pronunciation is easiest.

GALE

Cheerfulness	x
Activity	xxx
Toughness	xxxx
Unpleasantness	x
Sadness	xxxxx
Passivity	xxx
Gentleness	xxxx
Pleasantness	xxxxxx

Masculine sounds/feelings are medium low.
Feminine sounds/feelings are medium low.
Pronunciation is easiest.

GAY

Cheerfulness	x
Activity	xxx
Toughness	xxxx
Unpleasantness	x
Sadness	x
Passivity	x
Gentleness	x
Pleasantness	x

Masculine sounds/feelings are medium low.
Feminine sounds/feelings are very low.
Pronunciation is easiest.

GAYLE

Cheerfulness	x
Activity	xxx
Toughness	xxxx
Unpleasantness	x
Sadness	xxxxx
Passivity	xxx
Gentleness	xxxx
Pleasantness	xxxxxx

Masculine sounds/feelings are medium low.
Feminine sounds/feelings are medium low.
Pronunciation is average.

GENA

Cheerfulness	xxxxx
Activity	xxx
Toughness	x
Unpleasantness	x
Sadness	xxxxx
Passivity	xxxxx
Gentleness	xxxx
Pleasantness	x

Masculine sounds/feelings are medium.
Feminine sounds/feelings are low.
Pronunciation is more difficult.

GENEVA

Sheerfulness	xxxxxxxxxxxx
Activity	xxx
Toughness	x
Unpleasantness	x
Sadness	xxxxx
Passivity	xxxxx
Gentleness	xxxxxxxxxxx
Pleasantness	xxxxxxxxxxxx

Masculine sounds/feelings are medium low.
Feminine sounds/feelings are very high.
Pronunciation is most difficult.

GENEVIEVE

Cheerfulness	xxxxxxxxxxxxxxxxxxxx
Activity	xxx
Toughness	x
Unpleasantness	x
Sadness	xxxxx
Passivity	xxxxx
Gentleness	xxxxxxxxxxxxxxxxxxxx
Pleasantness	xxxxxxxxxxxxxxxxxxxx

Masculine sounds/feelings are medium high.
Feminine sounds/feelings are very high.
Pronunciation is most difficult.

GEORGETTE

Cheerfulness	xxxxxxxxx
Activity	xxxxxxxxxxxxxx
Toughness	xxxxxxxxxxxx
Unpleasantness	xxxxxxxxxxxx
Sadness	x
Passivity	xxxxx
Gentleness	xxxxxxxxxxx
Pleasantness	xxxxx

Masculine sounds/feelings are very high.
Feminine sounds/feelings are medium.
Pronunciation is most difficult.

GEORGIA

Cheerfulness	xxxxxxxxxxxx
Activity	xxxxxxxxxxxx
Toughness	xxxxxxx
Unpleasantness	xxxxx
Sadness	x
Passivity	xxx
Gentleness	xxxxxxx
Pleasantness	xxxxx

Masculine sounds/feelings are very high.
Feminine sounds/feelings are medium low.
Pronunciation is most difficult.

GEORGINA

Cheerfulness	xxxxxxxxxxx
Activity	xxxxxxxxxxx
Toughness	xxxxxxx
Unpleasantness	xxxxx
Sadness	xxxxx
Passivity	xxxxx
Gentleness	xxxxxxx
Pleasantness	xxxxx

Masculine sounds/feelings are very high.
Feminine sounds/feelings are medium.
Pronunciation is most difficult.

GERALDINE

Cheerfulness	xxxxxxxx
Activity	xxxxxxxx
Toughness	xxxxxxxxx
Unpleasantness	xxxxxxxx
Sadness	xxxxxxxxxxxx
Passivity	xxxxxxxxxx
Gentleness	xxxxxxxxx
Pleasantness	xxxxxx

Masculine sounds/feelings are very high.
Feminine sounds/feelings are very high.
Pronunciation is most difficult.

GERTRUDE

Cheerfulness	xxxxx
Activity	xxxxxxxxxxxxxx
Toughness	xxxxxxxxxxxxxxxx
Unpleasantness	xxxxxxxxxxxx
Sadness	xxxxx
Passivity	xxx
Gentleness	x
Pleasantness	x

Masculine sounds/feelings are very high.
Feminine sounds/feelings are very low.
Pronunciation is most difficult.

GINA

Cheerfulness	xxx
Activity	xxxxxx
Toughness	xxxxxxx
Unpleasantness	x
Sadness	xxxxx
Passivity	xxx
Gentleness	x
Pleasantness	x

Masculine sounds/feelings are medium high.
Feminine sounds/feelings are very low.
Pronunciation is easier.

GINGER

Cheerfulness	xxxxxxxxx
Activity	xxxxxxxxxxxxxx
Toughness	xxxxxxxxxxxxxx
Unpleasantness	x
Sadness	x
Passivity	x
Gentleness	x
Pleasantness	x

Masculine sounds/feelings are very high.
Feminine sounds/feelings are very low.
Pronunciation is average.

GLADYS

Cheerfulness	xxx
Activity	xxxxxx
Toughness	xxxxxxxxxx
Unpleasantness	xxxxx
Sadness	xxxxxxxxx
Passivity	xxxxxxx
Gentleness	xxxx
Pleasantness	xxxxxx

Masculine sounds/feelings are medium.
Feminine sounds/feelings are medium high.
Pronunciation is average.

GLENDA

Cheerfulness	xxx
Activity	xxx
Toughness	xxxxxxx
Unpleasantness	xxxxx
Sadness	xxxxxxxxxxxx
Passivity	xxxxxxxxx
Gentleness	xxxxxxx
Pleasantness	xxxxxx

Masculine sounds/feelings are medium.
Feminine sounds/feelings are very high.
Pronunciation is more difficult.

GLENNA

Cheerfulness	xxx
Activity	xxx
Toughness	xxxx
Unpleasantness	x
Sadness	xxxxxxxxxxx
Passivity	xxxxxxxx
Gentleness	xxxxxx
Pleasantness	xxxxxx

Masculine sounds/feelings are very low.
Feminine sounds/feelings are very high.
Pronunciation is more difficult.

GLORIA

Cheerfulness	xxx
Activity	xxxxxxxx
Toughness	xxxxxxxxx
Unpleasantness	xxxxx
Sadness	xxxxx
Passivity	xxxxx
Gentleness	xxxxxx
Pleasantness	xxxxxx

Masculine sounds/feelings are medium high.
Feminine sounds/feelings are medium.
Pronunciation is most difficult.

GOLDIE

Cheerfulness	xxx
Activity	xxx
Toughness	xxxxxxx
Unpleasantness	xxxxxxxx
Sadness	xxxxxxxxxxxx
Passivity	xxxxxxx
Gentleness	xxxxxxx
Pleasantness	xxxxxxxxxxx

Masculine sounds/feelings are medium.
Feminine sounds/feelings are very high.
Pronunciation is easier.

GRACE

Cheerfulness	x
Activity	xxxxx
Toughness	xxxxxxx
Unpleasantness	xxxxx
Sadness	x
Passivity	x
Gentleness	x
Pleasantness	x

Masculine sounds/feelings are medium high.
Feminine sounds/feelings are very low.
Pronunciation is easier.

GRACIE

Cheerfulness	xxx
Activity	xxxxxx
Toughness	xxxxxxx
Unpleasantness	xxxxx
Sadness	x
Passivity	x
Gentleness	xxxx
Pleasantness	xxxxxx

Masculine sounds/feelings are medium.
Feminine sounds/feelings are very low.
Pronunciation is easier.

GRACIELA

Cheerfulness	xxxxxx
Activity	xxxxx
Toughness	xxxxxxx
Unpleasantness	xxxxx
Sadness	xxxxx
Passivity	xxxxx
Gentleness	xxxxxxxxxx
Pleasantness	xxxxxxxxxxx

Masculine sounds/feelings are medium.
Feminine sounds/feelings are very high.
Pronunciation is most difficult.

Women's And Girls' Names

GRETA

Cheerfulness	xxx
Activity	xxxxxxxx
Toughness	xxxxxxxxxx
Unpleasantness	xxxxxxxx
Sadness	x
Passivity	xxx
Gentleness	xxxx
Pleasantness	x

Masculine sounds/feelings are very high.
Feminine sounds/feelings are very low.
Pronunciation is more difficult.

GRETCHEN

Cheerfulness	xxxxxxxx
Activity	xxxxxxxxxxxx
Toughness	xxxxxxxxxx
Unpleasantness	xxxxxxxxx
Sadness	xxxxx
Passivity	xxxxxxx
Gentleness	xxxxxxx
Pleasantness	x

Masculine sounds/feelings are very high.
Feminine sounds/feelings are medium.
Pronunciation is most difficult.

GUADALUPE

Cheerfulness	x
Activity	xxxxxxxx
Toughness	xxxxxxxxxxxx
Unpleasantness	xxxxx
Sadness	xxxxxxxxx
Passivity	xxxxxxxxx
Gentleness	xxxx
Pleasantness	xxxxxx

Masculine sounds/feelings are medium high.
Feminine sounds/feelings are medium high.
Pronunciation is more difficult.

GWEN

Cheerfulness	xxxxxx
Activity	xxx
Toughness	xxxx
Unpleasantness	x
Sadness	xxxxx
Passivity	xxxxx
Gentleness	xxxx
Pleasantness	xxxxxx

Masculine sounds/feelings are medium.
Feminine sounds/feelings are medium.
Pronunciation is easiest.

GWENDOLYN

Cheerfulness	xxxxxxxxxxxx
Activity	xxxxxxxxx
Toughness	xxxxxxxxxx
Unpleasantness	xxxxx
Sadness	xxxxxxxxxxxxxxxxx
Passivity	xxxxxxxxxxx
Gentleness	xxxxxxx
Pleasantness	xxxxxxxxxxxx

Masculine sounds/feelings are very high.
Feminine sounds/feelings are very high.
Pronunciation is most difficult.

HALEY

Cheerfulness	xxx
Activity	x
Toughness	x
Unpleasantness	x
Sadness	xxxxx
Passivity	xxx
Gentleness	xxxxxxx
Pleasantness	xxxxxxxxxxx

Masculine sounds/feelings are low.
Feminine sounds/feelings are medium high.
Pronunciation is easier.

HANNAH

Cheerfulness	x
Activity	x
Toughness	x
Unpleasantness	x

Sadness	xxxxxxxx
Passivity	xxxxxxxx
Gentleness	x
Pleasantness	x

Masculine sounds/feelings are very low.
Feminine sounds/feelings are medium.
Pronunciation is easiest.

HARRIET

Cheerfulness	xxxxxx
Activity	xxxxxx
Toughness	xxxxxxx
Unpleasantness	xxxxxxxxx

Sadness	x
Passivity	xxxxx
Gentleness	xxxxxxx
Pleasantness	xxxxxx

Masculine sounds/feelings are high.
Feminine sounds/feelings are medium.
Pronunciation is more difficult.

HARRIETT

Cheerfulness	xxxxxx
Activity	xxxxxxxxx
Toughness	xxxxxxxxxx
Unpleasantness	xxxxxxxxxxxx

Sadness	x
Passivity	xxxxx
Gentleness	xxxxxxx
Pleasantness	xxxxxx

Masculine sounds/feelings are very high.
Feminine sounds/feelings are medium.
Pronunciation is more difficult.

HATTIE

Cheerfulness	xxx
Activity	xxxxxx
Toughness	xxxxxx
Unpleasantness	xxxxxxxx

Sadness	x
Passivity	xxx
Gentleness	xxxx
Pleasantness	xxxxx

Masculine sounds/feelings are medium high.
Feminine sounds/feelings are low.
Pronunciation is easier.

HAZEL

Cheerfulness	xxx
Activity	x
Toughness	x
Unpleasantness	x

Sadness	xxxxx
Passivity	xxxxxx
Gentleness	xxxxxxxxxx
Pleasantness	xxxxxxxxxxx

Masculine sounds/feelings are very low.
Feminine sounds/feelings are very high.
Pronunciation is average.

HEATHER

Cheerfulness	xxxxxx
Activity	xxx
Toughness	xxxx
Unpleasantness	x

Sadness	x
Passivity	xxx
Gentleness	xxxxxxx
Pleasantness	xxxxxxxxxxx

Masculine sounds/feelings are medium.
Feminine sounds/feelings are medium.
Pronunciation is easier.

Women's And Girls' Names

HEIDI

Cheerfulness	xxxxx
Activity	xxx
Toughness	xxxxxxx
Unpleasantness	xxxxx
Sadness	xxxxx
Passivity	xxx
Gentleness	xxxx
Pleasantness	xxxxxx

Masculine sounds/feelings are high.
Feminine sounds/feelings are medium low.
Pronunciation is easiest.

HELEN

Cheerfulness	xxxxx
Activity	x
Toughness	x
Unpleasantness	x
Sadness	xxxxxxxxx
Passivity	xxxxxxx
Gentleness	xxxxxxxxxxx
Pleasantness	xxxxxxxxxxxx

Masculine sounds/feelings are very low.
Feminine sounds/feelings are very high.
Pronunciation is easier.

HELENA

Cheerfulness	xxxxx
Activity	x
Toughness	x
Unpleasantness	x
Sadness	xxxxxxxxx
Passivity	xxxxxxx
Gentleness	xxxxxxxxxxx
Pleasantness	xxxxxxxxxxxx

Masculine sounds/feelings are very low.
Feminine sounds/feelings are very high.
Pronunciation is more difficult.

HELENE

Cheerfulness	xxxxx
Activity	x
Toughness	x
Unpleasantness	x
Sadness	xxxxxxxxx
Passivity	xxxxx
Gentleness	xxxxxxxxxxx
Pleasantness	xxxxxxxxxxxxxxxxx

Masculine sounds/feelings are very low.
Feminine sounds/feelings are very high.
Pronunciation is easiest.

HENRIETTA

Cheerfulness	xxxxxxxxx
Activity	xxxxxxxxx
Toughness	xxxxxxxxx
Unpleasantness	xxxxxxxxxxxxx
Sadness	xxxxx
Passivity	xxxxxxx
Gentleness	xxxxxxxxxxx
Pleasantness	xxxxxx

Masculine sounds/feelings are very high.
Feminine sounds/feelings are high.
Pronunciation is most difficult.

HILARY

Cheerfulness	xxxxxxxxx
Activity	xxxxxxxxx
Toughness	xxxxxxx
Unpleasantness	xxxxx
Sadness	xxxxx
Passivity	xxx
Gentleness	xxxxxxx
Pleasantness	xxxxxxxxxxxx

Masculine sounds/feelings are high.
Feminine sounds/feelings are medium high.
Pronunciation is average.

HILDA

Cheerfulness	xxx
Activity	x
Toughness	xxxx
Unpleasantness	xxxxx
Sadness	xxxxxxxx
Passivity	xxxxx
Gentleness	xxxxxx
Pleasantness	xxxxxxxxxxx

Masculine sounds/feelings are low.
Feminine sounds/feelings are very high.
Pronunciation is more difficult.

HILLARY

Cheerfulness	xxxxxxxx
Activity	xxxxxxxx
Toughness	xxxxxxx
Unpleasantness	xxxxx
Sadness	xxxxx
Passivity	xxx
Gentleness	xxxxxxx
Pleasantness	xxxxxxxxxxx

Masculine sounds/feelings are high.
Feminine sounds/feelings are medium high.
Pronunciation is average.

HOLLY

Cheerfulness	xxxxxx
Activity	xxx
Toughness	x
Unpleasantness	x
Sadness	xxxxx
Passivity	xxx
Gentleness	xxxxxxx
Pleasantness	xxxxxxxxxxx

Masculine sounds/feelings are medium.
Feminine sounds/feelings are medium high.
Pronunciation is easiest.

HOPE

Cheerfulness	x
Activity	xxx
Toughness	xxxx
Unpleasantness	xxxxx
Sadness	xxxxx
Passivity	xxx
Gentleness	x
Pleasantness	x

Masculine sounds/feelings are medium.
Feminine sounds/feelings are very low.
Pronunciation is easiest.

IDA

Cheerfulness	xxx
Activity	xxx
Toughness	xxxxxxx
Unpleasantness	xxxxx
Sadness	xxxxx
Passivity	xxx
Gentleness	x
Pleasantness	x

Masculine sounds/feelings are medium high.
Feminine sounds/feelings are very low.
Pronunciation is easier.

ILA

Cheerfulness	xxx
Activity	xxx
Toughness	xxxx
Unpleasantness	x
Sadness	xxxxx
Passivity	xxx
Gentleness	xxxx
Pleasantness	xxxxxx

Masculine sounds/feelings are medium.
Feminine sounds/feelings are medium low.
Pronunciation is easier.

Women's And Girls' Names

ILENE

Cheerfulness	xxxxxx
Activity	xxx
Toughness	xxxx
Unpleasantness	x
Sadness	xxxxxxxxx
Passivity	xxxxx
Gentleness	xxxxxxx
Pleasantness	xxxxxxxxxxxx

Masculine sounds/feelings are medium.
Feminine sounds/feelings are very high.
Pronunciation is easiest.

IMELDA

Cheerfulness	xxxxx
Activity	xxx
Toughness	xxxxxxx
Unpleasantness	xxxxx
Sadness	xxxxxxxxx
Passivity	xxxxxxxxx
Gentleness	xxxxxxxxxxx
Pleasantness	xxxxxx

Masculine sounds/feelings are medium.
Feminine sounds/feelings are very high.
Pronunciation is most difficult.

IMOGENE

Cheerfulness	xxxxxxxxx
Activity	xxxxxx
Toughness	xxxx
Unpleasantness	xxxxx
Sadness	xxxxxxxxx
Passivity	xxxxxxx
Gentleness	xxxxxxx
Pleasantness	xxxxxx

Masculine sounds/feelings are medium.
Feminine sounds/feelings are high.
Pronunciation is average.

INA

Cheerfulness	xxx
Activity	xxx
Toughness	xxxx
Unpleasantness	x
Sadness	xxxxx
Passivity	xxx
Gentleness	x
Pleasantness	x

Masculine sounds/feelings are medium.
Feminine sounds/feelings are very low.
Pronunciation is easiest.

INEZ

Cheerfulness	xxxxxx
Activity	xxx
Toughness	xxxx
Unpleasantness	x
Sadness	xxxxx
Passivity	xxxxxxx
Gentleness	xxxxxxx
Pleasantness	xxxxxx

Masculine sounds/feelings are medium.
Feminine sounds/feelings are medium.
Pronunciation is easiest.

INGRID

Cheerfulness	xxxxxxxxx
Activity	xxxxxxxxxxx
Toughness	xxxxxxxxxxxxxxxx
Unpleasantness	xxxxxxxxx
Sadness	xxxxx
Passivity	xxx
Gentleness	x
Pleasantness	x

Masculine sounds/feelings are very high.
Feminine sounds/feelings are very low.
Pronunciation is more difficult.

IRENE

Cheerfulness	xxxxx
Activity	xxxxxx
Toughness	xxxxxxx
Unpleasantness	xxxxx
Sadness	xxxxx
Passivity	xxx
Gentleness	xxxx
Pleasantness	xxxxxx

Masculine sounds/feelings are very high.
Feminine sounds/feelings are medium low.
Pronunciation is easiest.

IRIS

Cheerfulness	xxxxxx
Activity	xxxxxx
Toughness	xxxxxxx
Unpleasantness	xxxxx
Sadness	x
Passivity	x
Gentleness	xxxx
Pleasantness	xxxxxx

Masculine sounds/feelings are very high.
Feminine sounds/feelings are very low.
Pronunciation is easier.

IRMA

Cheerfulness	xxx
Activity	xxx
Toughness	xxxx
Unpleasantness	x
Sadness	x
Passivity	xxx
Gentleness	xxxx
Pleasantness	x

Masculine sounds/feelings are medium.
Feminine sounds/feelings are very low.
Pronunciation is easier.

ISABEL

Cheerfulness	xxxxxx
Activity	xxx
Toughness	xxxx
Unpleasantness	xxxxx
Sadness	xxxxxxxxx
Passivity	xxxxxxx
Gentleness	xxxxxxxxxx
Pleasantness	xxxxxxxxxxx

Masculine sounds/feelings are medium.
Feminine sounds/feelings are very high.
Pronunciation is average.

ISABELLE

Cheerfulness	xxxxxx
Activity	xxx
Toughness	xxxx
Unpleasantness	xxxxx
Sadness	xxxxxxxxx
Passivity	xxxxxxxxx
Gentleness	xxxxxxxxxx
Pleasantness	xxxxxxxxxxxx

Masculine sounds/feelings are medium.
Feminine sounds/feelings are very high.
Pronunciation is average.

IVA

Cheerfulness	xxxxxx
Activity	xxx
Toughness	xxxx
Unpleasantness	x
Sadness	x
Passivity	x
Gentleness	xxxx
Pleasantness	xxxxxx

Masculine sounds/feelings are medium.
Feminine sounds/feelings are very low.
Pronunciation is easier.

Women's And Girls' Names

IVY

Cheerfulness	xxxxxxxx
Activity	x
Toughness	x
Unpleasantness	x
Sadness	x
Passivity	x
Gentleness	xxxxxxxxxx
Pleasantness	xxxxxxxxxxxxxx

Masculine sounds/feelings are medium.
Feminine sounds/feelings are high.
Pronunciation is easiest.

JACKIE

Cheerfulness	xxxxx
Activity	xxx
Toughness	xxxx
Unpleasantness	xxxxx
Sadness	x
Passivity	xxxxx
Gentleness	xxxx
Pleasantness	xxxxxx

Masculine sounds/feelings are medium high.
Feminine sounds/feelings are low.
Pronunciation is easiest.

JACLYN

Cheerfulness	xxxxxx
Activity	xxxxxx
Toughness	xxxxxxx
Unpleasantness	xxxxx
Sadness	xxxxxxxxx
Passivity	xxxxxxxxx
Gentleness	xxxx
Pleasantness	xxxxxx

Masculine sounds/feelings are medium.
Feminine sounds/feelings are medium high.
Pronunciation is more difficult.

JACQUELINE

Cheerfulness	xxxxxxxxxxx
Activity	xxxxx
Toughness	xxxxxxxxxx
Unpleasantness	xxxxxxxxx
Sadness	xxxxxxxxx
Passivity	xxxxxxxxxxxxxx
Gentleness	xxxxxxx
Pleasantness	xxxxxxxxxxx

Masculine sounds/feelings are very high.
Feminine sounds/feelings are very high.
Pronunciation is most difficult.

JACQUELYN

Cheerfulness	xxxxxxxxxxx
Activity	xxxxxx
Toughness	xxxxxxxxxx
Unpleasantness	xxxxxxxxx
Sadness	xxxxxxxxx
Passivity	xxxxxxxxxxxxxx
Gentleness	xxxxxxx
Pleasantness	xxxxxxxxxxx

Masculine sounds/feelings are very high.
Feminine sounds/feelings are very high.
Pronunciation is most difficult.

JAIME

Cheerfulness	xxx
Activity	xxx
Toughness	x
Unpleasantness	x
Sadness	x
Passivity	xxx
Gentleness	xxxx
Pleasantness	x

Masculine sounds/feelings are low.
Feminine sounds/feelings are very low.
Pronunciation is easier.

JAMI

Cheerfulness	xxxxx
Activity	xxxxxx
Toughness	xxxx
Unpleasantness	x
Sadness	x
Passivity	xxx
Gentleness	xxxx
Pleasantness	x

Masculine sounds/feelings are medium.
Feminine sounds/feelings are very low.
Pronunciation is easier.

JAMIE

Cheerfulness	xxxxxx
Activity	xxx
Toughness	x
Unpleasantness	x
Sadness	x
Passivity	xxx
Gentleness	xxxxxxx
Pleasantness	xxxxxx

Masculine sounds/feelings are medium.
Feminine sounds/feelings are medium low.
Pronunciation is easier.

JAN

Cheerfulness	xxx
Activity	xxx
Toughness	x
Unpleasantness	x
Sadness	xxxxx
Passivity	xxxxx
Gentleness	x
Pleasantness	x

Masculine sounds/feelings are low.
Feminine sounds/feelings are very low.
Pronunciation is easiest.

JANA

Cheerfulness	xxx
Activity	xxx
Toughness	x
Unpleasantness	x
Sadness	xxxxx
Passivity	xxxxx
Gentleness	x
Pleasantness	x

Masculine sounds/feelings are low.
Feminine sounds/feelings are very low.
Pronunciation is average.

JANE

Cheerfulness	xxx
Activity	xxx
Toughness	x
Unpleasantness	x
Sadness	xxxxx
Passivity	xxx
Gentleness	x
Pleasantness	x

Masculine sounds/feelings are low.
Feminine sounds/feelings are very low.
Pronunciation is easier.

JANELLE

Cheerfulness	xxxxxx
Activity	xxx
Toughness	x
Unpleasantness	x
Sadness	xxxxxxxx
Passivity	xxxxxxxx
Gentleness	xxxxxxx
Pleasantness	xxxxxx

Masculine sounds/feelings are very low.
Feminine sounds/feelings are very high.
Pronunciation is more difficult.

Women's And Girls' Names

JANET

Cheerfulness	xxxxxx
Activity	xxxxxx
Toughness	xxxx
Unpleasantness	xxxxx
Sadness	xxxxx
Passivity	xxxxx
Gentleness	xxxx
Pleasantness	x

Masculine sounds/feelings are medium.
Feminine sounds/feelings are low.
Pronunciation is more difficult.

JANETTE

Cheerfulness	xxxxxx
Activity	xxxxxxxxx
Toughness	xxxxxxx
Unpleasantness	xxxxxxxxx
Sadness	xxxxx
Passivity	xxxxxxx
Gentleness	xxxx
Pleasantness	x

Masculine sounds/feelings are very high.
Feminine sounds/feelings are medium low.
Pronunciation is more difficult.

JANICE

Cheerfulness	xxxxxx
Activity	xxxxxx
Toughness	xxxx
Unpleasantness	x
Sadness	xxxxx
Passivity	xxxxx
Gentleness	x
Pleasantness	x

Masculine sounds/feelings are medium low.
Feminine sounds/feelings are very low.
Pronunciation is average.

JANIE

Cheerfulness	xxxxxx
Activity	xxx
Toughness	x
Unpleasantness	x
Sadness	xxxxx
Passivity	xxx
Gentleness	xxxx
Pleasantness	xxxxxx

Masculine sounds/feelings are medium.
Feminine sounds/feelings are medium low.
Pronunciation is easier.

JANINE

Cheerfulness	xxxxxx
Activity	xxxxxx
Toughness	xxxx
Unpleasantness	x
Sadness	xxxxxxxxx
Passivity	xxxxxxx
Gentleness	x
Pleasantness	x

Masculine sounds/feelings are medium low.
Feminine sounds/feelings are medium low.
Pronunciation is easier.

JANIS

Cheerfulness	xxxxxx
Activity	xxxxxx
Toughness	xxxx
Unpleasantness	x
Sadness	xxxxx
Passivity	xxxxx
Gentleness	x
Pleasantness	x

Masculine sounds/feelings are medium low.
Feminine sounds/feelings are very low.
Pronunciation is average.

JANNA

Cheerfulness	xxx
Activity	xxx
Toughness	x
Unpleasantness	x
Sadness	xxxxxxxx
Passivity	xxxxxxx
Gentleness	x
Pleasantness	x

Masculine sounds/feelings are very low.
Feminine sounds/feelings are medium low.
Pronunciation is more difficult.

JASMINE

Cheerfulness	xxxxxx
Activity	xxxxxx
Toughness	xxxx
Unpleasantness	x
Sadness	xxxxx
Passivity	xxxxxxxxx
Gentleness	xxxxxxx
Pleasantness	xxxxxx

Masculine sounds/feelings are medium low.
Feminine sounds/feelings are medium high.
Pronunciation is average.

JAYNE

Cheerfulness	xxx
Activity	xxx
Toughness	x
Unpleasantness	x
Sadness	xxxxx
Passivity	xxx
Gentleness	x
Pleasantness	x

Masculine sounds/feelings are low.
Feminine sounds/feelings are very low.
Pronunciation is easier.

JEAN

Cheerfulness	xxxxxx
Activity	xxx
Toughness	x
Unpleasantness	x
Sadness	xxxxx
Passivity	xxx
Gentleness	xxxx
Pleasantness	xxxxxx

Masculine sounds/feelings are medium.
Feminine sounds/feelings are medium low.
Pronunciation is easiest.

JEANETTE

Cheerfulness	xxxxxxxxx
Activity	xxxxxxxxx
Toughness	xxxxxxx
Unpleasantness	xxxxxxxxx
Sadness	xxxxx
Passivity	xxxxx
Gentleness	xxxxxxx
Pleasantness	xxxxxx

Masculine sounds/feelings are very high.
Feminine sounds/feelings are medium.
Pronunciation is more difficult.

JEANIE

Cheerfulness	xxxxxxxxx
Activity	xxx
Toughness	x
Unpleasantness	x
Sadness	xxxxx
Passivity	xxx
Gentleness	xxxxxxx
Pleasantness	xxxxxxxxxxx

Masculine sounds/feelings are medium.
Feminine sounds/feelings are medium high.
Pronunciation is easiest.

JEANINE

Cheerfulness	xxxxxxxx
Activity	xxxxx
Toughness	xxxx
Unpleasantness	x
Sadness	xxxxxxxx
Passivity	xxxxx
Gentleness	xxxx
Pleasantness	xxxxxx

Masculine sounds/feelings are medium.
Feminine sounds/feelings are medium.
Pronunciation is easier.

JEANNE

Cheerfulness	xxxxxx
Activity	xxx
Toughness	x
Unpleasantness	x
Sadness	xxxxxxxxx
Passivity	xxxxx
Gentleness	xxxx
Pleasantness	xxxxxx

Masculine sounds/feelings are medium.
Feminine sounds/feelings are medium.
Pronunciation is easiest.

JEANNETTE

Cheerfulness	xxxxxxxxx
Activity	xxxxxxxxx
Toughness	xxxxxxx
Unpleasantness	xxxxxxxxx
Sadness	xxxxxxxxx
Passivity	xxxxxxx
Gentleness	xxxxxxx
Pleasantness	xxxxxx

Masculine sounds/feelings are very high.
Feminine sounds/feelings are high.
Pronunciation is more difficult.

JEANNIE

Cheerfulness	xxxxxxxxx
Activity	xxx
Toughness	x
Unpleasantness	x
Sadness	xxxxxxxxx
Passivity	xxxxx
Gentleness	xxxxxxx
Pleasantness	xxxxxxxxxxx

Masculine sounds/feelings are low.
Feminine sounds/feelings are very high.
Pronunciation is easier.

JEANNINE

Cheerfulness	xxxxxxxxx
Activity	xxxxxx
Toughness	xxxx
Unpleasantness	x
Sadness	xxxxxxxxxxxx
Passivity	xxxxxxx
Gentleness	xxxx
Pleasantness	xxxxxx

Masculine sounds/feelings are medium.
Feminine sounds/feelings are high.
Pronunciation is easier.

JENIFER

Cheerfulness	xxxxxxxxxxxxxxx
Activity	xxxxxxxxxxxx
Toughness	xxxxxxx
Unpleasantness	x
Sadness	xxxxx
Passivity	xxxxx
Gentleness	xxxx
Pleasantness	x

Masculine sounds/feelings are very high.
Feminine sounds/feelings are low.
Pronunciation is more difficult.

JENNA

Cheerfulness	xxxxx
Activity	xxx
Toughness	x
Unpleasantness	x
Sadness	xxxxxxxx
Passivity	xxxxxx
Gentleness	xxxx
Pleasantness	x

Masculine sounds/feelings are very low.
Feminine sounds/feelings are medium.
Pronunciation is more difficult.

JENNIE

Cheerfulness	xxxxxxxx
Activity	xxx
Toughness	x
Unpleasantness	x
Sadness	xxxxxxxx
Passivity	xxxxxx
Gentleness	xxxxxx
Pleasantness	xxxxx

Masculine sounds/feelings are low.
Feminine sounds/feelings are high.
Pronunciation is easier.

JENNIFER

Cheerfulness	xxxxxxxxxxxxx
Activity	xxxxxxxxxxx
Toughness	xxxxxx
Unpleasantness	x
Sadness	xxxxxxxx
Passivity	xxxxxx
Gentleness	xxxx
Pleasantness	x

Masculine sounds/feelings are very high.
Feminine sounds/feelings are medium.
Pronunciation is most difficult.

JENNY

Cheerfulness	xxxxxxxxx
Activity	xxx
Toughness	x
Unpleasantness	x
Sadness	xxxxxxxxx
Passivity	xxxxxx
Gentleness	xxxxxxx
Pleasantness	xxxxx

Masculine sounds/feelings are low.
Feminine sounds/feelings are high.
Pronunciation is easier.

JERI

Cheerfulness	xxxxxxxxx
Activity	xxxxxxxxx
Toughness	xxxxxxx
Unpleasantness	xxxxx
Sadness	x
Passivity	xxx
Gentleness	xxxx
Pleasantness	x

Masculine sounds/feelings are very high.
Feminine sounds/feelings are very low.
Pronunciation is average.

JERRI

Cheerfulness	xxxxxxxxx
Activity	xxxxxxxxxxx
Toughness	xxxxxxxxx
Unpleasantness	xxxxx
Sadness	x
Passivity	x
Gentleness	x
Pleasantness	x

Masculine sounds/feelings are very high.
Feminine sounds/feelings are very low.
Pronunciation is more difficult.

JERRY

Cheerfulness	xxxxxxxx
Activity	xxxxxxxx
Toughness	xxxxxxx
Unpleasantness	xxxxx
Sadness	x
Passivity	x
Gentleness	xxxx
Pleasantness	xxxxxx

Masculine sounds/feelings are very high.
Feminine sounds/feelings are very low.
Pronunciation is average.

JESSICA

Cheerfulness	xxxxxxxx
Activity	xxxxxx
Toughness	xxxxxxx
Unpleasantness	xxxxx
Sadness	x
Passivity	xxxxx
Gentleness	xxxx
Pleasantness	x

Masculine sounds/feelings are medium high.
Feminine sounds/feelings are very low.
Pronunciation is most difficult.

JESSIE

Cheerfulness	xxxxxxxxx
Activity	xxx
Toughness	x
Unpleasantness	x
Sadness	x
Passivity	xxx
Gentleness	xxxxxxx
Pleasantness	xxxxxx

Masculine sounds/feelings are medium.
Feminine sounds/feelings are medium low.
Pronunciation is easier.

JEWEL

Cheerfulness	xxxxxxxxxxx
Activity	xxx
Toughness	x
Unpleasantness	x
Sadness	xxxxx
Passivity	xxxxx
Gentleness	xxxxxxxxxx
Pleasantness	xxxxxxxxxxxxxxxx

Masculine sounds/feelings are medium low.
Feminine sounds/feelings are very high.
Pronunciation is more difficult.

JEWELL

Cheerfulness	xxxxxxxxxxx
Activity	xxx
Toughness	x
Unpleasantness	x
Sadness	xxxxx
Passivity	xxxxx
Gentleness	xxxxxxxxxx
Pleasantness	xxxxxxxxxxxxxxxxx

Masculine sounds/feelings are medium low.
Feminine sounds/feelings are very high.
Pronunciation is more difficult.

JILL

Cheerfulness	xxxxxx
Activity	xxxxxx
Toughness	xxxx
Unpleasantness	x
Sadness	xxxxx
Passivity	xxx
Gentleness	xxxx
Pleasantness	xxxxxx

Masculine sounds/feelings are medium.
Feminine sounds/feelings are medium low.
Pronunciation is easier.

JILLIAN

Cheerfulness	xxxxxxxx
Activity	xxxxxxxx
Toughness	xxxxxxx
Unpleasantness	x
Sadness	xxxxxxxx
Passivity	xxxxxxx
Gentleness	xxxx
Pleasantness	xxxxx

Masculine sounds/feelings are medium high.
Feminine sounds/feelings are medium high.
Pronunciation is more difficult.

JIMMIE

Cheerfulness	xxxxxxxxx
Activity	xxxxxx
Toughness	xxxx
Unpleasantness	x
Sadness	x
Passivity	xxxxx
Gentleness	xxxxxxxxxxx
Pleasantness	xxxxxx

Masculine sounds/feelings are medium.
Feminine sounds/feelings are medium.
Pronunciation is easier.

JO

Cheerfulness	xxx
Activity	xxx
Toughness	x
Unpleasantness	xxxxx
Sadness	xxxxx
Passivity	xxx
Gentleness	x
Pleasantness	x

Masculine sounds/feelings are medium.
Feminine sounds/feelings are very low.
Pronunciation is easiest.

JOAN

Cheerfulness	xxx
Activity	xxx
Toughness	x
Unpleasantness	xxxxx
Sadness	xxxxxxxx
Passivity	xxxxx
Gentleness	x
Pleasantness	x

Masculine sounds/feelings are medium.
Feminine sounds/feelings are low.
Pronunciation is easiest.

JOANN

Cheerfulness	xxx
Activity	xxx
Toughness	x
Unpleasantness	xxxxx
Sadness	xxxxxxxxxxxx
Passivity	xxxxxxx
Gentleness	x
Pleasantness	x

Masculine sounds/feelings are medium.
Feminine sounds/feelings are medium.
Pronunciation is easier.

JOANNA

Cheerfulness	xxx
Activity	xxx
Toughness	x
Unpleasantness	xxxxx
Sadness	xxxxxxxxxxxx
Passivity	xxxxxxx
Gentleness	x
Pleasantness	x

Masculine sounds/feelings are low.
Feminine sounds/feelings are medium.
Pronunciation is more difficult.

Women's And Girls' Names

JOANNE

Cheerfulness	xxx
Activity	xxx
Toughness	x
Unpleasantness	xxxxx
Sadness	xxxxxxxxxxxx
Passivity	xxxxxxx
Gentleness	x
Pleasantness	x

Masculine sounds/feelings are medium.
Feminine sounds/feelings are medium.
Pronunciation is easier.

JOCELYN

Cheerfulness	xxxxxxxxx
Activity	xxxxxx
Toughness	xxxx
Unpleasantness	xxxxx
Sadness	xxxxxxxxxxxxx
Passivity	xxxxxxxxx
Gentleness	xxxxxxx
Pleasantness	xxxxxx

Masculine sounds/feelings are medium.
Feminine sounds/feelings are very high.
Pronunciation is most difficult.

JODI

Cheerfulness	xxxxxxxxx
Activity	xxxxxxxxx
Toughness	xxxxxxx
Unpleasantness	xxxxx
Sadness	xxxxx
Passivity	xxx
Gentleness	x
Pleasantness	x

Masculine sounds/feelings are very high.
Feminine sounds/feelings are very low.
Pronunciation is easier.

JODIE

Cheerfulness	xxxxx
Activity	xxx
Toughness	xxxx
Unpleasantness	xxxxxxxx
Sadness	xxxxxxxx
Passivity	xxxxx
Gentleness	xxxx
Pleasantness	xxxxx

Masculine sounds/feelings are high.
Feminine sounds/feelings are medium.
Pronunciation is easier.

JODY

Cheerfulness	xxxxxxxxx
Activity	xxxxxx
Toughness	xxxx
Unpleasantness	xxxxx
Sadness	xxxxx
Passivity	xxx
Gentleness	xxxx
Pleasantness	xxxxxx

Masculine sounds/feelings are very high.
Feminine sounds/feelings are medium low.
Pronunciation is easier.

JOHANNA

Cheerfulness	xxxxx
Activity	xxxxxx
Toughness	x
Unpleasantness	x
Sadness	xxxxxxxxx
Passivity	xxxxxxx
Gentleness	x
Pleasantness	x

Masculine sounds/feelings are low.
Feminine sounds/feelings are medium low.
Pronunciation is most difficult.

JOLENE

Cheerfulness	xxxxx
Activity	xxx
Toughness	x
Unpleasantness	xxxxx
Sadness	xxxxxxxxxxxx
Passivity	xxxxxxx
Gentleness	xxxxxxx
Pleasantness	xxxxxxxxxxx

Masculine sounds/feelings are low.
Feminine sounds/feelings are very high.
Pronunciation is average.

JONI

Cheerfulness	xxxxxx
Activity	xxxxxx
Toughness	xxxx
Unpleasantness	x
Sadness	xxxxx
Passivity	xxxxx
Gentleness	x
Pleasantness	x

Masculine sounds/feelings are medium.
Feminine sounds/feelings are very low.
Pronunciation is easier.

JORDAN

Cheerfulness	xxx
Activity	xxxxxx
Toughness	xxxxxxx
Unpleasantness	xxxxxxxx
Sadness	xxxxxxxxx
Passivity	xxxxxxxxx
Gentleness	xxxx
Pleasantness	x

Masculine sounds/feelings are medium high.
Feminine sounds/feelings are medium.
Pronunciation is more difficult.

JOSEFA

Cheerfulness	xxxxxxxxx
Activity	xxxxxx
Toughness	x
Unpleasantness	xxxxx
Sadness	xxxxx
Passivity	xxxxxxx
Gentleness	xxxxxxx
Pleasantness	xxxxx

Masculine sounds/feelings are medium.
Feminine sounds/feelings are medium.
Pronunciation is most difficult.

JOSEFINA

Cheerfulness	xxxxxxxxxxx
Activity	xxxxxxxxx
Toughness	xxxx
Unpleasantness	xxxxx
Sadness	xxxxxxxxx
Passivity	xxxxxxxxx
Gentleness	xxxxxxx
Pleasantness	xxxxx

Masculine sounds/feelings are high.
Feminine sounds/feelings are very high.
Pronunciation is most difficult.

JOSEPHINE

Cheerfulness	xxxxxxxxxxx
Activity	xxxxxxxxx
Toughness	xxxx
Unpleasantness	xxxxx
Sadness	xxxxxxxxx
Passivity	xxxxxxxxx
Gentleness	xxxxxxx
Pleasantness	xxxxx

Masculine sounds/feelings are high.
Feminine sounds/feelings are very high.
Pronunciation is most difficult.

JOSIE

Cheerfulness	xxxxxx
Activity	xxx
Toughness	x
Unpleasantness	xxxxx
Sadness	xxxxx
Passivity	xxxxx
Gentleness	xxxxxxx
Pleasantness	xxxxxxxxxxx

Masculine sounds/feelings are medium.
Feminine sounds/feelings are high.
Pronunciation is easier.

JOY

Cheerfulness	xxxxxx
Activity	xxxxxx
Toughness	xxxx
Unpleasantness	x
Sadness	x
Passivity	x
Gentleness	x
Pleasantness	x

Masculine sounds/feelings are medium.
Feminine sounds/feelings are very low.
Pronunciation is easier.

JOYCE

Cheerfulness	xxxxxx
Activity	xxxxxx
Toughness	xxxx
Unpleasantness	x
Sadness	x
Passivity	x
Gentleness	x
Pleasantness	x

Masculine sounds/feelings are medium.
Feminine sounds/feelings are very low.
Pronunciation is average.

JUANA

Cheerfulness	xxx
Activity	xxxxxx
Toughness	xxxx
Unpleasantness	x
Sadness	xxxxx
Passivity	xxxxx
Gentleness	x
Pleasantness	x

Masculine sounds/feelings are low.
Feminine sounds/feelings are very low.
Pronunciation is more difficult.

JUANITA

Cheerfulness	xxxxxx
Activity	xxxxxxxxxxx
Toughness	xxxxxxxxxx
Unpleasantness	xxxxx
Sadness	xxxxx
Passivity	xxxxx
Gentleness	x
Pleasantness	x

Masculine sounds/feelings are very high.
Feminine sounds/feelings are very low.
Pronunciation is most difficult.

JUDITH

Cheerfulness	xxxxxxxxx
Activity	xxxxxxxxx
Toughness	xxxxxxxxxx
Unpleasantness	xxxxx
Sadness	xxxxx
Passivity	xxx
Gentleness	xxxx
Pleasantness	xxxxxx

Masculine sounds/feelings are very high.
Feminine sounds/feelings are medium low.
Pronunciation is more difficult.

JUDY

Cheerfulness	xxxxx
Activity	xxx
Toughness	xxxx
Unpleasantness	xxxxx
Sadness	xxxxx
Passivity	xxxxx
Gentleness	xxxx
Pleasantness	xxxxxx

Masculine sounds/feelings are medium high.
Feminine sounds/feelings are medium.
Pronunciation is easier.

JULIA

Cheerfulness	xxxxxx
Activity	xxxxxxxxx
Toughness	xxxxxxx
Unpleasantness	x
Sadness	xxxxx
Passivity	xxx
Gentleness	xxxx
Pleasantness	xxxxxx

Masculine sounds/feelings are medium.
Feminine sounds/feelings are medium low.
Pronunciation is most difficult.

JULIANA

Cheerfulness	xxxxxx
Activity	xxxxxxxxx
Toughness	xxxxxxx
Unpleasantness	x
Sadness	xxxxxxxxx
Passivity	xxxxxxx
Gentleness	xxxx
Pleasantness	xxxxxx

Masculine sounds/feelings are medium.
Feminine sounds/feelings are medium high.
Pronunciation is most difficult.

JULIANNE

Cheerfulness	xxxxx
Activity	xxxxxxxxx
Toughness	xxxxxxx
Unpleasantness	x
Sadness	xxxxxxxxxxxx
Passivity	xxxxxxxxx
Gentleness	xxxx
Pleasantness	xxxxx

Masculine sounds/feelings are medium.
Feminine sounds/feelings are very high.
Pronunciation is more difficult.

JULIE

Cheerfulness	xxxxxx
Activity	xxxxxx
Toughness	xxxx
Unpleasantness	x
Sadness	xxxxx
Passivity	xxx
Gentleness	xxxxxxx
Pleasantness	xxxxxxxxxxx

Masculine sounds/feelings are medium.
Feminine sounds/feelings are medium high.
Pronunciation is easier.

JULIETTE

Cheerfulness	xxxxxxxxx
Activity	xxxxxxxxxxx
Toughness	xxxxxxxxxx
Unpleasantness	xxxxxxxxx
Sadness	xxxxx
Passivity	xxxxx
Gentleness	xxxxxxxxxxx
Pleasantness	xxxxxxxxxxx

Masculine sounds/feelings are very high.
Feminine sounds/feelings are very high.
Pronunciation is most difficult.

Women's And Girls' Names

JUNE

Cheerfulness	xxx
Activity	xxxxxx
Toughness	xxxx
Unpleasantness	x
Sadness	xxxxx
Passivity	xxx
Gentleness	x
Pleasantness	x

Masculine sounds/feelings are medium.
Feminine sounds/feelings are very low.
Pronunciation is easiest.

JUSTINE

Cheerfulness	xxxxx
Activity	xxxxxxxxx
Toughness	xxxxxxx
Unpleasantness	xxxxx
Sadness	xxxxx
Passivity	xxxxx
Gentleness	x
Pleasantness	x

Masculine sounds/feelings are medium high.
Feminine sounds/feelings are very low.
Pronunciation is more difficult.

KARA

Cheerfulness	xxx
Activity	xxx
Toughness	xxxxxxx
Unpleasantness	xxxxxxxxx
Sadness	x
Passivity	xxxxx
Gentleness	xxxx
Pleasantness	x

Masculine sounds/feelings are high.
Feminine sounds/feelings are very low.
Pronunciation is average.

KAREN

Cheerfulness	xxxxxx
Activity	xxx
Toughness	xxxxxxx
Unpleasantness	xxxxxxxx
Sadness	xxxxx
Passivity	xxxxxxxxx
Gentleness	xxxxxxx
Pleasantness	x

Masculine sounds/feelings are medium high.
Feminine sounds/feelings are medium.
Pronunciation is average.

KARI

Cheerfulness	xxxxxx
Activity	xxxxxx
Toughness	xxxxxxxxxx
Unpleasantness	xxxxxxxxx
Sadness	x
Passivity	xxxxx
Gentleness	xxxx
Pleasantness	x

Masculine sounds/feelings are very high.
Feminine sounds/feelings are very low.
Pronunciation is easier.

KARIN

Cheerfulness	xxxxxx
Activity	xxxxxx
Toughness	xxxxxxxxxx
Unpleasantness	xxxxxxxx
Sadness	xxxxx
Passivity	xxxxxxx
Gentleness	xxxx
Pleasantness	x

Masculine sounds/feelings are very high.
Feminine sounds/feelings are medium low.
Pronunciation is easier.

KARINA

Cheerfulness	xxxxx
Activity	xxxxxx
Toughness	xxxxxxxxx
Unpleasantness	xxxxxxxx
Sadness	xxxxx
Passivity	xxxxxxx
Gentleness	xxxx
Pleasantness	x

Masculine sounds/feelings are very high.
Feminine sounds/feelings are medium low.
Pronunciation is more difficult.

KARLA

Cheerfulness	xxx
Activity	xxxxxx
Toughness	xxxxxxx
Unpleasantness	xxxxxxxxx
Sadness	xxxxx
Passivity	xxxxx
Gentleness	xxxx
Pleasantness	xxxxxx

Masculine sounds/feelings are medium high.
Feminine sounds/feelings are medium.
Pronunciation is more difficult.

KASEY

Cheerfulness	xxx
Activity	x
Toughness	xxxx
Unpleasantness	xxxxx
Sadness	x
Passivity	xxx
Gentleness	xxxx
Pleasantness	xxxxxx

Masculine sounds/feelings are medium.
Feminine sounds/feelings are low.
Pronunciation is easiest.

KATE

Cheerfulness	x
Activity	xxx
Toughness	xxxxxx
Unpleasantness	xxxxxxxxx
Sadness	x
Passivity	xxx
Gentleness	x
Pleasantness	x

Masculine sounds/feelings are medium high.
Feminine sounds/feelings are very low.
Pronunciation is easiest.

KATELYN

Cheerfulness	xxxxx
Activity	xxxxxx
Toughness	xxxxxxxxxx
Unpleasantness	xxxxxxxxx
Sadness	xxxxxxxxx
Passivity	xxxxxxxxx
Gentleness	xxxxxxx
Pleasantness	xxxxx

Masculine sounds/feelings are very high.
Feminine sounds/feelings are very high.
Pronunciation is more difficult.

KATHARINE

Cheerfulness	xxxxxxxxx
Activity	xxxxxx
Toughness	xxxxxxxxxx
Unpleasantness	xxxxxxxxx
Sadness	xxxxx
Passivity	xxxxxxxxx
Gentleness	xxxxxxx
Pleasantness	xxxxx

Masculine sounds/feelings are very high.
Feminine sounds/feelings are medium high.
Pronunciation is most difficult.

Women's And Girls' Names

KATHERINE

Cheerfulness	xxxxx
Activity	xxxxx
Toughness	xxxxxxxxx
Unpleasantness	xxxxx
Sadness	xxxxx
Passivity	xxxxxxxx
Gentleness	xxxx
Pleasantness	xxxxxx

Masculine sounds/feelings are medium high.
Feminine sounds/feelings are medium.
Pronunciation is more difficult.

KATHRINE

Cheerfulness	xxxxx
Activity	xxxxx
Toughness	xxxxxxxxx
Unpleasantness	xxxxxxxx
Sadness	xxxxx
Passivity	xxxxxxx
Gentleness	xxxx
Pleasantness	xxxxxx

Masculine sounds/feelings are very high.
Feminine sounds/feelings are medium.
Pronunciation is more difficult.

KATHIE

Cheerfulness	xxxxx
Activity	x
Toughness	xxxx
Unpleasantness	xxxxx
Sadness	x
Passivity	xxxxx
Gentleness	xxxxxxx
Pleasantness	xxxxxxxxxxx

Masculine sounds/feelings are medium.
Feminine sounds/feelings are medium.
Pronunciation is easiest.

KATHRYN

Cheerfulness	xxxxx
Activity	xxxxx
Toughness	xxxxxxxxx
Unpleasantness	xxxxxxxx
Sadness	xxxxx
Passivity	xxxxxxx
Gentleness	xxxx
Pleasantness	xxxxxx

Masculine sounds/feelings are very high.
Feminine sounds/feelings are medium.
Pronunciation is more difficult.

KATHLEEN

Cheerfulness	xxxxx
Activity	x
Toughness	xxxx
Unpleasantness	xxxxx
Sadness	xxxxxxxxx
Passivity	xxxxxxxxx
Gentleness	xxxxxxxxxx
Pleasantness	xxxxxxxxxxxxxxx

Masculine sounds/feelings are low.
Feminine sounds/feelings are very high.
Pronunciation is most difficult.

KATHY

Cheerfulness	xxxxx
Activity	x
Toughness	xxxx
Unpleasantness	xxxxx
Sadness	x
Passivity	xxxxx
Gentleness	xxxxxxx
Pleasantness	xxxxxxxxxxx

Masculine sounds/feelings are medium.
Feminine sounds/feelings are medium.
Pronunciation is easiest.

KATIE

Cheerfulness	xxx
Activity	xxx
Toughness	xxxxxxx
Unpleasantness	xxxxxxxx
Sadness	x
Passivity	xxx
Gentleness	xxxx
Pleasantness	xxxxxx

Masculine sounds/feelings are high.
Feminine sounds/feelings are low.
Pronunciation is easiest.

KATRINA

Cheerfulness	xxx
Activity	xxxxxxxxx
Toughness	xxxxxxxxxxxx
Unpleasantness	xxxxxxxxxxxx
Sadness	xxxxx
Passivity	xxxxxxx
Gentleness	x
Pleasantness	x

Masculine sounds/feelings are very high.
Feminine sounds/feelings are very low.
Pronunciation is most difficult.

KATY

Cheerfulness	xxx
Activity	xxx
Toughness	xxxxxxx
Unpleasantness	xxxxxxxx
Sadness	x
Passivity	xxx
Gentleness	xxxx
Pleasantness	xxxxxx

Masculine sounds/feelings are high.
Feminine sounds/feelings are low.
Pronunciation is easiest.

KAY

Cheerfulness	x
Activity	x
Toughness	xxxx
Unpleasantness	xxxxx
Sadness	x
Passivity	xxx
Gentleness	x
Pleasantness	x

Masculine sounds/feelings are medium low.
Feminine sounds/feelings are very low.
Pronunciation is easiest.

KAYE

Cheerfulness	xxx
Activity	xxx
Toughness	xxxxxxx
Unpleasantness	xxxxx
Sadness	x
Passivity	xxx
Gentleness	x
Pleasantness	x

Masculine sounds/feelings are medium high.
Feminine sounds/feelings are very low.
Pronunciation is easiest.

KAYLA

Cheerfulness	x
Activity	x
Toughness	xxxx
Unpleasantness	xxxxx
Sadness	xxxxx
Passivity	xxxxx
Gentleness	xxxx
Pleasantness	xxxxxx

Masculine sounds/feelings are medium low.
Feminine sounds/feelings are medium.
Pronunciation is average.

Women's And Girls' Names

KEISHA

Cheerfulness	xxx
Activity	xxx
Toughness	xxxxxxx
Unpleasantness	xxxxx
Sadness	x
Passivity	xxx
Gentleness	xxxx
Pleasantness	xxxxxx

Masculine sounds/feelings are medium high.
Feminine sounds/feelings are low.
Pronunciation is easier.

KELLEY

Cheerfulness	xxxxxx
Activity	x
Toughness	xxxx
Unpleasantness	xxxxx
Sadness	xxxxx
Passivity	xxxxxxx
Gentleness	xxxxxxxxxx
Pleasantness	xxxxxxxxxxx

Masculine sounds/feelings are medium.
Feminine sounds/feelings are very high.
Pronunciation is easiest.

KELLI

Cheerfulness	xxxxxx
Activity	xxx
Toughness	xxxxxxx
Unpleasantness	xxxxx
Sadness	xxxxx
Passivity	xxxxxxx
Gentleness	xxxxxxx
Pleasantness	xxxxxx

Masculine sounds/feelings are high.
Feminine sounds/feelings are medium.
Pronunciation is easier.

KELLIE

Cheerfulness	xxxxxx
Activity	x
Toughness	xxxx
Unpleasantness	xxxxx
Sadness	xxxxx
Passivity	xxxxxxx
Gentleness	xxxxxxxxxx
Pleasantness	xxxxxxxxxxx

Masculine sounds/feelings are medium.
Feminine sounds/feelings are very high.
Pronunciation is easiest.

KELLY

Cheerfulness	xxxxxx
Activity	x
Toughness	xxxx
Unpleasantness	xxxxx
Sadness	xxxxx
Passivity	xxxxxxx
Gentleness	xxxxxxxxxx
Pleasantness	xxxxxxxxxxx

Masculine sounds/feelings are medium.
Feminine sounds/feelings are very high.
Pronunciation is easiest.

KELSEY

Cheerfulness	xxxxxx
Activity	x
Toughness	xxxx
Unpleasantness	xxxxx
Sadness	xxxxx
Passivity	xxxxxxx
Gentleness	xxxxxxxxxx
Pleasantness	xxxxxxxxxxx

Masculine sounds/feelings are low.
Feminine sounds/feelings are very high.
Pronunciation is easier.

KENDRA

Cheerfulness	xxx
Activity	xxx
Toughness	xxxxxxxxx
Unpleasantness	xxxxxxxxxxxx
Sadness	xxxxxxxx
Passivity	xxxxxxxx
Gentleness	xxxx
Pleasantness	x

Masculine sounds/feelings are high.
Feminine sounds/feelings are medium.
Pronunciation is most difficult.

KENYA

Cheerfulness	xxxxxx
Activity	xxx
Toughness	xxxxxxx
Unpleasantness	xxxxx
Sadness	xxxxx
Passivity	xxxxxxx
Gentleness	xxxx
Pleasantness	x

Masculine sounds/feelings are medium.
Feminine sounds/feelings are medium low.
Pronunciation is average.

KERI

Cheerfulness	xxxxxx
Activity	xxxxxx
Toughness	xxxxxxxxxx
Unpleasantness	xxxxxxxxx
Sadness	x
Passivity	xxxxx
Gentleness	xxxx
Pleasantness	x

Masculine sounds/feelings are very high.
Feminine sounds/feelings are very low.
Pronunciation is easier.

KERRI

Cheerfulness	xxxxx
Activity	xxxxxxxxx
Toughness	xxxxxxxxxxxxx
Unpleasantness	xxxxxxxxx
Sadness	x
Passivity	xxx
Gentleness	x
Pleasantness	x

Masculine sounds/feelings are very high.
Feminine sounds/feelings are very low.
Pronunciation is easier.

KERRY

Cheerfulness	xxxxx
Activity	xxxxx
Toughness	xxxxxxxxx
Unpleasantness	xxxxxxxxx
Sadness	x
Passivity	xxx
Gentleness	xxxx
Pleasantness	xxxxx

Masculine sounds/feelings are very high.
Feminine sounds/feelings are low.
Pronunciation is easier.

KIM

Cheerfulness	xxx
Activity	xxx
Toughness	xxxxxxx
Unpleasantness	xxxxx
Sadness	x
Passivity	xxxxx
Gentleness	xxxx
Pleasantness	x

Masculine sounds/feelings are medium high.
Feminine sounds/feelings are very low.
Pronunciation is easiest.

Women's And Girls' Names

KIMBERLEY

Cheerfulness	xxxxxxxxx
Activity	xxxxxx
Toughness	xxxxxxxxxx
Unpleasantness	xxxxxxxxx
Sadness	xxxxxxxxx
Passivity	xxxxxxx
Gentleness	xxxxxxxxxxx
Pleasantness	xxxxxxxxxxxx

Masculine sounds/feelings are very high.
Feminine sounds/feelings are very high.
Pronunciation is most difficult.

KIMBERLY

Cheerfulness	xxxxxxxxx
Activity	xxxxxx
Toughness	xxxxxxxxxx
Unpleasantness	xxxxxxxxx
Sadness	xxxxxxxxx
Passivity	xxxxxxx
Gentleness	xxxxxxxxxxx
Pleasantness	xxxxxxxxxxxx

Masculine sounds/feelings are very high.
Feminine sounds/feelings are very high.
Pronunciation is average.

KIRSTEN

Cheerfulness	xxxxxx
Activity	xxxxxx
Toughness	xxxxxxxxxx
Unpleasantness	xxxxxxxxx
Sadness	xxxxx
Passivity	xxxxxxx
Gentleness	xxxx
Pleasantness	x

Masculine sounds/feelings are very high.
Feminine sounds/feelings are medium low.
Pronunciation is average.

KRIS

Cheerfulness	xxx
Activity	xxxxxx
Toughness	xxxxxxxxxx
Unpleasantness	xxxxxxxxx
Sadness	x
Passivity	xxxxx
Gentleness	xxxx
Pleasantness	xxxxx

Masculine sounds/feelings are very high.
Feminine sounds/feelings are low.
Pronunciation is easier.

KRISTA

Cheerfulness	xxx
Activity	xxxxxxxxx
Toughness	xxxxxxxxxxxx
Unpleasantness	xxxxxxxxxxxx
Sadness	x
Passivity	xxx
Gentleness	x
Pleasantness	x

Masculine sounds/feelings are very high.
Feminine sounds/feelings are very low.
Pronunciation is more difficult.

KRISTEN

Cheerfulness	xxxxxx
Activity	xxxxxxxxx
Toughness	xxxxxxxxxxxx
Unpleasantness	xxxxxxxxxxxx
Sadness	xxxxx
Passivity	xxxxxxx
Gentleness	xxxx
Pleasantness	x

Masculine sounds/feelings are very high.
Feminine sounds/feelings are medium low.
Pronunciation is more difficult.

KRISTI

Cheerfulness	xxxxx
Activity	xxxxxxxxxxx
Toughness	xxxxxxxxxxxxxxxx
Unpleasantness	xxxxxxxxxxxx
Sadness	x
Passivity	xxx
Gentleness	x
Pleasantness	x

Masculine sounds/feelings are very high.
Feminine sounds/feelings are very low.
Pronunciation is average.

KRISTIE

Cheerfulness	xxxxxx
Activity	xxxxxxxxx
Toughness	xxxxxxxxxxxx
Unpleasantness	xxxxxxxxxxxx
Sadness	x
Passivity	xxx
Gentleness	xxxx
Pleasantness	xxxxxx

Masculine sounds/feelings are very high.
Feminine sounds/feelings are low.
Pronunciation is average.

KRISTIN

Cheerfulness	xxxxxx
Activity	xxxxxxxxxxx
Toughness	xxxxxxxxxxxxxxxxx
Unpleasantness	xxxxxxxxxxxx
Sadness	xxxxx
Passivity	xxxxx
Gentleness	x
Pleasantness	x

Masculine sounds/feelings are very high.
Feminine sounds/feelings are very low.
Pronunciation is more difficult.

KRISTINA

Cheerfulness	xxxxxx
Activity	xxxxxxxxxxx
Toughness	xxxxxxxxxxxxxxxx
Unpleasantness	xxxxxxxxxxxx
Sadness	xxxxx
Passivity	xxxxx
Gentleness	x
Pleasantness	x

Masculine sounds/feelings are very high.
Feminine sounds/feelings are very low.
Pronunciation is most difficult.

KRISTINE

Cheerfulness	xxxxxx
Activity	xxxxxxxxxxx
Toughness	xxxxxxxxxxxxxxxxx
Unpleasantness	xxxxxxxxxxxx
Sadness	xxxxx
Passivity	xxxxx
Gentleness	x
Pleasantness	x

Masculine sounds/feelings are very high.
Feminine sounds/feelings are very low.
Pronunciation is more difficult.

KRISTY

Cheerfulness	xxxxxx
Activity	xxxxxxxxx
Toughness	xxxxxxxxxxxx
Unpleasantness	xxxxxxxxxxxx
Sadness	x
Passivity	xxx
Gentleness	xxxx
Pleasantness	xxxxx

Masculine sounds/feelings are very high.
Feminine sounds/feelings are low.
Pronunciation is average.

Women's And Girls' Names

KRYSTAL

Cheerfulness	xxx
Activity	xxxxxxxx
Toughness	xxxxxxxxxxxx
Unpleasantness	xxxxxxxxxxxx
Sadness	xxxxx
Passivity	xxxxxxx
Gentleness	xxxx
Pleasantness	xxxxxx

Masculine sounds/feelings are very high.
Feminine sounds/feelings are medium.
Pronunciation is more difficult.

LACEY

Cheerfulness	xxx
Activity	x
Toughness	x
Unpleasantness	x
Sadness	xxxxx
Passivity	xxx
Gentleness	xxxxxxx
Pleasantness	xxxxxxxxxxxx

Masculine sounds/feelings are low.
Feminine sounds/feelings are medium high.
Pronunciation is easier.

LADONNA

Cheerfulness	x
Activity	x
Toughness	xxxx
Unpleasantness	xxxxx
Sadness	xxxxxxxxxxxxxxxxx
Passivity	xxxxxxxxxx
Gentleness	xxxx
Pleasantness	xxxxxx

Masculine sounds/feelings are very low.
Feminine sounds/feelings are very high.
Pronunciation is most difficult.

LAKEISHA

Cheerfulness	xxx
Activity	xxx
Toughness	xxxxxxx
Unpleasantness	xxxxx
Sadness	xxxxx
Passivity	xxxxx
Gentleness	xxxxxxx
Pleasantness	xxxxxxxxxxx

Masculine sounds/feelings are medium.
Feminine sounds/feelings are high.
Pronunciation is more difficult.

LAKISHA

Cheerfulness	xxx
Activity	xxxxxx
Toughness	xxxxxxxxxx
Unpleasantness	xxxxx
Sadness	xxxxx
Passivity	xxxxxxx
Gentleness	xxxx
Pleasantness	xxxxxx

Masculine sounds/feelings are medium.
Feminine sounds/feelings are medium.
Pronunciation is more difficult.

LANA

Cheerfulness	x
Activity	x
Toughness	x
Unpleasantness	x
Sadness	xxxxxxxxx
Passivity	xxxxxxx
Gentleness	xxxx
Pleasantness	xxxxxx

Masculine sounds/feelings are very low.
Feminine sounds/feelings are medium high.
Pronunciation is easier.

LARA

Cheerfulness	xxx
Activity	xxx
Toughness	xxxx
Unpleasantness	xxxxx
Sadness	xxxxx
Passivity	xxxxx
Gentleness	xxxxxx
Pleasantness	xxxxxx

Masculine sounds/feelings are medium.
Feminine sounds/feelings are medium.
Pronunciation is more difficult.

LATASHA

Cheerfulness	x
Activity	xxxxxx
Toughness	xxxxxxx
Unpleasantness	xxxxx
Sadness	xxxxx
Passivity	xxxxxxx
Gentleness	xxxx
Pleasantness	xxxxxx

Masculine sounds/feelings are medium.
Feminine sounds/feelings are medium.
Pronunciation is more difficult.

LATISHA

Cheerfulness	xxx
Activity	xxxxxxxxx
Toughness	xxxxxxxxxx
Unpleasantness	xxxxx
Sadness	xxxxx
Passivity	xxxxx
Gentleness	xxxx
Pleasantness	xxxxxx

Masculine sounds/feelings are medium high.
Feminine sounds/feelings are medium.
Pronunciation is most difficult.

LATONYA

Cheerfulness	xxx
Activity	xxxxxx
Toughness	xxxxxxx
Unpleasantness	xxxxx
Sadness	xxxxxxxxx
Passivity	xxxxxxx
Gentleness	xxxx
Pleasantness	xxxxx

Masculine sounds/feelings are medium.
Feminine sounds/feelings are medium high.
Pronunciation is most difficult.

LATOYA

Cheerfulness	xxx
Activity	xxxxxx
Toughness	xxxxxxx
Unpleasantness	xxxxx
Sadness	xxxxx
Passivity	xxxxx
Gentleness	xxxx
Pleasantness	xxxxxx

Masculine sounds/feelings are medium.
Feminine sounds/feelings are medium.
Pronunciation is most difficult.

LAURA

Cheerfulness	x
Activity	xxx
Toughness	xxxx
Unpleasantness	xxxxx
Sadness	xxxxx
Passivity	xxxxx
Gentleness	xxxxxxx
Pleasantness	xxxxxx

Masculine sounds/feelings are medium.
Feminine sounds/feelings are medium.
Pronunciation is more difficult.

Women's And Girls' Names

LAUREL

Cheerfulness	xxx
Activity	xxx
Toughness	xxxx
Unpleasantness	xxxxx
Sadness	xxxxxxxx
Passivity	xxxxxxxx
Gentleness	xxxxxxxxxxxxx
Pleasantness	xxxxxxxxxxx

Masculine sounds/feelings are low.
Feminine sounds/feelings are very high.
Pronunciation is more difficult.

LAUREN

Cheerfulness	xxx
Activity	xxx
Toughness	xxxx
Unpleasantness	xxxxx
Sadness	xxxxxxxx
Passivity	xxxxxxxx
Gentleness	xxxxxxxxxxx
Pleasantness	xxxxxx

Masculine sounds/feelings are low.
Feminine sounds/feelings are very high.
Pronunciation is average.

LAURIE

Cheerfulness	xxx
Activity	xxx
Toughness	xxxx
Unpleasantness	xxxxx
Sadness	xxxxx
Passivity	xxxxx
Gentleness	xxxxxxxxxxx
Pleasantness	xxxxxxxxxxx

Masculine sounds/feelings are medium.
Feminine sounds/feelings are very high.
Pronunciation is easier.

LAVERNE

Cheerfulness	xxxxx
Activity	xxx
Toughness	xxxx
Unpleasantness	x
Sadness	xxxxxxxxx
Passivity	xxxxxxx
Gentleness	xxxxxxx
Pleasantness	xxxxxxxxxxx

Masculine sounds/feelings are low.
Feminine sounds/feelings are very high.
Pronunciation is average.

LAVONNE

Cheerfulness	xxx
Activity	x
Toughness	x
Unpleasantness	x
Sadness	xxxxxxxxxxxx
Passivity	xxxxxxxxx
Gentleness	xxxxxxx
Pleasantness	xxxxxxxxxxx

Masculine sounds/feelings are very low.
Feminine sounds/feelings are very high.
Pronunciation is more difficult.

LAWANDA

Cheerfulness	xxx
Activity	x
Toughness	xxxx
Unpleasantness	xxxxx
Sadness	xxxxxxxxxxxx
Passivity	xxxxxxxxx
Gentleness	xxxx
Pleasantness	xxxxxxxxxxx

Masculine sounds/feelings are low.
Feminine sounds/feelings are very high.
Pronunciation is most difficult.

LEA

Cheerfulness	xxx
Activity	x
Toughness	x
Unpleasantness	x
Sadness	xxxxx
Passivity	xxx
Gentleness	xxxxxxx
Pleasantness	xxxxxxxxxxx

Masculine sounds/feelings are low.
Feminine sounds/feelings are medium high.
Pronunciation is easiest.

LEAH

Cheerfulness	xxx
Activity	x
Toughness	x
Unpleasantness	x
Sadness	xxxxx
Passivity	xxx
Gentleness	xxxxxxx
Pleasantness	xxxxxxxxxxx

Masculine sounds/feelings are low.
Feminine sounds/feelings are medium high.
Pronunciation is easiest.

LEANN

Cheerfulness	xxx
Activity	x
Toughness	x
Unpleasantness	x
Sadness	xxxxxxxxxxx
Passivity	xxxxxxx
Gentleness	xxxxxxx
Pleasantness	xxxxxxxxxxx

Masculine sounds/feelings are low.
Feminine sounds/feelings are very high.
Pronunciation is easiest.

LEANNE

Cheerfulness	xxx
Activity	x
Toughness	x
Unpleasantness	x
Sadness	xxxxxxxxxxxx
Passivity	xxxxxxx
Gentleness	xxxxxxx
Pleasantness	xxxxxxxxxxx

Masculine sounds/feelings are low.
Feminine sounds/feelings are very high.
Pronunciation is easiest.

LEE

Cheerfulness	xxx
Activity	x
Toughness	x
Unpleasantness	x
Sadness	xxxxx
Passivity	xxx
Gentleness	xxxxxxx
Pleasantness	xxxxxxxxxxx

Masculine sounds/feelings are low.
Feminine sounds/feelings are medium high.
Pronunciation is easiest.

LEIGH

Cheerfulness	x
Activity	x
Toughness	x
Unpleasantness	x
Sadness	xxxxx
Passivity	xxx
Gentleness	xxxx
Pleasantness	xxxxx

Masculine sounds/feelings are very low.
Feminine sounds/feelings are medium low.
Pronunciation is easiest.

Women's And Girls' Names

LEILA

Cheerfulness	xxx
Activity	x
Toughness	x
Unpleasantness	x
Sadness	xxxxxxxx
Passivity	xxxxx
Gentleness	xxxxxxxxxx
Pleasantness	xxxxxxxxxxxxxxxx

Masculine sounds/feelings are low.
Feminine sounds/feelings are very high.
Pronunciation is average.

LELA

Cheerfulness	xxx
Activity	x
Toughness	x
Unpleasantness	x
Sadness	xxxxxxxx
Passivity	xxxxxx
Gentleness	xxxxxxxxxx
Pleasantness	xxxxxxxxxxx

Masculine sounds/feelings are low.
Feminine sounds/feelings are very high.
Pronunciation is more difficult.

LENA

Cheerfulness	xxx
Activity	x
Toughness	x
Unpleasantness	x
Sadness	xxxxxxxx
Passivity	xxxxxx
Gentleness	xxxxxx
Pleasantness	xxxxxx

Masculine sounds/feelings are low.
Feminine sounds/feelings are high.
Pronunciation is average.

LENORA

Cheerfulness	xxx
Activity	xxx
Toughness	xxxx
Unpleasantness	xxxxx
Sadness	xxxxxxxxx
Passivity	xxxxxxxxx
Gentleness	xxxxxxxxxx
Pleasantness	xxxxx

Masculine sounds/feelings are low.
Feminine sounds/feelings are very high.
Pronunciation is most difficult.

LENORE

Cheerfulness	xxx
Activity	xxx
Toughness	xxxx
Unpleasantness	xxxxx
Sadness	xxxxxxxxx
Passivity	xxxxxxxxx
Gentleness	xxxxxxxxxx
Pleasantness	xxxxx

Masculine sounds/feelings are low.
Feminine sounds/feelings are very high.
Pronunciation is average.

LEOLA

Cheerfulness	xxxxxx
Activity	xxx
Toughness	x
Unpleasantness	x
Sadness	xxxxxxxxx
Passivity	xxxxx
Gentleness	xxxxxxxxxx
Pleasantness	xxxxxxxxxxxxxxxx

Masculine sounds/feelings are very low.
Feminine sounds/feelings are very high.
Pronunciation is more difficult.

LEONA

Cheerfulness	xxxxx
Activity	xxx
Toughness	x
Unpleasantness	x

Sadness	xxxxxxxx
Passivity	xxxxx
Gentleness	xxxxxx
Pleasantness	xxxxxxxxxxx

Masculine sounds/feelings are very low.
Feminine sounds/feelings are very high.
Pronunciation is average.

LEONOR

Cheerfulness	xxxxxxxxx
Activity	xxxxxx
Toughness	xxxx
Unpleasantness	x

Sadness	xxxxxxxxx
Passivity	xxxxx
Gentleness	xxxxxx
Pleasantness	xxxxxxxxxxx

Masculine sounds/feelings are medium.
Feminine sounds/feelings are very high.
Pronunciation is easier.

LESLEY

Cheerfulness	xxxxx
Activity	x
Toughness	x
Unpleasantness	x

Sadness	xxxxxxxxx
Passivity	xxxxxx
Gentleness	xxxxxxxxxxxxx
Pleasantness	xxxxxxxxxxxxxxxx

Masculine sounds/feelings are very low.
Feminine sounds/feelings are very high.
Pronunciation is most difficult.

LESLIE

Cheerfulness	xxxxx
Activity	x
Toughness	x
Unpleasantness	x

Sadness	xxxxxxxxx
Passivity	xxxxxx
Gentleness	xxxxxxxxxxxxx
Pleasantness	xxxxxxxxxxxxxxxx

Masculine sounds/feelings are very low.
Feminine sounds/feelings are very high.
Pronunciation is average.

LESSIE

Cheerfulness	xxxxx
Activity	x
Toughness	x
Unpleasantness	x

Sadness	xxxxx
Passivity	xxxxx
Gentleness	xxxxxxxxxx
Pleasantness	xxxxxxxxxxx

Masculine sounds/feelings are low.
Feminine sounds/feelings are very high.
Pronunciation is easier.

LETHA

Cheerfulness	xxxxx
Activity	x
Toughness	x
Unpleasantness	x

Sadness	xxxxx
Passivity	xxxxx
Gentleness	xxxxxxxxxx
Pleasantness	xxxxxxxxxxx

Masculine sounds/feelings are low.
Feminine sounds/feelings are very high.
Pronunciation is more difficult.

Women's And Girls' Names

LETICIA

Cheerfulness	xxxxx
Activity	xxxxxxxx
Toughness	xxxxxxxxx
Unpleasantness	xxxxx
Sadness	xxxxx
Passivity	xxxxx
Gentleness	xxxxxxx
Pleasantness	xxxxxx

Masculine sounds/feelings are high.
Feminine sounds/feelings are medium.
Pronunciation is most difficult.

LIDIA

Cheerfulness	xxxxx
Activity	xxxxx
Toughness	xxxxxxxxxx
Unpleasantness	xxxxx
Sadness	xxxxxxxxx
Passivity	xxxxx
Gentleness	xxxx
Pleasantness	xxxxxx

Masculine sounds/feelings are medium high.
Feminine sounds/feelings are medium.
Pronunciation is more difficult.

LILA

Cheerfulness	xxx
Activity	xxx
Toughness	xxxx
Unpleasantness	x
Sadness	xxxxxxxxx
Passivity	xxxxx
Gentleness	xxxxxxx
Pleasantness	xxxxxxxxxxx

Masculine sounds/feelings are medium.
Feminine sounds/feelings are very high.
Pronunciation is more difficult.

LILIA

Cheerfulness	xxxxx
Activity	xxxxx
Toughness	xxxxxxx
Unpleasantness	x
Sadness	xxxxxxxxx
Passivity	xxxxx
Gentleness	xxxxxxx
Pleasantness	xxxxxxxxxxx

Masculine sounds/feelings are medium.
Feminine sounds/feelings are very high.
Pronunciation is more difficult.

LILIAN

Cheerfulness	xxxxxx
Activity	xxxxxx
Toughness	xxxxxxx
Unpleasantness	x
Sadness	xxxxxxxxxxxx
Passivity	xxxxxxxxx
Gentleness	xxxxxxx
Pleasantness	xxxxxxxxxxx

Masculine sounds/feelings are medium.
Feminine sounds/feelings are very high.
Pronunciation is average.

LILIANA

Cheerfulness	xxxxxx
Activity	xxxxxx
Toughness	xxxxxxx
Unpleasantness	x
Sadness	xxxxxxxxxxxx
Passivity	xxxxxxxxx
Gentleness	xxxxxxx
Pleasantness	xxxxxxxxxxx

Masculine sounds/feelings are medium.
Feminine sounds/feelings are very high.
Pronunciation is most difficult.

LILLIAN

Cheerfulness	xxxxx
Activity	xxxxxx
Toughness	xxxxxxx
Unpleasantness	x
Sadness	xxxxxxxxxxx
Passivity	xxxxxxxx
Gentleness	xxxxxxx
Pleasantness	xxxxxxxxxxx

Masculine sounds/feelings are medium.
Feminine sounds/feelings are very high.
Pronunciation is average.

LILLIE

Cheerfulness	xxxxxx
Activity	xxx
Toughness	xxxx
Unpleasantness	x
Sadness	xxxxxxxxx
Passivity	xxxxx
Gentleness	xxxxxxxxxxx
Pleasantness	xxxxxxxxxxxxxxxxx

Masculine sounds/feelings are medium.
Feminine sounds/feelings are very high.
Pronunciation is easier.

LILLY

Cheerfulness	xxxxxx
Activity	xxx
Toughness	xxxx
Unpleasantness	x
Sadness	xxxxxxxxx
Passivity	xxxxx
Gentleness	xxxxxxxxxxx
Pleasantness	xxxxxxxxxxxxxxxxx

Masculine sounds/feelings are medium.
Feminine sounds/feelings are very high.
Pronunciation is easier.

LILY

Cheerfulness	xxxxx
Activity	x
Toughness	x
Unpleasantness	x
Sadness	xxxxxxxx
Passivity	xxxxx
Gentleness	xxxxxxxxxxxx
Pleasantness	xxxxxxxxxxxxxxxxxxxx

Masculine sounds/feelings are low.
Feminine sounds/feelings are very high.
Pronunciation is easier.

LINA

Cheerfulness	xxx
Activity	xxx
Toughness	xxxx
Unpleasantness	x
Sadness	xxxxxxxx
Passivity	xxxxx
Gentleness	xxxx
Pleasantness	xxxxxx

Masculine sounds/feelings are medium.
Feminine sounds/feelings are medium.
Pronunciation is easier.

LINDA

Cheerfulness	xxx
Activity	x
Toughness	xxxx
Unpleasantness	xxxxx
Sadness	xxxxxxxxxxx
Passivity	xxxxxxx
Gentleness	xxxxxx
Pleasantness	xxxxxxxxxxx

Masculine sounds/feelings are low.
Feminine sounds/feelings are very high.
Pronunciation is more difficult.

Women's And Girls' Names

LINDSAY

Cheerfulness   xxx
Activity   x
Toughness   xxxx
Unpleasantness   xxxxx

Sadness   xxxxxxxxxxx
Passivity   xxxxxxx
Gentleness   xxxxxxx
Pleasantness   xxxxxxxxxxx

Masculine sounds/feelings are low.
Feminine sounds/feelings are very high.
Pronunciation is more difficult.

LINDSEY

Cheerfulness   xxxxx
Activity   x
Toughness   xxxx
Unpleasantness   xxxxx

Sadness   xxxxxxxxxxx
Passivity   xxxxxxx
Gentleness   xxxxxxxxxx
Pleasantness   xxxxxxxxxxxxxxxx

Masculine sounds/feelings are low.
Feminine sounds/feelings are very high.
Pronunciation is average.

LISA

Cheerfulness   xxx
Activity   xxx
Toughness   xxxx
Unpleasantness   x

Sadness   xxxxx
Passivity   xxxxx
Gentleness   xxxxxxx
Pleasantness   xxxxxxxxxxx

Masculine sounds/feelings are medium.
Feminine sounds/feelings are high.
Pronunciation is average.

LIZA

Cheerfulness   xxx
Activity   xxx
Toughness   xxxx
Unpleasantness   x

Sadness   xxxxx
Passivity   xxxxx
Gentleness   xxxxxxx
Pleasantness   xxxxxxxxxxx

Masculine sounds/feelings are medium.
Feminine sounds/feelings are high.
Pronunciation is average.

LIZZIE

Cheerfulness   xxxxxx
Activity   xxx
Toughness   xxxx
Unpleasantness   x

Sadness   xxxxx
Passivity   xxxxxxx
Gentleness   xxxxxxxxxxxxx
Pleasantness   xxxxxxxxxxxxxxxxxxx

Masculine sounds/feelings are low.
Feminine sounds/feelings are very high.
Pronunciation is easier.

LOIS

Cheerfulness   xxx
Activity   xxx
Toughness   xxxx
Unpleasantness   x

Sadness   xxxxx
Passivity   xxxxx
Gentleness   xxxxxxx
Pleasantness   xxxxxxxxxxx

Masculine sounds/feelings are medium.
Feminine sounds/feelings are high.
Pronunciation is easier.

LOLA

Cheerfulness	xxx
Activity	xxx
Toughness	x
Unpleasantness	x
Sadness	xxxxxxxx
Passivity	xxxxx
Gentleness	xxxxxx
Pleasantness	xxxxxxxxxxx

Masculine sounds/feelings are low.
Feminine sounds/feelings are very high.
Pronunciation is average.

LORA

Cheerfulness	x
Activity	xxx
Toughness	xxxx
Unpleasantness	xxxxx
Sadness	xxxxx
Passivity	xxxxx
Gentleness	xxxxxx
Pleasantness	xxxxxx

Masculine sounds/feelings are medium.
Feminine sounds/feelings are medium.
Pronunciation is more difficult.

LORAINE

Cheerfulness	x
Activity	xxx
Toughness	xxxx
Unpleasantness	xxxxx
Sadness	xxxxxxxx
Passivity	xxxxxxx
Gentleness	xxxxxxx
Pleasantness	xxxxxx

Masculine sounds/feelings are low.
Feminine sounds/feelings are high.
Pronunciation is average.

LORENA

Cheerfulness	xxx
Activity	xxx
Toughness	xxxx
Unpleasantness	xxxxx
Sadness	xxxxxxxx
Passivity	xxxxxxxx
Gentleness	xxxxxxxxxx
Pleasantness	xxxxx

Masculine sounds/feelings are low.
Feminine sounds/feelings are very high.
Pronunciation is most difficult.

LORENE

Cheerfulness	xxx
Activity	xxx
Toughness	xxxx
Unpleasantness	xxxxx
Sadness	xxxxxxxx
Passivity	xxxxxxx
Gentleness	xxxxxxxxxx
Pleasantness	xxxxxxxxxxx

Masculine sounds/feelings are low.
Feminine sounds/feelings are very high.
Pronunciation is easier.

LORETTA

Cheerfulness	xxx
Activity	xxxxxxxx
Toughness	xxxxxxxxx
Unpleasantness	xxxxxxxxxxx
Sadness	xxxxx
Passivity	xxxxxxx
Gentleness	xxxxxxxxxx
Pleasantness	xxxxx

Masculine sounds/feelings are very high.
Feminine sounds/feelings are high.
Pronunciation is most difficult.

Women's And Girls' Names

LORI

Cheerfulness	xxx
Activity	xxxxxx
Toughness	xxxxxxx
Unpleasantness	xxxxx
Sadness	xxxxx
Passivity	xxxxx
Gentleness	xxxxxxx
Pleasantness	xxxxxx

Masculine sounds/feelings are high.
Feminine sounds/feelings are medium.
Pronunciation is easier.

LORIE

Cheerfulness	xxx
Activity	xxx
Toughness	xxxx
Unpleasantness	xxxxx
Sadness	xxxxx
Passivity	xxxxx
Gentleness	xxxxxxxxxx
Pleasantness	xxxxxxxxxxxx

Masculine sounds/feelings are medium.
Feminine sounds/feelings are very high.
Pronunciation is easier.

LORNA

Cheerfulness	x
Activity	xxx
Toughness	xxxx
Unpleasantness	xxxxx
Sadness	xxxxxxxxx
Passivity	xxxxxxx
Gentleness	xxxxxxx
Pleasantness	xxxxxx

Masculine sounds/feelings are low.
Feminine sounds/feelings are high.
Pronunciation is more difficult.

LORRAINE

Cheerfulness	x
Activity	xxxxxx
Toughness	xxxxxxx
Unpleasantness	xxxxxxxxx
Sadness	xxxxxxxxx
Passivity	xxxxxxx
Gentleness	xxxxxxx
Pleasantness	xxxxxx

Masculine sounds/feelings are medium.
Feminine sounds/feelings are high.
Pronunciation is most difficult.

LORRIE

Cheerfulness	xxx
Activity	xxxxxx
Toughness	xxxxxxx
Unpleasantness	xxxxxxxxx
Sadness	xxxxx
Passivity	xxxxx
Gentleness	xxxxxxxxxx
Pleasantness	xxxxxxxxxxxx

Masculine sounds/feelings are medium high.
Feminine sounds/feelings are very high.
Pronunciation is more difficult.

LOTTIE

Cheerfulness	xxxxxx
Activity	xxxxxxxxx
Toughness	xxxxxxx
Unpleasantness	xxxxxxxxx
Sadness	xxxxx
Passivity	xxx
Gentleness	xxxxxxx
Pleasantness	xxxxxxxxxxxx

Masculine sounds/feelings are very high.
Feminine sounds/feelings are medium high.
Pronunciation is easier.

LOU

Cheerfulness	x
Activity	x
Toughness	x
Unpleasantness	xxxxx

Sadness	xxxxxxxx
Passivity	xxxxx
Gentleness	xxxx
Pleasantness	xxxxxx

Masculine sounds/feelings are low.
Feminine sounds/feelings are medium.
Pronunciation is easiest.

LOUISA

Cheerfulness	xxx
Activity	xxx
Toughness	xxxx
Unpleasantness	xxxxx

Sadness	xxxxxxxx
Passivity	xxxxxxx
Gentleness	xxxxxxx
Pleasantness	xxxxxxxxxxx

Masculine sounds/feelings are low.
Feminine sounds/feelings are very high.
Pronunciation is more difficult.

LOUISE

Cheerfulness	xxx
Activity	x
Toughness	x
Unpleasantness	xxxxx

Sadness	xxxxxxxx
Passivity	xxxxxxx
Gentleness	xxxxxxxxxxx
Pleasantness	xxxxxxxxxxxxxxxxx

Masculine sounds/feelings are medium low.
Feminine sounds/feelings are very high.
Pronunciation is easier.

LOURDES

Cheerfulness	x
Activity	xxx
Toughness	xxxxxx
Unpleasantness	xxxxxxxxx

Sadness	xxxxxxxxx
Passivity	xxxxxxxxx
Gentleness	xxxxxxxxxxx
Pleasantness	xxxxxxxxxxxx

Masculine sounds/feelings are medium.
Feminine sounds/feelings are very high.
Pronunciation is more difficult.

LUANN

Cheerfulness	x
Activity	xxx
Toughness	xxxx
Unpleasantness	x

Sadness	xxxxxxxxxxxx
Passivity	xxxxxxxxx
Gentleness	xxxx
Pleasantness	xxxxx

Masculine sounds/feelings are very low.
Feminine sounds/feelings are very high.
Pronunciation is easier.

LUCIA

Cheerfulness	x
Activity	xxxxxx
Toughness	xxxxxx
Unpleasantness	x

Sadness	xxxxx
Passivity	xxx
Gentleness	xxxx
Pleasantness	xxxxx

Masculine sounds/feelings are medium.
Feminine sounds/feelings are medium low.
Pronunciation is average.

Women's And Girls' Names

LUCILE

Cheerfulness	xxx
Activity	xxxxxx
Toughness	xxxxxxx
Unpleasantness	x
Sadness	xxxxxxxxx
Passivity	xxxxx
Gentleness	xxxxxxx
Pleasantness	xxxxxxxxxxx

Masculine sounds/feelings are medium low.
Feminine sounds/feelings are very high.
Pronunciation is average.

LUCILLE

Cheerfulness	xxx
Activity	xxxxxx
Toughness	xxxxxxx
Unpleasantness	x
Sadness	xxxxxxxxx
Passivity	xxxxx
Gentleness	xxxxxxx
Pleasantness	xxxxxxxxxxx

Masculine sounds/feelings are medium low.
Feminine sounds/feelings are very high.
Pronunciation is average.

LUCINDA

Cheerfulness	xxx
Activity	xxx
Toughness	xxxxxxx
Unpleasantness	xxxxx
Sadness	xxxxxxxxxxxx
Passivity	xxxxxxx
Gentleness	xxxxxxx
Pleasantness	xxxxxxxxxxx

Masculine sounds/feelings are medium.
Feminine sounds/feelings are very high.
Pronunciation is most difficult.

LUCY

Cheerfulness	xxx
Activity	x
Toughness	x
Unpleasantness	x
Sadness	xxxxx
Passivity	xxxxx
Gentleness	xxxxxxx
Pleasantness	xxxxxxxxxxx

Masculine sounds/feelings are low.
Feminine sounds/feelings are high.
Pronunciation is easiest.

LUELLA

Cheerfulness	xxx
Activity	xxx
Toughness	xxxx
Unpleasantness	x
Sadness	xxxxxxxxx
Passivity	xxxxxxx
Gentleness	xxxxxxxxxx
Pleasantness	xxxxxxxxxxx

Masculine sounds/feelings are very low.
Feminine sounds/feelings are very high.
Pronunciation is more difficult.

LUISA

Cheerfulness	xxx
Activity	xxxxxx
Toughness	xxxxxxx
Unpleasantness	x
Sadness	xxxxx
Passivity	xxxxx
Gentleness	xxxxxxx
Pleasantness	xxxxxxxxxxx

Masculine sounds/feelings are medium low.
Feminine sounds/feelings are high.
Pronunciation is more difficult.

LULA

Cheerfulness	x
Activity	xxx
Toughness	xxxx
Unpleasantness	x
Sadness	xxxxxxxx
Passivity	xxxxx
Gentleness	xxxxxx
Pleasantness	xxxxxxxxxxx

Masculine sounds/feelings are medium low.
Feminine sounds/feelings are very high.
Pronunciation is more difficult.

LUPE

Cheerfulness	x
Activity	xxxxxx
Toughness	xxxxxxx
Unpleasantness	x
Sadness	xxxxx
Passivity	xxx
Gentleness	xxxx
Pleasantness	xxxxxx

Masculine sounds/feelings are medium.
Feminine sounds/feelings are medium low.
Pronunciation is easiest.

LUZ

Cheerfulness	x
Activity	x
Toughness	x
Unpleasantness	x
Sadness	xxxxx
Passivity	xxxxxx
Gentleness	xxxxxx
Pleasantness	xxxxxxxxxxx

Masculine sounds/feelings are very low.
Feminine sounds/feelings are high.
Pronunciation is easiest.

LYDIA

Cheerfulness	xxxxx
Activity	xxxxx
Toughness	xxxxxxxxx
Unpleasantness	xxxxx
Sadness	xxxxxxxx
Passivity	xxxxx
Gentleness	xxxx
Pleasantness	xxxxx

Masculine sounds/feelings are medium high.
Feminine sounds/feelings are medium.
Pronunciation is more difficult.

LYNDA

Cheerfulness	xxx
Activity	xxx
Toughness	xxxxxx
Unpleasantness	xxxxx
Sadness	xxxxxxxxxxxx
Passivity	xxxxxxx
Gentleness	xxxx
Pleasantness	xxxxx

Masculine sounds/feelings are medium.
Feminine sounds/feelings are high.
Pronunciation is more difficult.

LYNETTE

Cheerfulness	xxxxx
Activity	xxxxxxxx
Toughness	xxxxxxxxxx
Unpleasantness	xxxxxxxx
Sadness	xxxxxxxxx
Passivity	xxxxxxx
Gentleness	xxxxxxx
Pleasantness	xxxxx

Masculine sounds/feelings are very high.
Feminine sounds/feelings are high.
Pronunciation is more difficult.

LYNN

Cheerfulness	xxx
Activity	xxx
Toughness	xxxx
Unpleasantness	x
Sadness	xxxxxxxxxxxx
Passivity	xxxxxx
Gentleness	xxxx
Pleasantness	xxxxxx

Masculine sounds/feelings are medium.
Feminine sounds/feelings are high.
Pronunciation is easiest.

LYNNE

Cheerfulness	xxxxxx
Activity	xxx
Toughness	xxxx
Unpleasantness	x
Sadness	xxxxxxxxxxxx
Passivity	xxxxxx
Gentleness	xxxxxx
Pleasantness	xxxxxxxxxxxx

Masculine sounds/feelings are low.
Feminine sounds/feelings are very high.
Pronunciation is easier.

LYNNETTE

Cheerfulness	xxxxxx
Activity	xxxxxxxxx
Toughness	xxxxxxxxxx
Unpleasantness	xxxxxxxxx
Sadness	xxxxxxxxxxxx
Passivity	xxxxxxxxx
Gentleness	xxxxxxx
Pleasantness	xxxxxx

Masculine sounds/feelings are very high.
Feminine sounds/feelings are very high.
Pronunciation is more difficult.

MABEL

Cheerfulness	xxx
Activity	x
Toughness	x
Unpleasantness	xxxxx
Sadness	xxxxxxxxx
Passivity	xxxxxxx
Gentleness	xxxxxxxxxx
Pleasantness	xxxxx

Masculine sounds/feelings are very low.
Feminine sounds/feelings are very high.
Pronunciation is easier.

MABLE

Cheerfulness	x
Activity	x
Toughness	x
Unpleasantness	xxxxx
Sadness	xxxxxxxxx
Passivity	xxxxx
Gentleness	xxxxxxx
Pleasantness	xxxxx

Masculine sounds/feelings are very low.
Feminine sounds/feelings are medium high.
Pronunciation is average.

MADELINE

Cheerfulness	xxxxxx
Activity	xxx
Toughness	xxxxxxx
Unpleasantness	xxxxx
Sadness	xxxxxxxxxxxx
Passivity	xxxxxxxxxxxxxx
Gentleness	xxxxxxxxxxx
Pleasantness	xxxxxx

Masculine sounds/feelings are medium.
Feminine sounds/feelings are very high.
Pronunciation is more difficult.

MADELYN

Cheerfulness	xxxxxx
Activity	xxx
Toughness	xxxxxxx
Unpleasantness	xxxxx
Sadness	xxxxxxxxxxxx
Passivity	xxxxxxxxxx
Gentleness	xxxxxxxxxx
Pleasantness	xxxxx

Masculine sounds/feelings are medium.
Feminine sounds/feelings are very high.
Pronunciation is more difficult.

MADGE

Cheerfulness	xxx
Activity	xxx
Toughness	xxxx
Unpleasantness	xxxxx
Sadness	xxxxx
Passivity	xxxxxxx
Gentleness	xxxx
Pleasantness	x

Masculine sounds/feelings are medium.
Feminine sounds/feelings are medium low.
Pronunciation is easier.

MAE

Cheerfulness	x
Activity	x
Toughness	x
Unpleasantness	x
Sadness	x
Passivity	xxxxx
Gentleness	xxxx
Pleasantness	x

Masculine sounds/feelings are very low.
Feminine sounds/feelings are very low.
Pronunciation is easiest.

MAGDALENA

Cheerfulness	xxx
Activity	xxx
Toughness	xxxxxxx
Unpleasantness	xxxxx
Sadness	xxxxxxxxxxx
Passivity	xxxxxxxxxxxxxxxx
Gentleness	xxxxxxxxxx
Pleasantness	xxxxx

Masculine sounds/feelings are medium.
Feminine sounds/feelings are very high.
Pronunciation is most difficult.

MAGGIE

Cheerfulness	xxx
Activity	xxx
Toughness	xxxx
Unpleasantness	x
Sadness	x
Passivity	xxxxx
Gentleness	xxxxxxx
Pleasantness	xxxxx

Masculine sounds/feelings are medium.
Feminine sounds/feelings are medium.
Pronunciation is easiest.

MALINDA

Cheerfulness	xxx
Activity	x
Toughness	xxxx
Unpleasantness	xxxxx
Sadness	xxxxxxxxxxxx
Passivity	xxxxxxxxxx
Gentleness	xxxxxxxxxx
Pleasantness	xxxxxxxxxx

Masculine sounds/feelings are low.
Feminine sounds/feelings are very high.
Pronunciation is most difficult.

Women's And Girls' Names

MALLORY

Cheerfulness	xxx
Activity	xxx
Toughness	xxxx
Unpleasantness	xxxxx
Sadness	xxxxx
Passivity	xxxxxxxx
Gentleness	xxxxxxxxxxxxxxxx
Pleasantness	xxxxxxxxxxx

Masculine sounds/feelings are low.
Feminine sounds/feelings are very high.
Pronunciation is average.

MAMIE

Cheerfulness	xxx
Activity	x
Toughness	x
Unpleasantness	x
Sadness	x
Passivity	xxxxx
Gentleness	xxxxxxxxxx
Pleasantness	xxxxxx

Masculine sounds/feelings are low.
Feminine sounds/feelings are medium.
Pronunciation is easiest.

MANDY

Cheerfulness	xxx
Activity	x
Toughness	xxxx
Unpleasantness	xxxxx
Sadness	xxxxxxxx
Passivity	xxxxxxxx
Gentleness	xxxxxxx
Pleasantness	xxxxxx

Masculine sounds/feelings are low.
Feminine sounds/feelings are very high.
Pronunciation is easiest.

MANUELA

Cheerfulness	xxx
Activity	xxx
Toughness	xxxx
Unpleasantness	x
Sadness	xxxxxxxx
Passivity	xxxxxxxxxx
Gentleness	xxxxxxxxxx
Pleasantness	xxxxx

Masculine sounds/feelings are very low.
Feminine sounds/feelings are very high.
Pronunciation is most difficult.

MARCELLA

Cheerfulness	xxxxxx
Activity	xxxxxx
Toughness	xxxx
Unpleasantness	xxxxx
Sadness	xxxxx
Passivity	xxxxxxx
Gentleness	xxxxxxxxxxx
Pleasantness	xxxxxx

Masculine sounds/feelings are medium.
Feminine sounds/feelings are high.
Pronunciation is most difficult.

MARCI

Cheerfulness	xxxxxx
Activity	xxxxxxxx
Toughness	xxxxxxx
Unpleasantness	xxxxx
Sadness	x
Passivity	xxx
Gentleness	xxxx
Pleasantness	x

Masculine sounds/feelings are medium high.
Feminine sounds/feelings are very low.
Pronunciation is easier.

182

MARCIA

Cheerfulness	xxx
Activity	xxxxxxxx
Toughness	xxxxxx
Unpleasantness	xxxxx
Sadness	x
Passivity	xxx
Gentleness	xxxx
Pleasantness	x

Masculine sounds/feelings are medium.
Feminine sounds/feelings are very low.
Pronunciation is more difficult.

MARCIE

Cheerfulness	xxxxxx
Activity	xxxxxx
Toughness	xxxx
Unpleasantness	xxxxx
Sadness	x
Passivity	xxx
Gentleness	xxxxxx
Pleasantness	xxxxxx

Masculine sounds/feelings are medium.
Feminine sounds/feelings are medium low.
Pronunciation is easier.

MARCY

Cheerfulness	xxxxxx
Activity	xxxxxx
Toughness	xxxx
Unpleasantness	xxxxx
Sadness	x
Passivity	xxx
Gentleness	xxxxxx
Pleasantness	xxxxxx

Masculine sounds/feelings are medium.
Feminine sounds/feelings are medium low.
Pronunciation is easier.

MARGARET

Cheerfulness	xxxxxxxx
Activity	xxxxxxxxxxxxxx
Toughness	xxxxxxxxxxxx
Unpleasantness	xxxxxxxxxxxx
Sadness	x
Passivity	xxxxxx
Gentleness	xxxxxxxxxx
Pleasantness	x

Masculine sounds/feelings are very high.
Feminine sounds/feelings are medium.
Pronunciation is most difficult.

MARGARITA

Cheerfulness	xxxxxxxx
Activity	xxxxxxxxxxxxxxxxx
Toughness	xxxxxxxxxxxxxxx
Unpleasantness	xxxxxxxxxxx
Sadness	x
Passivity	xxxxx
Gentleness	xxxxxx
Pleasantness	x

Masculine sounds/feelings are very high.
Feminine sounds/feelings are low.
Pronunciation is most difficult.

MARGERY

Cheerfulness	xxxxxxxxxxx
Activity	xxxxxxxxxxx
Toughness	xxxxxxx
Unpleasantness	xxxxx
Sadness	x
Passivity	xxx
Gentleness	xxxxxx
Pleasantness	xxxxx

Masculine sounds/feelings are very high.
Feminine sounds/feelings are medium low.
Pronunciation is more difficult.

Women's And Girls' Names

MARGIE

Cheerfulness	xxxxxxxx
Activity	xxxxxxxx
Toughness	xxxx
Unpleasantness	xxxxx
Sadness	x
Passivity	xxx
Gentleness	xxxxxxx
Pleasantness	xxxxxx

Masculine sounds/feelings are medium high.
Feminine sounds/feelings are medium low.
Pronunciation is average.

MARGO

Cheerfulness	xxx
Activity	xxxxxxxxx
Toughness	xxxxxxx
Unpleasantness	xxxxxxxx
Sadness	xxxxx
Passivity	xxxxx
Gentleness	xxxx
Pleasantness	x

Masculine sounds/feelings are high.
Feminine sounds/feelings are low.
Pronunciation is easier.

MARGRET

Cheerfulness	xxxxx
Activity	xxxxxxxxxxxxxx
Toughness	xxxxxxxxxxxx
Unpleasantness	xxxxxxxxxxxx
Sadness	x
Passivity	xxxxx
Gentleness	xxxxxxx
Pleasantness	x

Masculine sounds/feelings are very high.
Feminine sounds/feelings are low.
Pronunciation is most difficult.

MARGUERITE

Cheerfulness	xxxxxxxx
Activity	xxxxxxxxxxxxxxxxx
Toughness	xxxxxxxxxxxxxxx
Unpleasantness	xxxxxxxxxxxxx
Sadness	x
Passivity	xxxxx
Gentleness	xxxxxxx
Pleasantness	x

Masculine sounds/feelings are very high.
Feminine sounds/feelings are low.
Pronunciation is most difficult.

MARI

Cheerfulness	xxxxxx
Activity	xxxxxx
Toughness	xxxxxxx
Unpleasantness	xxxxx
Sadness	x
Passivity	xxxxx
Gentleness	xxxxxxx
Pleasantness	x

Masculine sounds/feelings are very high.
Feminine sounds/feelings are low.
Pronunciation is easier.

MARIA

Cheerfulness	xxxxxx
Activity	xxxxxx
Toughness	xxxxxxx
Unpleasantness	xxxxx
Sadness	x
Passivity	xxxxx
Gentleness	xxxxxxx
Pleasantness	x

Masculine sounds/feelings are medium.
Feminine sounds/feelings are low.
Pronunciation is more difficult.

MARIAN

Cheerfulness	xxxxx
Activity	xxxxx
Toughness	xxxxxxx
Unpleasantness	xxxxx
Sadness	xxxxx
Passivity	xxxxxxxx
Gentleness	xxxxxxx
Pleasantness	x

Masculine sounds/feelings are medium.
Feminine sounds/feelings are medium.
Pronunciation is average.

MARIANNE

Cheerfulness	xxxxx
Activity	xxxxx
Toughness	xxxxxxx
Unpleasantness	xxxxx
Sadness	xxxxxxxx
Passivity	xxxxxxxxxx
Gentleness	xxxxxxx
Pleasantness	x

Masculine sounds/feelings are medium.
Feminine sounds/feelings are medium high.
Pronunciation is more difficult.

MARIBEL

Cheerfulness	xxxxxxxx
Activity	xxxxx
Toughness	xxxxxx
Unpleasantness	xxxxxxxx
Sadness	xxxxxxxx
Passivity	xxxxxxxx
Gentleness	xxxxxxxxxxxx
Pleasantness	xxxxx

Masculine sounds/feelings are very high.
Feminine sounds/feelings are very high.
Pronunciation is most difficult.

MARICELA

Cheerfulness	xxxxxxxxx
Activity	xxxxx
Toughness	xxxxxx
Unpleasantness	xxxxx
Sadness	xxxxx
Passivity	xxxxxxxx
Gentleness	xxxxxxxxxxxx
Pleasantness	xxxxx

Masculine sounds/feelings are medium high.
Feminine sounds/feelings are very high.
Pronunciation is most difficult.

MARIE

Cheerfulness	xxxxx
Activity	xxx
Toughness	xxxx
Unpleasantness	xxxxx
Sadness	x
Passivity	xxxxx
Gentleness	xxxxxxxxxx
Pleasantness	xxxxx

Masculine sounds/feelings are medium high.
Feminine sounds/feelings are medium.
Pronunciation is easier.

MARIETTA

Cheerfulness	xxxxxxxx
Activity	xxxxxxxx
Toughness	xxxxxxxxx
Unpleasantness	xxxxxxxxxxx
Sadness	x
Passivity	xxxxxx
Gentleness	xxxxxxxxxxxx
Pleasantness	xxxxx

Masculine sounds/feelings are very high.
Feminine sounds/feelings are medium high.
Pronunciation is most difficult.

Women's And Girls' Names

MARILYN

Cheerfulness	xxxxxxxx
Activity	xxxxxxxx
Toughness	xxxxxxxxx
Unpleasantness	xxxxx
Sadness	xxxxxxxx
Passivity	xxxxxxxx
Gentleness	xxxxxxxxxx
Pleasantness	xxxxxx

Masculine sounds/feelings are very high.
Feminine sounds/feelings are very high.
Pronunciation is more difficult.

MARINA

Cheerfulness	xxxxx
Activity	xxxxx
Toughness	xxxxxxx
Unpleasantness	xxxxx
Sadness	xxxxx
Passivity	xxxxxxx
Gentleness	xxxxxxx
Pleasantness	x

Masculine sounds/feelings are medium.
Feminine sounds/feelings are medium.
Pronunciation is more difficult.

MARION

Cheerfulness	xxxxxx
Activity	xxxxxx
Toughness	xxxxxxx
Unpleasantness	xxxxx
Sadness	xxxxx
Passivity	xxxxxxx
Gentleness	xxxxxxx
Pleasantness	x

Masculine sounds/feelings are medium.
Feminine sounds/feelings are medium.
Pronunciation is more difficult.

MARISA

Cheerfulness	xxxxx
Activity	xxxxx
Toughness	xxxxxx
Unpleasantness	xxxxx
Sadness	x
Passivity	xxxxxxx
Gentleness	xxxxxxxxxx
Pleasantness	xxxxx

Masculine sounds/feelings are medium.
Feminine sounds/feelings are medium.
Pronunciation is most difficult.

MARISOL

Cheerfulness	xxxxxxxxx
Activity	xxxxxxxxx
Toughness	xxxxxxx
Unpleasantness	xxxxx
Sadness	xxxxx
Passivity	xxxxxxxxx
Gentleness	xxxxxxxxxxxxxx
Pleasantness	xxxxxxxxxxx

Masculine sounds/feelings are high.
Feminine sounds/feelings are very high.
Pronunciation is most difficult.

MARISSA

Cheerfulness	xxxxxx
Activity	xxxxxx
Toughness	xxxxxxx
Unpleasantness	xxxxx
Sadness	x
Passivity	xxxxx
Gentleness	xxxxxxx
Pleasantness	x

Masculine sounds/feelings are medium.
Feminine sounds/feelings are low.
Pronunciation is most difficult.

MARITZA

Cheerfulness	xxxxx
Activity	xxxxxxxx
Toughness	xxxxxxxxx
Unpleasantness	xxxxxxxx
Sadness	x
Passivity	xxxxxxx
Gentleness	xxxxxxxxxx
Pleasantness	xxxxx

Masculine sounds/feelings are very high.
Feminine sounds/feelings are medium.
Pronunciation is most difficult.

MARJORIE

Cheerfulness	xxxxxxxx
Activity	xxxxxxxxxxx
Toughness	xxxxxxx
Unpleasantness	xxxxxxxxx
Sadness	x
Passivity	xxxxx
Gentleness	xxxxxxxxxx
Pleasantness	xxxxxx

Masculine sounds/feelings are very high.
Feminine sounds/feelings are medium.
Pronunciation is most difficult.

MARLA

Cheerfulness	xxx
Activity	xxxxxx
Toughness	xxxx
Unpleasantness	xxxxx
Sadness	xxxxx
Passivity	xxxxx
Gentleness	xxxxxxx
Pleasantness	xxxxxx

Masculine sounds/feelings are medium.
Feminine sounds/feelings are medium.
Pronunciation is more difficult.

MARLENE

Cheerfulness	xxxxxx
Activity	xxxxxx
Toughness	xxxx
Unpleasantness	xxxxx
Sadness	xxxxxxxxx
Passivity	xxxxxxx
Gentleness	xxxxxxxxxx
Pleasantness	xxxxxxxxxxx

Masculine sounds/feelings are medium.
Feminine sounds/feelings are very high.
Pronunciation is most difficult.

MARSHA

Cheerfulness	xxx
Activity	xxxxxxxx
Toughness	xxxxxxx
Unpleasantness	xxxxx
Sadness	x
Passivity	xxx
Gentleness	xxxx
Pleasantness	x

Masculine sounds/feelings are medium.
Feminine sounds/feelings are very low.
Pronunciation is more difficult.

MARTA

Cheerfulness	xxx
Activity	xxxxxxxx
Toughness	xxxxxxx
Unpleasantness	xxxxxxxx
Sadness	x
Passivity	xxx
Gentleness	xxxx
Pleasantness	x

Masculine sounds/feelings are high.
Feminine sounds/feelings are very low.
Pronunciation is more difficult.

Women's And Girls' Names

MARTHA

Cheerfulness	xxxxx
Activity	xxxxx
Toughness	xxxx
Unpleasantness	xxxxx
Sadness	x
Passivity	xxx
Gentleness	xxxxxxx
Pleasantness	xxxxxx

Masculine sounds/feelings are medium.
Feminine sounds/feelings are medium low.
Pronunciation is more difficult.

MARTINA

Cheerfulness	xxxxx
Activity	xxxxxxxxxxx
Toughness	xxxxxxxxxx
Unpleasantness	xxxxxxxxx
Sadness	xxxxx
Passivity	xxxxx
Gentleness	xxxx
Pleasantness	x

Masculine sounds/feelings are very high.
Feminine sounds/feelings are low.
Pronunciation is most difficult.

MARVA

Cheerfulness	xxxxx
Activity	xxxxx
Toughness	xxxx
Unpleasantness	xxxxx
Sadness	x
Passivity	xxx
Gentleness	xxxxxxx
Pleasantness	xxxxxx

Masculine sounds/feelings are medium.
Feminine sounds/feelings are medium low.
Pronunciation is more difficult.

MARY

Cheerfulness	xxx
Activity	xxx
Toughness	xxxx
Unpleasantness	xxxxx
Sadness	x
Passivity	xxx
Gentleness	xxxxxxx
Pleasantness	xxxxxx

Masculine sounds/feelings are medium.
Feminine sounds/feelings are medium low.
Pronunciation is easiest.

MARYANN

Cheerfulness	xxx
Activity	xxxxxx
Toughness	xxxxxxx
Unpleasantness	xxxxx
Sadness	xxxxxxxxx
Passivity	xxxxxxxxx
Gentleness	xxxx
Pleasantness	x

Masculine sounds/feelings are medium.
Feminine sounds/feelings are medium.
Pronunciation is more difficult.

MARYANNE

Cheerfulness	xxx
Activity	xxxxxx
Toughness	xxxxxxx
Unpleasantness	xxxxx
Sadness	xxxxxxxxx
Passivity	xxxxxxxxx
Gentleness	xxxx
Pleasantness	x

Masculine sounds/feelings are medium.
Feminine sounds/feelings are medium.
Pronunciation is more difficult.

MARYLOU

Cheerfulness	xxx
Activity	xxxxxx
Toughness	xxxxxxx
Unpleasantness	xxxxxxxxx
Sadness	xxxxxxxxx
Passivity	xxxxxxxxx
Gentleness	xxxxxxx
Pleasantness	xxxxx

Masculine sounds/feelings are medium high.
Feminine sounds/feelings are very high.
Pronunciation is more difficult.

MATILDA

Cheerfulness	xxx
Activity	xxx
Toughness	xxxxxx
Unpleasantness	xxxxxxxxx
Sadness	xxxxxxxxx
Passivity	xxxxxxxxx
Gentleness	xxxxxxxxxxx
Pleasantness	xxxxxxxxxxxx

Masculine sounds/feelings are medium.
Feminine sounds/feelings are very high.
Pronunciation is most difficult.

MATTIE

Cheerfulness	xxx
Activity	xxxxxx
Toughness	xxxxxxx
Unpleasantness	xxxxxxxxx
Sadness	x
Passivity	xxxxx
Gentleness	xxxxxxx
Pleasantness	xxxxx

Masculine sounds/feelings are medium high.
Feminine sounds/feelings are medium.
Pronunciation is easier.

MAUDE

Cheerfulness	x
Activity	x
Toughness	xxxx
Unpleasantness	xxxxx
Sadness	xxxxx
Passivity	xxxxxx
Gentleness	xxxxxx
Pleasantness	x

Masculine sounds/feelings are medium low.
Feminine sounds/feelings are medium.
Pronunciation is easiest.

MAUREEN

Cheerfulness	xxx
Activity	xxx
Toughness	xxxx
Unpleasantness	xxxxx
Sadness	xxxxx
Passivity	xxxxxx
Gentleness	xxxxxxxxxx
Pleasantness	xxxxx

Masculine sounds/feelings are low.
Feminine sounds/feelings are high.
Pronunciation is easier.

MAVIS

Cheerfulness	xxxxx
Activity	xxx
Toughness	xxxx
Unpleasantness	x
Sadness	x
Passivity	xxxxx
Gentleness	xxxxxx
Pleasantness	xxxxx

Masculine sounds/feelings are low.
Feminine sounds/feelings are medium.
Pronunciation is easier.

Women's And Girls' Names

MAXINE

Cheerfulness	xxx
Activity	xxx
Toughness	xxxxxxx
Unpleasantness	xxxxx
Sadness	xxxxx
Passivity	xxxxxxxxx
Gentleness	xxxx
Pleasantness	x

Masculine sounds/feelings are medium.
Feminine sounds/feelings are medium.
Pronunciation is easier.

MAY

Cheerfulness	x
Activity	x
Toughness	x
Unpleasantness	x
Sadness	x
Passivity	xxx
Gentleness	xxxx
Pleasantness	x

Masculine sounds/feelings are very low.
Feminine sounds/feelings are very low.
Pronunciation is easiest.

MAYRA

Cheerfulness	x
Activity	xxx
Toughness	xxxx
Unpleasantness	xxxxx
Sadness	x
Passivity	xxx
Gentleness	xxxx
Pleasantness	x

Masculine sounds/feelings are medium.
Feminine sounds/feelings are very low.
Pronunciation is average.

MEAGAN

Cheerfulness	xxx
Activity	xxx
Toughness	xxxx
Unpleasantness	x
Sadness	xxxxx
Passivity	xxxxxxx
Gentleness	xxxxxxx
Pleasantness	xxxxxx

Masculine sounds/feelings are very low.
Feminine sounds/feelings are medium.
Pronunciation is easiest.

MEGAN

Cheerfulness	xxx
Activity	xxx
Toughness	xxxx
Unpleasantness	x
Sadness	xxxxx
Passivity	xxxxxxxxx
Gentleness	xxxxxxx
Pleasantness	x

Masculine sounds/feelings are very low.
Feminine sounds/feelings are medium.
Pronunciation is easiest.

MEGHAN

Cheerfulness	xxx
Activity	x
Toughness	x
Unpleasantness	x
Sadness	xxxxx
Passivity	xxxxxxxxx
Gentleness	xxxxxxx
Pleasantness	x

Masculine sounds/feelings are low.
Feminine sounds/feelings are medium.
Pronunciation is easiest.

MELANIE

Cheerfulness	xxxxxx
Activity	x
Toughness	x
Unpleasantness	x
Sadness	xxxxxxxx
Passivity	xxxxxxxx
Gentleness	xxxxxxxxxxxx
Pleasantness	xxxxxxxxxxx

Masculine sounds/feelings are very low.
Feminine sounds/feelings are very high.
Pronunciation is average.

MELBA

Cheerfulness	xxx
Activity	x
Toughness	x
Unpleasantness	xxxxx
Sadness	xxxxxxxxx
Passivity	xxxxxxx
Gentleness	xxxxxxxxxxx
Pleasantness	xxxxx

Masculine sounds/feelings are very low.
Feminine sounds/feelings are very high.
Pronunciation is average.

MELINDA

Cheerfulness	xxxxxx
Activity	x
Toughness	xxxx
Unpleasantness	xxxxx
Sadness	xxxxxxxxxxxx
Passivity	xxxxxxxxxx
Gentleness	xxxxxxxxxxxxx
Pleasantness	xxxxxxxxxxx

Masculine sounds/feelings are low.
Feminine sounds/feelings are very high.
Pronunciation is most difficult.

MELISA

Cheerfulness	xxxxxx
Activity	xxx
Toughness	xxxx
Unpleasantness	x
Sadness	xxxxx
Passivity	xxxxxxxxx
Gentleness	xxxxxxxxxxxxx
Pleasantness	xxxxxxxxxxx

Masculine sounds/feelings are low.
Feminine sounds/feelings are very high.
Pronunciation is more difficult.

MELISSA

Cheerfulness	xxxxxx
Activity	xxx
Toughness	xxxx
Unpleasantness	x
Sadness	xxxxx
Passivity	xxxxxxx
Gentleness	xxxxxxxxxx
Pleasantness	xxxxx

Masculine sounds/feelings are low.
Feminine sounds/feelings are high.
Pronunciation is more difficult.

MELODY

Cheerfulness	xxxxxxxxx
Activity	xxx
Toughness	xxxx
Unpleasantness	xxxxx
Sadness	xxxxxxxxx
Passivity	xxxxxxxxx
Gentleness	xxxxxxxxxxxxx
Pleasantness	xxxxxxxxxxx

Masculine sounds/feelings are medium.
Feminine sounds/feelings are very high.
Pronunciation is average.

MELVA

Cheerfulness	xxxxxx
Activity	x
Toughness	x
Unpleasantness	x

Sadness	xxxxx
Passivity	xxxxxxx
Gentleness	xxxxxxxxxxxxx
Pleasantness	xxxxxxxxxxx

Masculine sounds/feelings are very low.
Feminine sounds/feelings are very high.
Pronunciation is more difficult.

MERCEDES

Cheerfulness	xxxxxx
Activity	xxx
Toughness	xxxxxxx
Unpleasantness	xxxxx

Sadness	xxxxx
Passivity	xxxxxxx
Gentleness	xxxxxxxxxx
Pleasantness	xxxxxxxxxxx

Masculine sounds/feelings are medium.
Feminine sounds/feelings are very high.
Pronunciation is average.

MEREDITH

Cheerfulness	xxxxxxxxxxx
Activity	xxxxxx
Toughness	xxxxxxxxxx
Unpleasantness	xxxxxxxxx

Sadness	xxxxx
Passivity	xxxxxxx
Gentleness	xxxxxxxxxxxxx
Pleasantness	xxxxxxxxxxx

Masculine sounds/feelings are very high.
Feminine sounds/feelings are very high.
Pronunciation is most difficult.

MERLE

Cheerfulness	xxx
Activity	xxx
Toughness	xxxx
Unpleasantness	x

Sadness	xxxxx
Passivity	xxxxx
Gentleness	xxxxxxx
Pleasantness	xxxxx

Masculine sounds/feelings are medium.
Feminine sounds/feelings are medium.
Pronunciation is average.

MIA

Cheerfulness	xxx
Activity	xxx
Toughness	xxxx
Unpleasantness	x

Sadness	x
Passivity	xxx
Gentleness	xxxx
Pleasantness	x

Masculine sounds/feelings are medium.
Feminine sounds/feelings are very low.
Pronunciation is easiest.

MICHAELE

Cheerfulness	xxxxxxxxx
Activity	xxxxxx
Toughness	xxxx
Unpleasantness	x

Sadness	xxxxx
Passivity	xxxxxxxxx
Gentleness	xxxxxxxxxxx
Pleasantness	xxxxxx

Masculine sounds/feelings are medium.
Feminine sounds/feelings are high.
Pronunciation is more difficult.

MICHELE

Cheerfulness	xxxxxxxx
Activity	xxxxxx
Toughness	xxxx
Unpleasantness	x
Sadness	xxxxx
Passivity	xxxxx
Gentleness	xxxxxxxxxx
Pleasantness	xxxxxxxxxxx

Masculine sounds/feelings are medium.
Feminine sounds/feelings are very high.
Pronunciation is easier.

MICHELLE

Cheerfulness	xxxxxxxx
Activity	xxxxxx
Toughness	xxxx
Unpleasantness	x
Sadness	xxxxx
Passivity	xxxxxxx
Gentleness	xxxxxxxxxx
Pleasantness	xxxxxx

Masculine sounds/feelings are medium.
Feminine sounds/feelings are high.
Pronunciation is average.

MILAGROS

Cheerfulness	xxxxxx
Activity	xxxxxxxxxxx
Toughness	xxxxxxxxxx
Unpleasantness	xxxxx
Sadness	xxxxx
Passivity	xxxxxxx
Gentleness	xxxxxxx
Pleasantness	xxxxx

Masculine sounds/feelings are very high.
Feminine sounds/feelings are medium.
Pronunciation is most difficult.

MILDRED

Cheerfulness	xxx
Activity	xxx
Toughness	xxxxxxxxx
Unpleasantness	xxxxxxxxxxxx
Sadness	xxxxxxxxxxxx
Passivity	xxxxxxxxx
Gentleness	xxxxxxxxxx
Pleasantness	xxxxxxxxxxx

Masculine sounds/feelings are high.
Feminine sounds/feelings are very high.
Pronunciation is more difficult.

MILLIE

Cheerfulness	xxxxxx
Activity	xxx
Toughness	xxxx
Unpleasantness	x
Sadness	xxxxx
Passivity	xxxxx
Gentleness	xxxxxxxxxx
Pleasantness	xxxxxxxxxxx

Masculine sounds/feelings are medium.
Feminine sounds/feelings are very high.
Pronunciation is easiest.

MINDY

Cheerfulness	xxxxxx
Activity	x
Toughness	xxxx
Unpleasantness	xxxxx
Sadness	xxxxxxxxx
Passivity	xxxxxxx
Gentleness	xxxxxxxxxx
Pleasantness	xxxxxxxxxxx

Masculine sounds/feelings are low.
Feminine sounds/feelings are very high.
Pronunciation is easiest.

MINERVA

Cheerfulness	xxxxxxxx
Activity	xxxxxx
Toughness	xxxxxxx
Unpleasantness	x
Sadness	xxxxx
Passivity	xxxxx
Gentleness	xxxxxxx
Pleasantness	xxxxxx

Masculine sounds/feelings are medium.
Feminine sounds/feelings are medium.
Pronunciation is more difficult.

MINNIE

Cheerfulness	xxxxxx
Activity	xxx
Toughness	xxxx
Unpleasantness	x
Sadness	xxxxxxxxx
Passivity	xxxxxxx
Gentleness	xxxxxxx
Pleasantness	xxxxxx

Masculine sounds/feelings are low.
Feminine sounds/feelings are high.
Pronunciation is easiest.

MIRANDA

Cheerfulness	xxx
Activity	xxx
Toughness	xxxxxx
Unpleasantness	xxxxxxxxx
Sadness	xxxxxxxxx
Passivity	xxxxxxxxx
Gentleness	xxxxxxx
Pleasantness	xxxxxx

Masculine sounds/feelings are medium.
Feminine sounds/feelings are very high.
Pronunciation is most difficult.

MIRIAM

Cheerfulness	xxxxx
Activity	xxxxxxxx
Toughness	xxxxxxxxx
Unpleasantness	xxxxx
Sadness	x
Passivity	xxxxxxx
Gentleness	xxxxxxx
Pleasantness	x

Masculine sounds/feelings are high.
Feminine sounds/feelings are low.
Pronunciation is average.

MISTY

Cheerfulness	xxxxxx
Activity	xxxxxx
Toughness	xxxxxxx
Unpleasantness	xxxxx
Sadness	x
Passivity	xxx
Gentleness	xxxxxxx
Pleasantness	xxxxxx

Masculine sounds/feelings are medium.
Feminine sounds/feelings are medium low.
Pronunciation is easier.

MITZI

Cheerfulness	xxxxx
Activity	xxxxxxxx
Toughness	xxxxxxxxx
Unpleasantness	xxxxx
Sadness	x
Passivity	xxxxx
Gentleness	xxxxxxx
Pleasantness	xxxxxx

Masculine sounds/feelings are high.
Feminine sounds/feelings are medium.
Pronunciation is easier.

MOLLIE

Cheerfulness	xxxxxx
Activity	xxx
Toughness	x
Unpleasantness	x
Sadness	xxxxx
Passivity	xxxxx
Gentleness	xxxxxxxxxx
Pleasantness	xxxxxxxxxxx

Masculine sounds/feelings are medium.
Feminine sounds/feelings are very high.
Pronunciation is easiest.

MOLLY

Cheerfulness	xxxxxx
Activity	xxx
Toughness	x
Unpleasantness	x
Sadness	xxxxx
Passivity	xxxxx
Gentleness	xxxxxxxxxx
Pleasantness	xxxxxxxxxxx

Masculine sounds/feelings are medium.
Feminine sounds/feelings are very high.
Pronunciation is easiest.

MONA

Cheerfulness	x
Activity	x
Toughness	x
Unpleasantness	x
Sadness	xxxxx
Passivity	xxxxxxx
Gentleness	xxxx
Pleasantness	x

Masculine sounds/feelings are very low.
Feminine sounds/feelings are medium low.
Pronunciation is easier.

MONICA

Cheerfulness	xxx
Activity	xxx
Toughness	xxxxxxx
Unpleasantness	xxxxx
Sadness	xxxxx
Passivity	xxxxxxxxx
Gentleness	xxxx
Pleasantness	x

Masculine sounds/feelings are medium.
Feminine sounds/feelings are medium.
Pronunciation is average.

MONIQUE

Cheerfulness	xxx
Activity	x
Toughness	xxxx
Unpleasantness	xxxxx
Sadness	xxxxx
Passivity	xxxxxxxxx
Gentleness	xxxxxxx
Pleasantness	xxxxx

Masculine sounds/feelings are low.
Feminine sounds/feelings are medium high.
Pronunciation is easiest.

MORGAN

Cheerfulness	x
Activity	xxxxx
Toughness	xxxxxxx
Unpleasantness	xxxxx
Sadness	xxxxx
Passivity	xxxxxxxxx
Gentleness	xxxxxxx
Pleasantness	x

Masculine sounds/feelings are medium.
Feminine sounds/feelings are medium.
Pronunciation is easier.

MURIEL

Cheerfulness	xxxxxxxx
Activity	xxx
Toughness	xxxx
Unpleasantness	xxxxx
Sadness	xxxxx
Passivity	xxxxxxx
Gentleness	xxxxxxxxxxxxx
Pleasantness	xxxxxxxxxxxxxxxx

Masculine sounds/feelings are medium.
Feminine sounds/feelings are very high.
Pronunciation is most difficult.

MYRA

Cheerfulness	xxx
Activity	xxx
Toughness	xxxx
Unpleasantness	xxxxx
Sadness	x
Passivity	xxx
Gentleness	xxxxxxx
Pleasantness	xxxxxx

Masculine sounds/feelings are medium.
Feminine sounds/feelings are medium low.
Pronunciation is average.

MYRNA

Cheerfulness	xxx
Activity	xxxxxx
Toughness	xxxxxxx
Unpleasantness	xxxxx
Sadness	xxxxx
Passivity	xxxxx
Gentleness	xxxx
Pleasantness	x

Masculine sounds/feelings are medium.
Feminine sounds/feelings are low.
Pronunciation is average.

MYRTLE

Cheerfulness	xxxxx
Activity	xxxxxxxx
Toughness	xxxxxxxxxx
Unpleasantness	xxxxxxxxx
Sadness	xxxxx
Passivity	xxxxx
Gentleness	xxxxxxxxxx
Pleasantness	xxxxxxxxxxx

Masculine sounds/feelings are very high.
Feminine sounds/feelings are very high.
Pronunciation is more difficult.

NADIA

Cheerfulness	xxx
Activity	xxx
Toughness	xxxxxxx
Unpleasantness	xxxxx
Sadness	xxxxxxxxx
Passivity	xxxxx
Gentleness	x
Pleasantness	x

Masculine sounds/feelings are medium.
Feminine sounds/feelings are low.
Pronunciation is average.

NADINE

Cheerfulness	xxx
Activity	xxx
Toughness	xxxxxxx
Unpleasantness	xxxxx
Sadness	xxxxxxxxxxxxx
Passivity	xxxxxxxxx
Gentleness	x
Pleasantness	x

Masculine sounds/feelings are medium.
Feminine sounds/feelings are medium.
Pronunciation is easier.

NANCY

Cheerfulness	xxx
Activity	x
Toughness	x
Unpleasantness	x
Sadness	xxxxxxxx
Passivity	xxxxxxx
Gentleness	xxxx
Pleasantness	xxxxxx

Masculine sounds/feelings are very low.
Feminine sounds/feelings are medium high.
Pronunciation is easiest.

NANETTE

Cheerfulness	xxx
Activity	xxxxxx
Toughness	xxxxxxx
Unpleasantness	xxxxxxxxx
Sadness	xxxxxxxx
Passivity	xxxxxxxxx
Gentleness	xxxx
Pleasantness	x

Masculine sounds/feelings are medium high.
Feminine sounds/feelings are medium.
Pronunciation is average.

NANNIE

Cheerfulness	xxx
Activity	x
Toughness	x
Unpleasantness	x
Sadness	xxxxxxxxxxxx
Passivity	xxxxxxxxx
Gentleness	xxxx
Pleasantness	xxxxxx

Masculine sounds/feelings are very low.
Feminine sounds/feelings are very high.
Pronunciation is easiest.

NAOMI

Cheerfulness	xxxxx
Activity	xxxxxx
Toughness	xxxx
Unpleasantness	x
Sadness	xxxxx
Passivity	xxxxxxx
Gentleness	xxxx
Pleasantness	x

Masculine sounds/feelings are medium low.
Feminine sounds/feelings are medium low.
Pronunciation is easiest.

NATALIA

Cheerfulness	xxx
Activity	xxxxxx
Toughness	xxxxxxx
Unpleasantness	xxxxx
Sadness	xxxxxxxxx
Passivity	xxxxxxx
Gentleness	xxxx
Pleasantness	xxxxxx

Masculine sounds/feelings are medium.
Feminine sounds/feelings are medium high.
Pronunciation is most difficult.

NATALIE

Cheerfulness	xxx
Activity	xxx
Toughness	xxxx
Unpleasantness	xxxxx
Sadness	xxxxxxxxx
Passivity	xxxxxxx
Gentleness	xxxxxxx
Pleasantness	xxxxxxxxxxx

Masculine sounds/feelings are low.
Feminine sounds/feelings are very high.
Pronunciation is average.

Women's And Girls' Names

NATASHA

Cheerfulness	x
Activity	xxxxxx
Toughness	xxxxxxx
Unpleasantness	xxxxx
Sadness	xxxxx
Passivity	xxxxxxx
Gentleness	x
Pleasantness	x

Masculine sounds/feelings are medium.
Feminine sounds/feelings are very low.
Pronunciation is more difficult.

NELDA

Cheerfulness	xxx
Activity	x
Toughness	xxxx
Unpleasantness	xxxxx
Sadness	xxxxxxxxxxxx
Passivity	xxxxxxxxx
Gentleness	xxxxxxx
Pleasantness	xxxxxx

Masculine sounds/feelings are low.
Feminine sounds/feelings are very high.
Pronunciation is more difficult.

NELL

Cheerfulness	xxx
Activity	x
Toughness	x
Unpleasantness	x
Sadness	xxxxxxxxx
Passivity	xxxxxxx
Gentleness	xxxxxxx
Pleasantness	xxxxxx

Masculine sounds/feelings are low.
Feminine sounds/feelings are high.
Pronunciation is easiest.

NELLIE

Cheerfulness	xxxxxx
Activity	x
Toughness	x
Unpleasantness	x
Sadness	xxxxxxxxx
Passivity	xxxxxxx
Gentleness	xxxxxxxxxx
Pleasantness	xxxxxxxxxxxx

Masculine sounds/feelings are low.
Feminine sounds/feelings are very high.
Pronunciation is easiest.

NETTIE

Cheerfulness	xxxxxx
Activity	xxxxxx
Toughness	xxxxxxx
Unpleasantness	xxxxxxxxx
Sadness	xxxxx
Passivity	xxxxx
Gentleness	xxxxxxx
Pleasantness	xxxxxx

Masculine sounds/feelings are high.
Feminine sounds/feelings are medium.
Pronunciation is easier.

NEVA

Cheerfulness	xxxxxx
Activity	x
Toughness	x
Unpleasantness	x
Sadness	xxxxx
Passivity	xxxxx
Gentleness	xxxxxxx
Pleasantness	xxxxxx

Masculine sounds/feelings are low.
Feminine sounds/feelings are medium.
Pronunciation is average.

NICHOLE

Cheerfulness	xxxxx
Activity	xxxxxx
Toughness	xxxx
Unpleasantness	xxxxx
Sadness	xxxxxxxxxxxx
Passivity	xxxxxxx
Gentleness	xxxx
Pleasantness	xxxxxx

Masculine sounds/feelings are medium.
Feminine sounds/feelings are high.
Pronunciation is average.

NICOLE

Cheerfulness	xxx
Activity	xxx
Toughness	xxxxxxx
Unpleasantness	xxxxxxxxx
Sadness	xxxxxxxxxxxx
Passivity	xxxxxxxxx
Gentleness	xxxx
Pleasantness	xxxxxx

Masculine sounds/feelings are medium.
Feminine sounds/feelings are very high.
Pronunciation is easier.

NIKKI

Cheerfulness	xxxxx
Activity	xxxxxx
Toughness	xxxxxxxxxxxx
Unpleasantness	xxxxxxxxx
Sadness	xxxxx
Passivity	xxxxxxx
Gentleness	x
Pleasantness	x

Masculine sounds/feelings are very high.
Feminine sounds/feelings are very low.
Pronunciation is easiest.

NINA

Cheerfulness	xxx
Activity	xxx
Toughness	xxxx
Unpleasantness	x
Sadness	xxxxxxxxx
Passivity	xxxxx
Gentleness	x
Pleasantness	x

Masculine sounds/feelings are medium.
Feminine sounds/feelings are low.
Pronunciation is easier.

NITA

Cheerfulness	xxx
Activity	xxxxxx
Toughness	xxxxxxx
Unpleasantness	xxxxx
Sadness	xxxxx
Passivity	xxx
Gentleness	x
Pleasantness	x

Masculine sounds/feelings are high.
Feminine sounds/feelings are very low.
Pronunciation is easier.

NOEMI

Cheerfulness	xxxxx
Activity	xxx
Toughness	xxxx
Unpleasantness	xxxxx
Sadness	xxxxxxxxx
Passivity	xxxxxxxxx
Gentleness	xxxxxx
Pleasantness	x

Masculine sounds/feelings are medium.
Feminine sounds/feelings are medium high.
Pronunciation is easier.

Women's And Girls' Names

NOLA

Cheerfulness	xxx
Activity	xxx
Toughness	x
Unpleasantness	x
Sadness	xxxxxxxx
Passivity	xxxxx
Gentleness	xxxx
Pleasantness	xxxxxx

Masculine sounds/feelings are low.
Feminine sounds/feelings are medium.
Pronunciation is easier.

NONA

Cheerfulness	x
Activity	x
Toughness	x
Unpleasantness	x
Sadness	xxxxxxxx
Passivity	xxxxxxx
Gentleness	x
Pleasantness	x

Masculine sounds/feelings are very low.
Feminine sounds/feelings are medium low.
Pronunciation is easier.

NORA

Cheerfulness	x
Activity	xxx
Toughness	xxxx
Unpleasantness	xxxxx
Sadness	xxxxx
Passivity	xxxxx
Gentleness	xxxx
Pleasantness	x

Masculine sounds/feelings are medium.
Feminine sounds/feelings are low.
Pronunciation is average.

NOREEN

Cheerfulness	xxx
Activity	xxx
Toughness	xxxx
Unpleasantness	xxxxx
Sadness	xxxxxxxx
Passivity	xxxxxxx
Gentleness	xxxxxxx
Pleasantness	xxxxx

Masculine sounds/feelings are low.
Feminine sounds/feelings are high.
Pronunciation is easier.

NORMA

Cheerfulness	x
Activity	xxx
Toughness	xxxx
Unpleasantness	xxxxx
Sadness	xxxxx
Passivity	xxxxxxx
Gentleness	xxxxxxx
Pleasantness	x

Masculine sounds/feelings are low.
Feminine sounds/feelings are medium.
Pronunciation is average.

ODESSA

Cheerfulness	xxx
Activity	x
Toughness	xxxx
Unpleasantness	xxxxxxxx
Sadness	xxxxxxxx
Passivity	xxxxxxx
Gentleness	xxxx
Pleasantness	x

Masculine sounds/feelings are medium low.
Feminine sounds/feelings are medium.
Pronunciation is more difficult.

OFELIA

Cheerfulness	xxxxxxxx
Activity	xxxxxx
Toughness	xxxx
Unpleasantness	xxxxx
Sadness	xxxxxxxxx
Passivity	xxxxxxx
Gentleness	xxxxxxx
Pleasantness	xxxxxx

Masculine sounds/feelings are medium.
Feminine sounds/feelings are high.
Pronunciation is more difficult.

OLA

Cheerfulness	xxx
Activity	xxx
Toughness	x
Unpleasantness	x
Sadness	xxxxx
Passivity	xxx
Gentleness	xxxx
Pleasantness	xxxxxx

Masculine sounds/feelings are low.
Feminine sounds/feelings are medium low.
Pronunciation is easier.

OLGA

Cheerfulness	xxx
Activity	xxxxxx
Toughness	xxxx
Unpleasantness	x
Sadness	xxxxx
Passivity	xxx
Gentleness	xxxx
Pleasantness	xxxxxx

Masculine sounds/feelings are medium.
Feminine sounds/feelings are medium low.
Pronunciation is easier.

OLIVE

Cheerfulness	xxxxxxxxx
Activity	xxxxxx
Toughness	xxxx
Unpleasantness	x
Sadness	xxxxx
Passivity	xxx
Gentleness	xxxxxxx
Pleasantness	xxxxxxxxxxx

Masculine sounds/feelings are medium high.
Feminine sounds/feelings are medium high.
Pronunciation is easier.

OLIVIA

Cheerfulness	xxxxxxxxxxx
Activity	xxxxxxxxx
Toughness	xxxxxxx
Unpleasantness	x
Sadness	xxxxx
Passivity	xxx
Gentleness	xxxxxxx
Pleasantness	xxxxxxxxxxx

Masculine sounds/feelings are high.
Feminine sounds/feelings are medium high.
Pronunciation is most difficult.

OLLIE

Cheerfulness	xxxxxx
Activity	xxx
Toughness	x
Unpleasantness	x
Sadness	xxxxx
Passivity	xxx
Gentleness	xxxxxxx
Pleasantness	xxxxxxxxxxx

Masculine sounds/feelings are medium.
Feminine sounds/feelings are medium high.
Pronunciation is easiest.

Women's And Girls' Names

OPAL

Cheerfulness	xxx
Activity	xxxxxx
Toughness	xxxx
Unpleasantness	x
Sadness	xxxxx
Passivity	xxx
Gentleness	xxxx
Pleasantness	xxxxxx

Masculine sounds/feelings are medium.
Feminine sounds/feelings are medium low.
Pronunciation is easier.

OPHELIA

Cheerfulness	xxxxxxxxxxxx
Activity	xxxxxxxxx
Toughness	xxxx
Unpleasantness	x
Sadness	xxxxx
Passivity	xxxxx
Gentleness	xxxxxxx
Pleasantness	xxxxxx

Masculine sounds/feelings are medium high.
Feminine sounds/feelings are medium.
Pronunciation is more difficult.

ORA

Cheerfulness	x
Activity	xxx
Toughness	xxxx
Unpleasantness	xxxxx
Sadness	x
Passivity	xxx
Gentleness	xxxx
Pleasantness	x

Masculine sounds/feelings are medium.
Feminine sounds/feelings are very low.
Pronunciation is easier.

PAIGE

Cheerfulness	xxx
Activity	xxxxxx
Toughness	xxxx
Unpleasantness	x
Sadness	x
Passivity	x
Gentleness	x
Pleasantness	x

Masculine sounds/feelings are medium.
Feminine sounds/feelings are very low.
Pronunciation is easier.

PAM

Cheerfulness	x
Activity	xxx
Toughness	xxxx
Unpleasantness	x
Sadness	x
Passivity	xxxxx
Gentleness	xxxx
Pleasantness	x

Masculine sounds/feelings are medium low.
Feminine sounds/feelings are very low.
Pronunciation is easiest.

PAMELA

Cheerfulness	xxx
Activity	xxx
Toughness	xxxx
Unpleasantness	x
Sadness	xxxxx
Passivity	xxxxxxxxx
Gentleness	xxxxxxxxxxx
Pleasantness	xxxxxx

Masculine sounds/feelings are very low.
Feminine sounds/feelings are high.
Pronunciation is more difficult.

PAT

Cheerfulness	x
Activity	xxxxxx
Toughness	xxxxxxx
Unpleasantness	xxxxx
Sadness	x
Passivity	xxx
Gentleness	x
Pleasantness	x

Masculine sounds/feelings are medium high.
Feminine sounds/feelings are very low.
Pronunciation is easiest.

PATRICA

Cheerfulness	xxx
Activity	xxxxxxxxxxx
Toughness	xxxxxxxxxxxxxxxx
Unpleasantness	xxxxxxxxxxxx
Sadness	x
Passivity	xxxxx
Gentleness	x
Pleasantness	x

Masculine sounds/feelings are very high.
Feminine sounds/feelings are very low.
Pronunciation is most difficult.

PATRICE

Cheerfulness	xxx
Activity	xxxxxxxxxxx
Toughness	xxxxxxxxxxxx
Unpleasantness	xxxxxxxxx
Sadness	x
Passivity	xxx
Gentleness	x
Pleasantness	x

Masculine sounds/feelings are very high.
Feminine sounds/feelings are very low.
Pronunciation is average.

PATRICIA

Cheerfulness	xxx
Activity	xxxxxxxxxxxxxxx
Toughness	xxxxxxxxxxxxxxx
Unpleasantness	xxxxxxxxx
Sadness	x
Passivity	xxx
Gentleness	x
Pleasantness	x

Masculine sounds/feelings are very high.
Feminine sounds/feelings are very low.
Pronunciation is most difficult.

PATSY

Cheerfulness	xxx
Activity	xxxxxx
Toughness	xxxxxxx
Unpleasantness	xxxxx
Sadness	x
Passivity	xxx
Gentleness	xxxx
Pleasantness	xxxxxx

Masculine sounds/feelings are medium.
Feminine sounds/feelings are low.
Pronunciation is easiest.

PATTI

Cheerfulness	xxx
Activity	xxxxxxxxxxx
Toughness	xxxxxxxxxxxx
Unpleasantness	xxxxxxxxx
Sadness	x
Passivity	xxx
Gentleness	x
Pleasantness	x

Masculine sounds/feelings are very high.
Feminine sounds/feelings are very low.
Pronunciation is easier.

PATTY

Cheerfulness	xxx
Activity	xxxxxxxx
Toughness	xxxxxxxxxx
Unpleasantness	xxxxxxxx
Sadness	x
Passivity	xxx
Gentleness	xxxx
Pleasantness	xxxxxx

Masculine sounds/feelings are very high.
Feminine sounds/feelings are low.
Pronunciation is easier.

PAULA

Cheerfulness	x
Activity	xxx
Toughness	xxxx
Unpleasantness	x
Sadness	xxxxx
Passivity	xxxxx
Gentleness	xxxxxxx
Pleasantness	xxxxxx

Masculine sounds/feelings are medium low.
Feminine sounds/feelings are medium.
Pronunciation is average.

PAULETTE

Cheerfulness	xxx
Activity	xxxxxxxxx
Toughness	xxxxxxxxxx
Unpleasantness	xxxxxxxxx
Sadness	xxxxx
Passivity	xxxxxxx
Gentleness	xxxxxxxxxxx
Pleasantness	xxxxxx

Masculine sounds/feelings are very high.
Feminine sounds/feelings are high.
Pronunciation is more difficult.

PAULINE

Cheerfulness	xxx
Activity	xxxxx
Toughness	xxxxxx
Unpleasantness	x
Sadness	xxxxxxxx
Passivity	xxxxxxx
Gentleness	xxxxxxx
Pleasantness	xxxxx

Masculine sounds/feelings are medium low.
Feminine sounds/feelings are high.
Pronunciation is easier.

PEARL

Cheerfulness	xxx
Activity	xxxxxx
Toughness	xxxxxxx
Unpleasantness	xxxxx
Sadness	xxxxx
Passivity	xxx
Gentleness	xxxxxxx
Pleasantness	xxxxxxxxxxxx

Masculine sounds/feelings are high.
Feminine sounds/feelings are medium high.
Pronunciation is easier.

PEARLIE

Cheerfulness	xxxxxx
Activity	xxxxxx
Toughness	xxxxxxx
Unpleasantness	xxxxx
Sadness	xxxxx
Passivity	xxx
Gentleness	xxxxxxxxxxx
Pleasantness	xxxxxxxxxxxxxxxxx

Masculine sounds/feelings are medium.
Feminine sounds/feelings are very high.
Pronunciation is easier.

PEGGY

Cheerfulness	xxxxxx
Activity	xxxxxx
Toughness	xxxxxxx
Unpleasantness	x
Sadness	x
Passivity	xxx
Gentleness	xxxxxxx
Pleasantness	xxxxxx

Masculine sounds/feelings are medium high.
Feminine sounds/feelings are medium low.
Pronunciation is easiest.

PENELOPE

Cheerfulness	xxxxxx
Activity	xxxxxx
Toughness	xxxxxxx
Unpleasantness	xxxxx
Sadness	xxxxxxxxxxxx
Passivity	xxxxxxxxx
Gentleness	xxxxxxxxxxx
Pleasantness	xxxxxxxxxxxx

Masculine sounds/feelings are medium.
Feminine sounds/feelings are very high.
Pronunciation is average.

PENNY

Cheerfulness	xxxxxx
Activity	xxx
Toughness	xxxx
Unpleasantness	x
Sadness	xxxxxxxxx
Passivity	xxxxxxx
Gentleness	xxxxxxx
Pleasantness	xxxxxx

Masculine sounds/feelings are low.
Feminine sounds/feelings are high.
Pronunciation is easiest.

PETRA

Cheerfulness	xxx
Activity	xxxxxxxx
Toughness	xxxxxxxxx
Unpleasantness	xxxxxxxx
Sadness	x
Passivity	xxx
Gentleness	xxxx
Pleasantness	x

Masculine sounds/feelings are very high.
Feminine sounds/feelings are very low.
Pronunciation is more difficult.

PHYLLIS

Cheerfulness	xxxxxxxxx
Activity	xxxxxxxxx
Toughness	xxxxxxx
Unpleasantness	x
Sadness	xxxxx
Passivity	xxxxx
Gentleness	xxxxxxx
Pleasantness	xxxxxxxxxxx

Masculine sounds/feelings are medium high.
Feminine sounds/feelings are high.
Pronunciation is average.

POLLY

Cheerfulness	xxxxx
Activity	xxxxxx
Toughness	xxxx
Unpleasantness	x
Sadness	xxxxx
Passivity	xxx
Gentleness	xxxxxxx
Pleasantness	xxxxxxxxxxx

Masculine sounds/feelings are medium.
Feminine sounds/feelings are medium high.
Pronunciation is easiest.

PRISCILLA

Cheerfulness	xxxxx
Activity	xxxxxxxxxxx
Toughness	xxxxxxxxxxxx
Unpleasantness	xxxxx
Sadness	xxxxx
Passivity	xxx
Gentleness	xxxx
Pleasantness	xxxxxx

Masculine sounds/feelings are very high.
Feminine sounds/feelings are medium low.
Pronunciation is most difficult.

RACHAEL

Cheerfulness	xxxxx
Activity	xxxxxx
Toughness	xxxx
Unpleasantness	xxxxx
Sadness	xxxxx
Passivity	xxxxxxxx
Gentleness	xxxxxxx
Pleasantness	xxxxxx

Masculine sounds/feelings are medium.
Feminine sounds/feelings are medium high.
Pronunciation is more difficult.

RACHEL

Cheerfulness	xxxxxx
Activity	xxxxxx
Toughness	xxxx
Unpleasantness	xxxxx
Sadness	xxxxx
Passivity	xxxxxxx
Gentleness	xxxxxxx
Pleasantness	xxxxxx

Masculine sounds/feelings are medium.
Feminine sounds/feelings are medium.
Pronunciation is more difficult.

RACHELLE

Cheerfulness	xxxxx
Activity	xxxxx
Toughness	xxxx
Unpleasantness	xxxxx
Sadness	xxxxx
Passivity	xxxxxxx
Gentleness	xxxxxxx
Pleasantness	xxxxx

Masculine sounds/feelings are medium.
Feminine sounds/feelings are medium.
Pronunciation is more difficult.

RAE

Cheerfulness	x
Activity	xxx
Toughness	xxxx
Unpleasantness	xxxxx
Sadness	x
Passivity	xxx
Gentleness	x
Pleasantness	x

Masculine sounds/feelings are medium.
Feminine sounds/feelings are very low.
Pronunciation is easiest.

RAMONA

Cheerfulness	x
Activity	xxx
Toughness	xxxx
Unpleasantness	xxxxx
Sadness	xxxxx
Passivity	xxxxxxx
Gentleness	xxxx
Pleasantness	x

Masculine sounds/feelings are low.
Feminine sounds/feelings are medium low.
Pronunciation is most difficult.

RANDI

Cheerfulness	xxx
Activity	xxxxxx
Toughness	xxxxxxxxxx
Unpleasantness	xxxxxxxxx
Sadness	xxxxxxxxx
Passivity	xxxxxxx
Gentleness	x
Pleasantness	x

Masculine sounds/feelings are high.
Feminine sounds/feelings are medium low.
Pronunciation is easier.

RAQUEL

Cheerfulness	xxxxxx
Activity	xxx
Toughness	xxxxxxx
Unpleasantness	xxxxxxxxx
Sadness	xxxxx
Passivity	xxxxxxxxx
Gentleness	xxxxxxx
Pleasantness	xxxxxxxxxxx

Masculine sounds/feelings are medium high.
Feminine sounds/feelings are very high.
Pronunciation is more difficult.

REBA

Cheerfulness	xxx
Activity	xxx
Toughness	xxxx
Unpleasantness	xxxxxxxxx
Sadness	xxxxx
Passivity	x
Gentleness	xxxx
Pleasantness	xxxxxx

Masculine sounds/feelings are medium high.
Feminine sounds/feelings are low.
Pronunciation is easier.

REBECCA

Cheerfulness	xxxxxx
Activity	xxx
Toughness	xxxxxxxxx
Unpleasantness	xxxxxxxxxxxxxxxxx
Sadness	xxxxx
Passivity	xxxxxxx
Gentleness	xxxxxx
Pleasantness	xxxxx

Masculine sounds/feelings are very high.
Feminine sounds/feelings are medium.
Pronunciation is more difficult.

REBEKAH

Cheerfulness	xxxxx
Activity	xxx
Toughness	xxxxxxx
Unpleasantness	xxxxxxxxxxxxx
Sadness	xxxxx
Passivity	xxxxxxx
Gentleness	xxxxxxx
Pleasantness	xxxxx

Masculine sounds/feelings are high.
Feminine sounds/feelings are medium.
Pronunciation is easier.

REGINA

Cheerfulness	xxxxxxxxx
Activity	xxxxxxxxx
Toughness	xxxxxxx
Unpleasantness	xxxxx
Sadness	xxxxx
Passivity	xxx
Gentleness	xxxx
Pleasantness	xxxxx

Masculine sounds/feelings are high.
Feminine sounds/feelings are medium low.
Pronunciation is most difficult.

Women's And Girls' Names

RENA

Cheerfulness	xxx
Activity	xxx
Toughness	xxxx
Unpleasantness	xxxxx
Sadness	xxxxx
Passivity	xxx
Gentleness	xxxx
Pleasantness	xxxxxx

Masculine sounds/feelings are medium.
Feminine sounds/feelings are medium low.
Pronunciation is easier.

RENE

Cheerfulness	xxx
Activity	xxx
Toughness	xxxx
Unpleasantness	xxxxx
Sadness	xxxxx
Passivity	xxx
Gentleness	xxxx
Pleasantness	xxxxxx

Masculine sounds/feelings are medium.
Feminine sounds/feelings are medium low.
Pronunciation is easiest.

RENEE

Cheerfulness	xxxxxx
Activity	xxx
Toughness	xxxx
Unpleasantness	xxxxx
Sadness	xxxxx
Passivity	xxx
Gentleness	xxxxxxx
Pleasantness	xxxxxxxxxxx

Masculine sounds/feelings are medium high.
Feminine sounds/feelings are medium high.
Pronunciation is easiest.

REVA

Cheerfulness	xxxxxx
Activity	xxx
Toughness	xxxx
Unpleasantness	xxxxx
Sadness	x
Passivity	x
Gentleness	xxxxxxx
Pleasantness	xxxxxxxxxxx

Masculine sounds/feelings are medium high.
Feminine sounds/feelings are medium.
Pronunciation is average.

RHODA

Cheerfulness	xxx
Activity	xxxxxx
Toughness	xxxxxxx
Unpleasantness	xxxxxxxxx
Sadness	xxxxx
Passivity	xxx
Gentleness	x
Pleasantness	x

Masculine sounds/feelings are medium high.
Feminine sounds/feelings are very low.
Pronunciation is more difficult.

RHONDA

Cheerfulness	x
Activity	xxx
Toughness	xxxxxxx
Unpleasantness	xxxxxxxxx
Sadness	xxxxxxxxx
Passivity	xxxxxxx
Gentleness	x
Pleasantness	x

Masculine sounds/feelings are medium.
Feminine sounds/feelings are medium low.
Pronunciation is most difficult.

208

RITA

Cheerfulness	xxx
Activity	xxxxxxxx
Toughness	xxxxxxxxxx
Unpleasantness	xxxxxxxx

Sadness	x
Passivity	x
Gentleness	x
Pleasantness	x

Masculine sounds/feelings are very high.
Feminine sounds/feelings are very low.
Pronunciation is average.

ROBBIE

Cheerfulness	xxxxxx
Activity	xxxxxx
Toughness	xxxx
Unpleasantness	xxxxxxxxxxxx

Sadness	xxxxxxxx
Passivity	x
Gentleness	xxxx
Pleasantness	xxxxxx

Masculine sounds/feelings are high.
Feminine sounds/feelings are medium.
Pronunciation is easiest.

ROBERTA

Cheerfulness	xxx
Activity	xxxxxxxxx
Toughness	xxxxxxxxxx
Unpleasantness	xxxxxxxxxxxxxxxxxx

Sadness	xxxxxxxx
Passivity	xxx
Gentleness	x
Pleasantness	x

Masculine sounds/feelings are very high.
Feminine sounds/feelings are very low.
Pronunciation is most difficult.

ROBIN

Cheerfulness	xxxxx
Activity	xxxxxxxx
Toughness	xxxxxx
Unpleasantness	xxxxxxxx

Sadness	xxxxxxxx
Passivity	xxx
Gentleness	x
Pleasantness	x

Masculine sounds/feelings are very high.
Feminine sounds/feelings are very low.
Pronunciation is easier.

ROBYN

Cheerfulness	xxxxx
Activity	xxxxxxxx
Toughness	xxxxxx
Unpleasantness	xxxxxxxx

Sadness	xxxxxxxx
Passivity	xxx
Gentleness	x
Pleasantness	x

Masculine sounds/feelings are very high.
Feminine sounds/feelings are very low.
Pronunciation is easier.

ROCHELLE

Cheerfulness	xxxxxxxx
Activity	xxxxxxxx
Toughness	xxxx
Unpleasantness	xxxxx

Sadness	xxxxx
Passivity	xxxxx
Gentleness	xxxxxx
Pleasantness	xxxxx

Masculine sounds/feelings are medium high.
Feminine sounds/feelings are medium.
Pronunciation is more difficult.

RONDA

Cheerfulness	x
Activity	xxx
Toughness	xxxxxxx
Unpleasantness	xxxxxxxxx
Sadness	xxxxxxxxx
Passivity	xxxxxxx
Gentleness	x
Pleasantness	x

Masculine sounds/feelings are medium.
Feminine sounds/feelings are medium low.
Pronunciation is more difficult.

ROSA

Cheerfulness	xxx
Activity	xxxxxx
Toughness	xxxx
Unpleasantness	xxxxx
Sadness	x
Passivity	xxx
Gentleness	xxxx
Pleasantness	xxxxxx

Masculine sounds/feelings are medium high.
Feminine sounds/feelings are low.
Pronunciation is average.

ROSALIE

Cheerfulness	xxxxxx
Activity	xxxxxx
Toughness	xxxx
Unpleasantness	xxxxx
Sadness	xxxxx
Passivity	xxxxx
Gentleness	xxxxxxxxxx
Pleasantness	xxxxxxxxxxxxxxxx

Masculine sounds/feelings are medium.
Feminine sounds/feelings are very high.
Pronunciation is more difficult.

ROSALIND

Cheerfulness	xxxxxx
Activity	xxxxxx
Toughness	xxxxxxx
Unpleasantness	xxxxxxxxx
Sadness	xxxxxxxxxxxx
Passivity	xxxxxxxxxxx
Gentleness	xxxxxxxxxxx
Pleasantness	xxxxxxxxxxxxxxxx

Masculine sounds/feelings are high.
Feminine sounds/feelings are very high.
Pronunciation is most difficult.

ROSALINDA

Cheerfulness	xxxxxx
Activity	xxxxxx
Toughness	xxxxxxx
Unpleasantness	xxxxxxxxx
Sadness	xxxxxxxxxxxx
Passivity	xxxxxxxxxxx
Gentleness	xxxxxxxxxxx
Pleasantness	xxxxxxxxxxxxxxxxx

Masculine sounds/feelings are high.
Feminine sounds/feelings are very high.
Pronunciation is most difficult.

ROSALYN

Cheerfulness	xxxxxx
Activity	xxxxxxxxx
Toughness	xxxxxxx
Unpleasantness	xxxxx
Sadness	xxxxxxxxx
Passivity	xxxxxxxxx
Gentleness	xxxxxxxxxxx
Pleasantness	xxxxxxxxxxx

Masculine sounds/feelings are medium high.
Feminine sounds/feelings are very high.
Pronunciation is more difficult.

ROSANNE

Cheerfulness	xxx
Activity	xxxxxx
Toughness	xxxx
Unpleasantness	xxxxx
Sadness	xxxxxxxx
Passivity	xxxxxxxx
Gentleness	xxxx
Pleasantness	xxxxx

Masculine sounds/feelings are medium.
Feminine sounds/feelings are medium high.
Pronunciation is average.

ROSARIO

Cheerfulness	xxxxxxxx
Activity	xxxxxxxxxxx
Toughness	xxxxxxxxxx
Unpleasantness	xxxxxxxxxxxx
Sadness	xxxxx
Passivity	xxxxxxx
Gentleness	xxxxxxx
Pleasantness	xxxxx

Masculine sounds/feelings are very high.
Feminine sounds/feelings are medium.
Pronunciation is most difficult.

ROSE

Cheerfulness	x
Activity	xxx
Toughness	xxxx
Unpleasantness	xxxxxxxx
Sadness	xxxxx
Passivity	xxxxx
Gentleness	xxxx
Pleasantness	xxxxx

Masculine sounds/feelings are medium.
Feminine sounds/feelings are medium.
Pronunciation is easiest.

ROSEANN

Cheerfulness	xxx
Activity	xxx
Toughness	xxxx
Unpleasantness	xxxxxxxx
Sadness	xxxxxxxxxxxx
Passivity	xxxxxxxx
Gentleness	xxxxxx
Pleasantness	xxxxxxxxxxx

Masculine sounds/feelings are medium.
Feminine sounds/feelings are very high.
Pronunciation is easier.

ROSELLA

Cheerfulness	xxx
Activity	xxx
Toughness	xxxx
Unpleasantness	xxxxxxxx
Sadness	xxxxxxxx
Passivity	xxxxxxxx
Gentleness	xxxxxxxxxx
Pleasantness	xxxxxxxxxxx

Masculine sounds/feelings are medium.
Feminine sounds/feelings are very high.
Pronunciation is most difficult.

ROSEMARIE

Cheerfulness	xxxxxxxx
Activity	xxxxx
Toughness	xxxxxxx
Unpleasantness	xxxxxxxxxxxx
Sadness	xxxxx
Passivity	xxxxxxxxxx
Gentleness	xxxxxxxxxxxxxxxxxx
Pleasantness	xxxxxxxxxxx

Masculine sounds/feelings are very high.
Feminine sounds/feelings are very high.
Pronunciation is most difficult.

Women's And Girls' Names

ROSEMARY

Cheerfulness	xxxxxxxx
Activity	xxxxxxxx
Toughness	xxxxxxx
Unpleasantness	xxxxxxxxxxxx
Sadness	xxxxx
Passivity	xxxxxxxxx
Gentleness	xxxxxxxxxxxxx
Pleasantness	xxxxxxxxxxx

Masculine sounds/feelings are very high.
Feminine sounds/feelings are very high.
Pronunciation is most difficult.

ROSETTA

Cheerfulness	xxx
Activity	xxxxxxxxx
Toughness	xxxxxxxxxx
Unpleasantness	xxxxxxxxxxxxxxxxxx
Sadness	xxxxx
Passivity	xxxxxxx
Gentleness	xxxxxxx
Pleasantness	xxxxxx

Masculine sounds/feelings are very high.
Feminine sounds/feelings are medium.
Pronunciation is most difficult.

ROSIE

Cheerfulness	xxx
Activity	xxx
Toughness	xxxx
Unpleasantness	xxxxxxxxx
Sadness	xxxxx
Passivity	xxxxx
Gentleness	xxxxxxx
Pleasantness	xxxxxxxxxxx

Masculine sounds/feelings are medium high.
Feminine sounds/feelings are high.
Pronunciation is easier.

ROSLYN

Cheerfulness	xxxxx
Activity	xxxxxxxx
Toughness	xxxxxxx
Unpleasantness	xxxxx
Sadness	xxxxxxxxx
Passivity	xxxxx
Gentleness	xxxx
Pleasantness	xxxxx

Masculine sounds/feelings are medium high.
Feminine sounds/feelings are medium.
Pronunciation is more difficult.

ROXANNE

Cheerfulness	xxx
Activity	xxxxxx
Toughness	xxxxxxx
Unpleasantness	xxxxxxxxx
Sadness	xxxxxxxxx
Passivity	xxxxxxxxx
Gentleness	x
Pleasantness	x

Masculine sounds/feelings are medium high.
Feminine sounds/feelings are medium.
Pronunciation is average.

ROXIE

Cheerfulness	xxx
Activity	xxx
Toughness	xxxxxxx
Unpleasantness	xxxxxxxxxxxx
Sadness	xxxxx
Passivity	xxxxx
Gentleness	xxxx
Pleasantness	xxxxxx

Masculine sounds/feelings are medium high.
Feminine sounds/feelings are medium.
Pronunciation is easier.

RUBY

Cheerfulness	xxx
Activity	xxx
Toughness	xxxx
Unpleasantness	xxxxxxxx
Sadness	xxxxx
Passivity	xxx
Gentleness	xxxx
Pleasantness	xxxxxx

Masculine sounds/feelings are medium high.
Feminine sounds/feelings are medium low.
Pronunciation is easiest.

RUTH

Cheerfulness	xxx
Activity	xxx
Toughness	xxxx
Unpleasantness	xxxxx
Sadness	x
Passivity	xxx
Gentleness	xxxx
Pleasantness	xxxxxx

Masculine sounds/feelings are medium.
Feminine sounds/feelings are low.
Pronunciation is easier.

RUTHIE

Cheerfulness	xxxxxx
Activity	xxx
Toughness	xxxx
Unpleasantness	xxxxx
Sadness	x
Passivity	xxx
Gentleness	xxxxxxx
Pleasantness	xxxxxxxxxxx

Masculine sounds/feelings are medium high.
Feminine sounds/feelings are medium.
Pronunciation is easier.

SABRINA

Cheerfulness	xxx
Activity	xxxxxx
Toughness	xxxxxxx
Unpleasantness	xxxxxxxxx
Sadness	xxxxxxxxx
Passivity	xxxxx
Gentleness	x
Pleasantness	x

Masculine sounds/feelings are medium high.
Feminine sounds/feelings are low.
Pronunciation is more difficult.

SADIE

Cheerfulness	xxx
Activity	x
Toughness	xxxx
Unpleasantness	xxxxx
Sadness	xxxxx
Passivity	xxx
Gentleness	xxxx
Pleasantness	xxxxxx

Masculine sounds/feelings are medium.
Feminine sounds/feelings are medium low.
Pronunciation is easiest.

SALLIE

Cheerfulness	xxx
Activity	x
Toughness	x
Unpleasantness	x
Sadness	xxxxx
Passivity	xxxxx
Gentleness	xxxxxxxxxx
Pleasantness	xxxxxxxxxxx

Masculine sounds/feelings are low.
Feminine sounds/feelings are very high.
Pronunciation is easiest.

Women's And Girls' Names

SALLY

Cheerfulness	xxx
Activity	x
Toughness	x
Unpleasantness	x
Sadness	xxxxx
Passivity	xxxxx
Gentleness	xxxxxxxxxx
Pleasantness	xxxxxxxxxxxx

Masculine sounds/feelings are low.
Feminine sounds/feelings are very high.
Pronunciation is easiest.

SAMANTHA

Cheerfulness	xxx
Activity	x
Toughness	x
Unpleasantness	x
Sadness	xxxxx
Passivity	xxxxxxxxx
Gentleness	xxxxxxx
Pleasantness	xxxxxx

Masculine sounds/feelings are very low.
Feminine sounds/feelings are medium high.
Pronunciation is most difficult.

SANDRA

Cheerfulness	x
Activity	xxx
Toughness	xxxxxxx
Unpleasantness	xxxxxxxxx
Sadness	xxxxxxxxx
Passivity	xxxxxxx
Gentleness	x
Pleasantness	x

Masculine sounds/feelings are medium.
Feminine sounds/feelings are medium low.
Pronunciation is more difficult.

SANDY

Cheerfulness	xxx
Activity	x
Toughness	xxxx
Unpleasantness	xxxxx
Sadness	xxxxxxxxx
Passivity	xxxxxxx
Gentleness	xxxx
Pleasantness	xxxxx

Masculine sounds/feelings are low.
Feminine sounds/feelings are medium high.
Pronunciation is easier.

SARA

Cheerfulness	xxx
Activity	xxx
Toughness	xxxx
Unpleasantness	xxxxx
Sadness	x
Passivity	xxx
Gentleness	xxxx
Pleasantness	x

Masculine sounds/feelings are medium.
Feminine sounds/feelings are very low.
Pronunciation is more difficult.

SARAH

Cheerfulness	xxx
Activity	xxx
Toughness	xxxx
Unpleasantness	xxxxx
Sadness	x
Passivity	xxxxx
Gentleness	xxxx
Pleasantness	x

Masculine sounds/feelings are medium.
Feminine sounds/feelings are very low.
Pronunciation is easier.

SASHA

Cheerfulness	x
Activity	xxx
Toughness	xxxx
Unpleasantness	x
Sadness	x
Passivity	xxx
Gentleness	x
Pleasantness	x

Masculine sounds/feelings are medium low.
Feminine sounds/feelings are very low.
Pronunciation is easier.

SAUNDRA

Cheerfulness	x
Activity	xxx
Toughness	xxxxxxx
Unpleasantness	xxxxxxxxx
Sadness	xxxxxxxxx
Passivity	xxxxxxx
Gentleness	xxxx
Pleasantness	x

Masculine sounds/feelings are medium.
Feminine sounds/feelings are medium.
Pronunciation is most difficult.

SAVANNAH

Cheerfulness	xxx
Activity	x
Toughness	x
Unpleasantness	x
Sadness	xxxxxxxxx
Passivity	xxxxxxxxxxx
Gentleness	xxxx
Pleasantness	xxxxxx

Masculine sounds/feelings are very low.
Feminine sounds/feelings are high.
Pronunciation is average.

SELENA

Cheerfulness	xxxxxx
Activity	x
Toughness	x
Unpleasantness	x
Sadness	xxxxxxxx
Passivity	xxxxxx
Gentleness	xxxxxxxxxx
Pleasantness	xxxxxxxxxxx

Masculine sounds/feelings are very low.
Feminine sounds/feelings are very high.
Pronunciation is more difficult.

SELMA

Cheerfulness	xxx
Activity	x
Toughness	x
Unpleasantness	x
Sadness	xxxxx
Passivity	xxxxxxx
Gentleness	xxxxxxxxxxx
Pleasantness	xxxxx

Masculine sounds/feelings are very low.
Feminine sounds/feelings are high.
Pronunciation is more difficult.

SERENA

Cheerfulness	xxxxxx
Activity	xxx
Toughness	xxxx
Unpleasantness	xxxxx
Sadness	xxxxx
Passivity	xxxxx
Gentleness	xxxxxxx
Pleasantness	xxxxx

Masculine sounds/feelings are medium.
Feminine sounds/feelings are medium.
Pronunciation is more difficult.

SHANA

Cheerfulness	x
Activity	xxx
Toughness	xxxx
Unpleasantness	x
Sadness	xxxxx
Passivity	xxxxx
Gentleness	x
Pleasantness	x

Masculine sounds/feelings are medium low.
Feminine sounds/feelings are very low.
Pronunciation is easier.

SHANNA

Cheerfulness	x
Activity	xxx
Toughness	xxxx
Unpleasantness	x
Sadness	xxxxxxxxx
Passivity	xxxxxxx
Gentleness	x
Pleasantness	x

Masculine sounds/feelings are very low.
Feminine sounds/feelings are medium low.
Pronunciation is average.

SHANNON

Cheerfulness	x
Activity	xxx
Toughness	xxxx
Unpleasantness	x
Sadness	xxxxxxxxxxxxx
Passivity	xxxxxxxxx
Gentleness	x
Pleasantness	x

Masculine sounds/feelings are very low.
Feminine sounds/feelings are medium.
Pronunciation is average.

SHARI

Cheerfulness	xxxxx
Activity	xxxxxxxxx
Toughness	xxxxxxxxxx
Unpleasantness	xxxxx
Sadness	x
Passivity	xxx
Gentleness	xxxx
Pleasantness	x

Masculine sounds/feelings are very high.
Feminine sounds/feelings are very low.
Pronunciation is average.

SHARON

Cheerfulness	xxx
Activity	xxxxxx
Toughness	xxxxxxx
Unpleasantness	xxxxx
Sadness	xxxxx
Passivity	xxxxx
Gentleness	xxxx
Pleasantness	x

Masculine sounds/feelings are medium.
Feminine sounds/feelings are low.
Pronunciation is more difficult.

SHARRON

Cheerfulness	x
Activity	xxxxx
Toughness	xxxxxxx
Unpleasantness	xxxxx
Sadness	xxxxx
Passivity	xxxxx
Gentleness	x
Pleasantness	x

Masculine sounds/feelings are medium.
Feminine sounds/feelings are very low.
Pronunciation is more difficult.

SHAUNA

Cheerfulness	x
Activity	xxx
Toughness	xxxx
Unpleasantness	x
Sadness	xxxxx
Passivity	xxxxx
Gentleness	xxxx
Pleasantness	x

Masculine sounds/feelings are medium low.
Feminine sounds/feelings are low.
Pronunciation is easier.

SHAWN

Cheerfulness	x
Activity	xxx
Toughness	xxxx
Unpleasantness	x
Sadness	xxxxx
Passivity	xxxxx
Gentleness	xxxx
Pleasantness	x

Masculine sounds/feelings are medium low.
Feminine sounds/feelings are low.
Pronunciation is easiest.

SHAWNA

Cheerfulness	x
Activity	xxx
Toughness	xxxx
Unpleasantness	x
Sadness	xxxxx
Passivity	xxxxx
Gentleness	xxxx
Pleasantness	x

Masculine sounds/feelings are medium low.
Feminine sounds/feelings are low.
Pronunciation is easier.

SHEENA

Cheerfulness	xxx
Activity	xxx
Toughness	xxxx
Unpleasantness	x
Sadness	xxxxx
Passivity	xxx
Gentleness	xxxx
Pleasantness	xxxxx

Masculine sounds/feelings are medium.
Feminine sounds/feelings are medium low.
Pronunciation is easier.

SHEILA

Cheerfulness	xxx
Activity	xxx
Toughness	xxxx
Unpleasantness	x
Sadness	xxxxx
Passivity	xxx
Gentleness	xxxxxxx
Pleasantness	xxxxxxxxxxx

Masculine sounds/feelings are medium.
Feminine sounds/feelings are medium high.
Pronunciation is average.

SHELBY

Cheerfulness	xxxxx
Activity	xxx
Toughness	xxxx
Unpleasantness	xxxxx
Sadness	xxxxxxxxx
Passivity	xxxxx
Gentleness	xxxxxxxxxx
Pleasantness	xxxxxxxxxxx

Masculine sounds/feelings are medium.
Feminine sounds/feelings are very high.
Pronunciation is easier.

SHELIA

Cheerfulness	xxxxxx
Activity	xxxxxx
Toughness	xxxxxxx
Unpleasantness	x
Sadness	xxxxx
Passivity	xxxxx
Gentleness	xxxxxxx
Pleasantness	xxxxxx

Masculine sounds/feelings are medium.
Feminine sounds/feelings are medium.
Pronunciation is more difficult.

SHELLEY

Cheerfulness	xxxxxx
Activity	xxx
Toughness	xxxx
Unpleasantness	x
Sadness	xxxxx
Passivity	xxxxx
Gentleness	xxxxxxxxxx
Pleasantness	xxxxxxxxxxx

Masculine sounds/feelings are medium.
Feminine sounds/feelings are very high.
Pronunciation is easier.

SHELLY

Cheerfulness	xxxxxx
Activity	xxx
Toughness	xxxx
Unpleasantness	x
Sadness	xxxxx
Passivity	xxxxx
Gentleness	xxxxxxxxxx
Pleasantness	xxxxxxxxxxx

Masculine sounds/feelings are medium.
Feminine sounds/feelings are very high.
Pronunciation is easier.

SHEREE

Cheerfulness	xxxxx
Activity	xxxxxx
Toughness	xxxxxxx
Unpleasantness	xxxxx
Sadness	x
Passivity	x
Gentleness	xxxxxxx
Pleasantness	xxxxxxxxxxx

Masculine sounds/feelings are very high.
Feminine sounds/feelings are medium.
Pronunciation is easiest.

SHERI

Cheerfulness	xxxxxx
Activity	xxxxxxxxx
Toughness	xxxxxxxxxx
Unpleasantness	xxxxx
Sadness	x
Passivity	xxx
Gentleness	xxxx
Pleasantness	x

Masculine sounds/feelings are very high.
Feminine sounds/feelings are very low.
Pronunciation is average.

SHERRI

Cheerfulness	xxxxxx
Activity	xxxxxxxxxxx
Toughness	xxxxxxxxxxxx
Unpleasantness	xxxxx
Sadness	x
Passivity	x
Gentleness	x
Pleasantness	x

Masculine sounds/feelings are very high.
Feminine sounds/feelings are very low.
Pronunciation is average.

SHERRIE

Cheerfulness	xxxxx
Activity	xxxxxxxxx
Toughness	xxxxxxxxxx
Unpleasantness	xxxxx
Sadness	x
Passivity	x
Gentleness	xxxx
Pleasantness	xxxxxx

Masculine sounds/feelings are very high.
Feminine sounds/feelings are very low.
Pronunciation is easier.

SHERRY

Cheerfulness	xxxxxx
Activity	xxxxxxxxx
Toughness	xxxxxxxxxx
Unpleasantness	xxxxx
Sadness	x
Passivity	x
Gentleness	xxxx
Pleasantness	xxxxxx

Masculine sounds/feelings are very high.
Feminine sounds/feelings are very low.
Pronunciation is easier.

SHERYL

Cheerfulness	xxxxxx
Activity	xxxxxxxxx
Toughness	xxxxxxxxxx
Unpleasantness	x
Sadness	xxxxx
Passivity	xxx
Gentleness	xxxx
Pleasantness	xxxxxx

Masculine sounds/feelings are very high.
Feminine sounds/feelings are medium low.
Pronunciation is average.

SHIRLEY

Cheerfulness	xxxxx
Activity	xxxxx
Toughness	xxxxxxx
Unpleasantness	x
Sadness	xxxxx
Passivity	xxx
Gentleness	xxxxxx
Pleasantness	xxxxxxxxxxx

Masculine sounds/feelings are medium.
Feminine sounds/feelings are medium high.
Pronunciation is more difficult.

SILVIA

Cheerfulness	xxxxxxxxx
Activity	xxxxxx
Toughness	xxxxxxx
Unpleasantness	x
Sadness	xxxxx
Passivity	xxx
Gentleness	xxxxxx
Pleasantness	xxxxxxxxxxx

Masculine sounds/feelings are medium.
Feminine sounds/feelings are medium high.
Pronunciation is most difficult.

SIMONE

Cheerfulness	xxx
Activity	xxx
Toughness	xxxx
Unpleasantness	xxxxx
Sadness	xxxxxxxxx
Passivity	xxxxxxx
Gentleness	xxxx
Pleasantness	x

Masculine sounds/feelings are low.
Feminine sounds/feelings are medium.
Pronunciation is easier.

SOCORRO

Cheerfulness	xxx
Activity	xxxxxxxx
Toughness	xxxxxxxxx
Unpleasantness	xxxxxxxxxxxxxxxxx
Sadness	xxxxx
Passivity	xxxxxxx
Gentleness	xxxx
Pleasantness	x

Masculine sounds/feelings are very high.
Feminine sounds/feelings are medium low.
Pronunciation is more difficult.

SOFIA

Cheerfulness	xxxxxx
Activity	xxxxxx
Toughness	xxxx
Unpleasantness	xxxxx
Sadness	xxxxx
Passivity	xxx
Gentleness	x
Pleasantness	x

Masculine sounds/feelings are medium.
Feminine sounds/feelings are very low.
Pronunciation is average.

SONDRA

Cheerfulness	x
Activity	xxx
Toughness	xxxxxxx
Unpleasantness	xxxxxxxxx
Sadness	xxxxxxxxx
Passivity	xxxxxxx
Gentleness	x
Pleasantness	x

Masculine sounds/feelings are medium.
Feminine sounds/feelings are medium low.
Pronunciation is most difficult.

SONIA

Cheerfulness	xxx
Activity	xxx
Toughness	xxxx
Unpleasantness	xxxxx
Sadness	xxxxxxxxx
Passivity	xxxxx
Gentleness	x
Pleasantness	x

Masculine sounds/feelings are low.
Feminine sounds/feelings are low.
Pronunciation is average.

SONJA

Cheerfulness	xxx
Activity	xxx
Toughness	x
Unpleasantness	x
Sadness	xxxxx
Passivity	xxxxx
Gentleness	x
Pleasantness	x

Masculine sounds/feelings are very low.
Feminine sounds/feelings are very low.
Pronunciation is more difficult.

SONYA

Cheerfulness	xxx
Activity	xxx
Toughness	xxxx
Unpleasantness	x
Sadness	xxxxx
Passivity	xxxxx
Gentleness	x
Pleasantness	x

Masculine sounds/feelings are very low.
Feminine sounds/feelings are very low.
Pronunciation is average.

SOPHIA

Cheerfulness	xxxxxxxx
Activity	xxxxxxxx
Toughness	xxxx
Unpleasantness	x
Sadness	x
Passivity	x
Gentleness	x
Pleasantness	x

Masculine sounds/feelings are medium.
Feminine sounds/feelings are very low.
Pronunciation is average.

SOPHIE

Cheerfulness	xxxxxxxxx
Activity	xxxxxx
Toughness	x
Unpleasantness	x
Sadness	x
Passivity	x
Gentleness	xxxx
Pleasantness	xxxxxx

Masculine sounds/feelings are medium.
Feminine sounds/feelings are very low.
Pronunciation is easiest.

STACEY

Cheerfulness	xxx
Activity	xxx
Toughness	xxxx
Unpleasantness	xxxxx
Sadness	x
Passivity	x
Gentleness	xxxx
Pleasantness	xxxxxx

Masculine sounds/feelings are low.
Feminine sounds/feelings are very low.
Pronunciation is easier.

STACI

Cheerfulness	xxx
Activity	xxxxxx
Toughness	xxxxxxx
Unpleasantness	xxxxx
Sadness	x
Passivity	x
Gentleness	x
Pleasantness	x

Masculine sounds/feelings are medium.
Feminine sounds/feelings are very low.
Pronunciation is easier.

STACIE

Cheerfulness	xxx
Activity	xxx
Toughness	xxxx
Unpleasantness	xxxxx
Sadness	x
Passivity	x
Gentleness	xxxx
Pleasantness	xxxxxx

Masculine sounds/feelings are low.
Feminine sounds/feelings are very low.
Pronunciation is easier.

STACY

Cheerfulness	xxx
Activity	xxx
Toughness	xxxx
Unpleasantness	xxxxx
Sadness	x
Passivity	x
Gentleness	xxxx
Pleasantness	xxxxxx

Masculine sounds/feelings are low.
Feminine sounds/feelings are very low.
Pronunciation is easier.

STEFANIE

Cheerfulness	xxxxxxxx
Activity	xxxxxx
Toughness	xxxx
Unpleasantness	xxxxx
Sadness	xxxxx
Passivity	xxxxx
Gentleness	xxxxxxx
Pleasantness	xxxxxx

Masculine sounds/feelings are medium.
Feminine sounds/feelings are medium.
Pronunciation is average.

STELLA

Cheerfulness	xxx
Activity	xxx
Toughness	xxxx
Unpleasantness	xxxxx
Sadness	xxxxx
Passivity	xxxxx
Gentleness	xxxxxxx
Pleasantness	xxxxxx

Masculine sounds/feelings are low.
Feminine sounds/feelings are medium.
Pronunciation is more difficult.

STEPHANIE

Cheerfulness	xxxxxxxx
Activity	xxxxxx
Toughness	xxxx
Unpleasantness	xxxxx
Sadness	xxxxx
Passivity	xxxxx
Gentleness	xxxxxxx
Pleasantness	xxxxxx

Masculine sounds/feelings are medium.
Feminine sounds/feelings are medium.
Pronunciation is average.

SUE

Cheerfulness	x
Activity	xxx
Toughness	xxxx
Unpleasantness	x
Sadness	x
Passivity	x
Gentleness	x
Pleasantness	x

Masculine sounds/feelings are medium low.
Feminine sounds/feelings are very low.
Pronunciation is easiest.

SUMMER

Cheerfulness	xxx
Activity	xxx
Toughness	xxxx
Unpleasantness	x
Sadness	x
Passivity	xxxxxxx
Gentleness	xxxxxxx
Pleasantness	x

Masculine sounds/feelings are very low.
Feminine sounds/feelings are low.
Pronunciation is easier.

SUSAN

Cheerfulness	x
Activity	xxx
Toughness	xxxx
Unpleasantness	x
Sadness	xxxxx
Passivity	xxxxxxx
Gentleness	xxxx
Pleasantness	xxxxxx

Masculine sounds/feelings are very low.
Feminine sounds/feelings are medium.
Pronunciation is easier.

SUSANA

Cheerfulness	x
Activity	xxx
Toughness	xxxx
Unpleasantness	x
Sadness	xxxxx
Passivity	xxxxxxx
Gentleness	xxxx
Pleasantness	xxxxxx

Masculine sounds/feelings are very low.
Feminine sounds/feelings are medium.
Pronunciation is more difficult.

SUSANNA

Cheerfulness	x
Activity	xxx
Toughness	xxxx
Unpleasantness	x
Sadness	xxxxxxxx
Passivity	xxxxxxxxx
Gentleness	xxxx
Pleasantness	xxxxxx

Masculine sounds/feelings are very low.
Feminine sounds/feelings are medium high.
Pronunciation is more difficult.

SUSANNE

Cheerfulness	x
Activity	xxx
Toughness	xxxx
Unpleasantness	x
Sadness	xxxxxxxx
Passivity	xxxxxxxxx
Gentleness	xxxx
Pleasantness	xxxxxx

Masculine sounds/feelings are very low.
Feminine sounds/feelings are medium high.
Pronunciation is easier.

SUSIE

Cheerfulness	xxx
Activity	xxx
Toughness	xxxx
Unpleasantness	x
Sadness	x
Passivity	xxx
Gentleness	xxxxxxx
Pleasantness	xxxxxxxxxxx

Masculine sounds/feelings are medium.
Feminine sounds/feelings are medium.
Pronunciation is easiest.

SUZANNE

Cheerfulness	x
Activity	xxx
Toughness	xxxx
Unpleasantness	x
Sadness	xxxxxxxx
Passivity	xxxxxxxxx
Gentleness	xxxx
Pleasantness	xxxxxx

Masculine sounds/feelings are very low.
Feminine sounds/feelings are medium high.
Pronunciation is easier.

SUZETTE

Cheerfulness	xxx
Activity	xxxxxxxx
Toughness	xxxxxxxxx
Unpleasantness	xxxxxxxx
Sadness	x
Passivity	xxxxx
Gentleness	xxxxxxx
Pleasantness	xxxxxx

Masculine sounds/feelings are very high.
Feminine sounds/feelings are medium.
Pronunciation is more difficult.

Women's And Girls' Names

SYBIL

Cheerfulness	xxxxxx
Activity	xxx
Toughness	xxxx
Unpleasantness	xxxxx
Sadness	xxxxxxxxx
Passivity	xxx
Gentleness	xxxxxxx
Pleasantness	xxxxxxxxxxxx

Masculine sounds/feelings are medium.
Feminine sounds/feelings are high.
Pronunciation is easier.

SYLVIA

Cheerfulness	xxxxxxxxx
Activity	xxxxxx
Toughness	xxxxxxx
Unpleasantness	x
Sadness	xxxxx
Passivity	xxx
Gentleness	xxxxxxx
Pleasantness	xxxxxxxxxxxx

Masculine sounds/feelings are medium.
Feminine sounds/feelings are medium high.
Pronunciation is most difficult.

TABATHA

Cheerfulness	xxx
Activity	xxx
Toughness	xxxx
Unpleasantness	xxxxxxxxx
Sadness	xxxxx
Passivity	xxxxx
Gentleness	xxxx
Pleasantness	xxxxxx

Masculine sounds/feelings are medium.
Feminine sounds/feelings are medium.
Pronunciation is more difficult.

TABITHA

Cheerfulness	xxxxxx
Activity	xxxxxx
Toughness	xxxxxxx
Unpleasantness	xxxxxxxxx
Sadness	xxxxx
Passivity	xxx
Gentleness	xxxx
Pleasantness	xxxxx

Masculine sounds/feelings are high.
Feminine sounds/feelings are medium low.
Pronunciation is more difficult.

TAMARA

Cheerfulness	xxx
Activity	xxxxxx
Toughness	xxxxxxx
Unpleasantness	xxxxxxxxx
Sadness	x
Passivity	xxxxxxx
Gentleness	xxxxxxx
Pleasantness	x

Masculine sounds/feelings are medium high.
Feminine sounds/feelings are low.
Pronunciation is more difficult.

TAMEKA

Cheerfulness	xxx
Activity	xxx
Toughness	xxxxxxx
Unpleasantness	xxxxxxxxx
Sadness	x
Passivity	xxxxxxxxx
Gentleness	xxxxxxx
Pleasantness	x

Masculine sounds/feelings are medium.
Feminine sounds/feelings are medium low.
Pronunciation is more difficult.

TAMI

Cheerfulness	xxx
Activity	xxxxxx
Toughness	xxxxxxx
Unpleasantness	xxxxx
Sadness	x
Passivity	xxx
Gentleness	xxxx
Pleasantness	x

Masculine sounds/feelings are high.
Feminine sounds/feelings are very low.
Pronunciation is easiest.

TAMIKA

Cheerfulness	xxx
Activity	xxxxxx
Toughness	xxxxxxxxxx
Unpleasantness	xxxxxxxxx
Sadness	x
Passivity	xxxxxxx
Gentleness	xxxx
Pleasantness	x

Masculine sounds/feelings are high.
Feminine sounds/feelings are very low.
Pronunciation is average.

TAMMI

Cheerfulness	xxx
Activity	xxxxxx
Toughness	xxxxxxx
Unpleasantness	xxxxx
Sadness	x
Passivity	xxxxxxx
Gentleness	xxxxxxx
Pleasantness	x

Masculine sounds/feelings are medium.
Feminine sounds/feelings are low.
Pronunciation is easier.

TAMMIE

Cheerfulness	xxx
Activity	xxx
Toughness	xxxx
Unpleasantness	xxxxx
Sadness	x
Passivity	xxxxxxx
Gentleness	xxxxxxxxxx
Pleasantness	xxxxx

Masculine sounds/feelings are low.
Feminine sounds/feelings are medium.
Pronunciation is easiest.

TAMMY

Cheerfulness	xxx
Activity	xxx
Toughness	xxxx
Unpleasantness	xxxxx
Sadness	x
Passivity	xxxxxxx
Gentleness	xxxxxxxxxx
Pleasantness	xxxxx

Masculine sounds/feelings are low.
Feminine sounds/feelings are medium.
Pronunciation is easiest.

TANIA

Cheerfulness	xxx
Activity	xxxxx
Toughness	xxxxxxx
Unpleasantness	xxxxx
Sadness	xxxxx
Passivity	xxx
Gentleness	x
Pleasantness	x

Masculine sounds/feelings are medium.
Feminine sounds/feelings are very low.
Pronunciation is average.

TANISHA

Cheerfulness	xxx
Activity	xxxxxxxx
Toughness	xxxxxxxxxx
Unpleasantness	xxxxx
Sadness	xxxxx
Passivity	xxxxx
Gentleness	x
Pleasantness	x

Masculine sounds/feelings are medium high.
Feminine sounds/feelings are very low.
Pronunciation is more difficult.

TANYA

Cheerfulness	xxxxxx
Activity	xxx
Toughness	xxxx
Unpleasantness	xxxxx
Sadness	xxxxx
Passivity	xxxxx
Gentleness	xxxxxxx
Pleasantness	xxxxxx

Masculine sounds/feelings are medium.
Feminine sounds/feelings are medium.
Pronunciation is average.

TARA

Cheerfulness	xxx
Activity	xxxxxx
Toughness	xxxxxxx
Unpleasantness	xxxxxxxxx
Sadness	x
Passivity	xxx
Gentleness	xxxx
Pleasantness	x

Masculine sounds/feelings are very high.
Feminine sounds/feelings are very low.
Pronunciation is more difficult.

TASHA

Cheerfulness	x
Activity	xxxxx
Toughness	xxxxxx
Unpleasantness	xxxxx
Sadness	x
Passivity	xxx
Gentleness	x
Pleasantness	x

Masculine sounds/feelings are medium high.
Feminine sounds/feelings are very low.
Pronunciation is average.

TAYLOR

Cheerfulness	xxx
Activity	xxxxxx
Toughness	xxxxxxx
Unpleasantness	xxxxx
Sadness	xxxxx
Passivity	xxx
Gentleness	xxxx
Pleasantness	xxxxxx

Masculine sounds/feelings are high.
Feminine sounds/feelings are medium low.
Pronunciation is average.

TERESA

Cheerfulness	xxxxxx
Activity	xxxxxx
Toughness	xxxxxxx
Unpleasantness	xxxxxxxxx
Sadness	x
Passivity	xxxxx
Gentleness	xxxxxxxxxxx
Pleasantness	xxxxxxxxxxx

Masculine sounds/feelings are high.
Feminine sounds/feelings are medium high.
Pronunciation is most difficult.

TERI

Cheerfulness	xxxxx
Activity	xxxxxxxxx
Toughness	xxxxxxxxxx
Unpleasantness	xxxxxxxxx
Sadness	x
Passivity	xxx
Gentleness	xxxx
Pleasantness	x

Masculine sounds/feelings are very high.
Feminine sounds/feelings are very low.
Pronunciation is easier.

TERRY

Cheerfulness	xxxxx
Activity	xxxxxxxxx
Toughness	xxxxxxxxxx
Unpleasantness	xxxxxxxxx
Sadness	x
Passivity	x
Gentleness	xxxx
Pleasantness	xxxxx

Masculine sounds/feelings are very high.
Feminine sounds/feelings are very low.
Pronunciation is easier.

TERRI

Cheerfulness	xxxxx
Activity	xxxxxxxxxxx
Toughness	xxxxxxxxxxxx
Unpleasantness	xxxxxxxxx
Sadness	x
Passivity	x
Gentleness	x
Pleasantness	x

Masculine sounds/feelings are very high.
Feminine sounds/feelings are very low.
Pronunciation is average.

TESSA

Cheerfulness	xxx
Activity	xxx
Toughness	xxxx
Unpleasantness	xxxxx
Sadness	x
Passivity	xxx
Gentleness	xxxx
Pleasantness	x

Masculine sounds/feelings are medium.
Feminine sounds/feelings are very low.
Pronunciation is average.

TERRIE

Cheerfulness	xxxxx
Activity	xxxxxxxxx
Toughness	xxxxxxxxxx
Unpleasantness	xxxxxxxxx
Sadness	x
Passivity	x
Gentleness	xxxx
Pleasantness	xxxxx

Masculine sounds/feelings are very high.
Feminine sounds/feelings are very low.
Pronunciation is easier.

THELMA

Cheerfulness	xxxxx
Activity	x
Toughness	x
Unpleasantness	x
Sadness	xxxxx
Passivity	xxxxxxx
Gentleness	xxxxxxxxxxxxxx
Pleasantness	xxxxxxxxxxx

Masculine sounds/feelings are very low.
Feminine sounds/feelings are very high.
Pronunciation is most difficult.

Women's And Girls' Names

THERESA

Cheerfulness	xxx
Activity	xxx
Toughness	xxxx
Unpleasantness	xxxxx
Sadness	x
Passivity	xxxxxx
Gentleness	xxxxxxxxxx
Pleasantness	xxxxxxxxxxx

Masculine sounds/feelings are low.
Feminine sounds/feelings are high.
Pronunciation is most difficult.

THERESE

Cheerfulness	xxx
Activity	xxx
Toughness	xxxx
Unpleasantness	xxxxx
Sadness	x
Passivity	xxxxxx
Gentleness	xxxxxxxxxx
Pleasantness	xxxxxxxxxxx

Masculine sounds/feelings are medium.
Feminine sounds/feelings are high.
Pronunciation is more difficult.

TIA

Cheerfulness	x
Activity	xxx
Toughness	xxxx
Unpleasantness	x
Sadness	x
Passivity	x
Gentleness	x
Pleasantness	x

Masculine sounds/feelings are medium low.
Feminine sounds/feelings are very low.
Pronunciation is easiest.

TIFFANY

Cheerfulness	xxxxxxxxxxx
Activity	xxxxxxxxxxx
Toughness	xxxxxxx
Unpleasantness	xxxxx
Sadness	xxxxx
Passivity	xxxxx
Gentleness	xxxx
Pleasantness	xxxxx

Masculine sounds/feelings are very high.
Feminine sounds/feelings are medium.
Pronunciation is easier.

TINA

Cheerfulness	xxx
Activity	xxxxxx
Toughness	xxxxxxx
Unpleasantness	xxxxx
Sadness	xxxxx
Passivity	xxx
Gentleness	x
Pleasantness	x

Masculine sounds/feelings are high.
Feminine sounds/feelings are very low.
Pronunciation is easier.

TOMMIE

Cheerfulness	xxxxxx
Activity	xxxxxx
Toughness	xxxx
Unpleasantness	xxxxx
Sadness	x
Passivity	xxxxx
Gentleness	xxxxxxxxxx
Pleasantness	xxxxxx

Masculine sounds/feelings are medium.
Feminine sounds/feelings are medium.
Pronunciation is easiest.

TONI

Cheerfulness	xxx
Activity	xxxxx
Toughness	xxxxxxx
Unpleasantness	xxxxx
Sadness	xxxxx
Passivity	xxxxx
Gentleness	x
Pleasantness	x

Masculine sounds/feelings are high.
Feminine sounds/feelings are very low.
Pronunciation is easiest.

TONIA

Cheerfulness	xxx
Activity	xxxxx
Toughness	xxxxxx
Unpleasantness	xxxxxxxxx
Sadness	xxxxxxxxx
Passivity	xxxxx
Gentleness	x
Pleasantness	x

Masculine sounds/feelings are medium high.
Feminine sounds/feelings are low.
Pronunciation is average.

TONYA

Cheerfulness	xxx
Activity	xxxxx
Toughness	xxxxxxx
Unpleasantness	xxxxx
Sadness	xxxxx
Passivity	xxxxx
Gentleness	x
Pleasantness	x

Masculine sounds/feelings are medium.
Feminine sounds/feelings are very low.
Pronunciation is average.

TRACEY

Cheerfulness	xxx
Activity	xxxxx
Toughness	xxxxxx
Unpleasantness	xxxxxxxxx
Sadness	x
Passivity	x
Gentleness	xxxx
Pleasantness	xxxxx

Masculine sounds/feelings are medium high.
Feminine sounds/feelings are very low.
Pronunciation is average.

TRACI

Cheerfulness	xxx
Activity	xxxxxxxxx
Toughness	xxxxxxxxxx
Unpleasantness	xxxxxxxxx
Sadness	x
Passivity	x
Gentleness	x
Pleasantness	x

Masculine sounds/feelings are very high.
Feminine sounds/feelings are very low.
Pronunciation is average.

TRACIE

Cheerfulness	xxx
Activity	xxxxx
Toughness	xxxxxx
Unpleasantness	xxxxxxxxx
Sadness	x
Passivity	x
Gentleness	xxxx
Pleasantness	xxxxx

Masculine sounds/feelings are medium high.
Feminine sounds/feelings are very low.
Pronunciation is average.

Women's And Girls' Names

TRACY

Cheerfulness	xxx
Activity	xxxxxx
Toughness	xxxxxxx
Unpleasantness	xxxxxxxx

Sadness	x
Passivity	x
Gentleness	xxxx
Pleasantness	xxxxxx

Masculine sounds/feelings are medium high.
Feminine sounds/feelings are very low.
Pronunciation is average.

TRICIA

Cheerfulness	xxx
Activity	xxxxxxxxxxx
Toughness	xxxxxxxxxxxxx
Unpleasantness	xxxxxxxxx

Sadness	x
Passivity	x
Gentleness	x
Pleasantness	x

Masculine sounds/feelings are very high.
Feminine sounds/feelings are very low.
Pronunciation is more difficult.

TRINA

Cheerfulness	xxx
Activity	xxxxxxxxx
Toughness	xxxxxxxxxx
Unpleasantness	xxxxxxxxx

Sadness	xxxxx
Passivity	xxx
Gentleness	x
Pleasantness	x

Masculine sounds/feelings are very high.
Feminine sounds/feelings are very low.
Pronunciation is more difficult.

TRISHA

Cheerfulness	xxx
Activity	xxxxxxxxxxxx
Toughness	xxxxxxxxxxxx
Unpleasantness	xxxxxxxxx

Sadness	x
Passivity	x
Gentleness	x
Pleasantness	x

Masculine sounds/feelings are very high.
Feminine sounds/feelings are very low.
Pronunciation is more difficult.

TRUDY

Cheerfulness	xxx
Activity	xxxxxx
Toughness	xxxxxxxxxx
Unpleasantness	xxxxxxxxxxxx

Sadness	xxxxx
Passivity	xxxxx
Gentleness	xxxx
Pleasantness	xxxxxx

Masculine sounds/feelings are very high.
Feminine sounds/feelings are medium.
Pronunciation is average.

URSULA

Cheerfulness	xxx
Activity	xxxxxx
Toughness	xxxxxxx
Unpleasantness	x

Sadness	xxxxx
Passivity	xxx
Gentleness	xxxx
Pleasantness	xxxxxx

Masculine sounds/feelings are medium low.
Feminine sounds/feelings are medium low.
Pronunciation is more difficult.

VALARIE

Cheerfulness	xxxxxxxx
Activity	xxx
Toughness	xxxx
Unpleasantness	xxxxx
Sadness	xxxxx
Passivity	xxxxxxx
Gentleness	xxxxxxxxxxxx
Pleasantness	xxxxxxxxxxxxxxxx

Masculine sounds/feelings are medium.
Feminine sounds/feelings are very high.
Pronunciation is more difficult.

VALERIA

Cheerfulness	xxxxxxxx
Activity	xxx
Toughness	xxxx
Unpleasantness	xxxxx
Sadness	xxxxx
Passivity	xxxxx
Gentleness	xxxxxxxxxxxx
Pleasantness	xxxxxxxxxxxxxxxxxx

Masculine sounds/feelings are medium.
Feminine sounds/feelings are very high.
Pronunciation is most difficult.

VALERIE

Cheerfulness	xxxxxxxx
Activity	xxx
Toughness	xxxx
Unpleasantness	xxxxx
Sadness	xxxxx
Passivity	xxxxx
Gentleness	xxxxxxxxxxxx
Pleasantness	xxxxxxxxxxxxxxxxxxx

Masculine sounds/feelings are medium.
Feminine sounds/feelings are very high.
Pronunciation is more difficult.

VANESSA

Cheerfulness	xxxxx
Activity	x
Toughness	x
Unpleasantness	x
Sadness	xxxxx
Passivity	xxxxxx
Gentleness	xxxxxx
Pleasantness	xxxxx

Masculine sounds/feelings are very low.
Feminine sounds/feelings are medium.
Pronunciation is more difficult.

VELMA

Cheerfulness	xxxxx
Activity	x
Toughness	x
Unpleasantness	x
Sadness	xxxxx
Passivity	xxxxxx
Gentleness	xxxxxxxxxxxx
Pleasantness	xxxxxxxxxxx

Masculine sounds/feelings are very low.
Feminine sounds/feelings are very high.
Pronunciation is more difficult.

VERA

Cheerfulness	xxxxx
Activity	xxx
Toughness	xxxx
Unpleasantness	xxxxx
Sadness	x
Passivity	xxx
Gentleness	xxxxxxx
Pleasantness	xxxxx

Masculine sounds/feelings are medium high.
Feminine sounds/feelings are medium low.
Pronunciation is more difficult.

Women's And Girls' Names

VERNA

Cheerfulness	xxxxxx
Activity	xxx
Toughness	xxxx
Unpleasantness	x
Sadness	xxxxx
Passivity	xxx
Gentleness	xxxx
Pleasantness	xxxxxx

Masculine sounds/feelings are medium.
Feminine sounds/feelings are medium low.
Pronunciation is average.

VERONICA

Cheerfulness	xxxxxxxxx
Activity	xxxxxx
Toughness	xxxxxxxxxx
Unpleasantness	xxxxxxxxx
Sadness	xxxxx
Passivity	xxxxxxx
Gentleness	xxxxxxx
Pleasantness	xxxxxx

Masculine sounds/feelings are very high.
Feminine sounds/feelings are medium.
Pronunciation is most difficult.

VICKI

Cheerfulness	xxxxxxxxx
Activity	xxxxxx
Toughness	xxxxxxxxxx
Unpleasantness	xxxxx
Sadness	x
Passivity	xxx
Gentleness	xxxx
Pleasantness	xxxxxx

Masculine sounds/feelings are very high.
Feminine sounds/feelings are low.
Pronunciation is easier.

VICKIE

Cheerfulness	xxxxxxxxx
Activity	xxx
Toughness	xxxxxxx
Unpleasantness	xxxxx
Sadness	x
Passivity	xxx
Gentleness	xxxxxxx
Pleasantness	xxxxxxxxxxx

Masculine sounds/feelings are very high.
Feminine sounds/feelings are medium.
Pronunciation is easiest.

VICKY

Cheerfulness	xxxxxxxxx
Activity	xxx
Toughness	xxxxxxx
Unpleasantness	xxxxx
Sadness	x
Passivity	xxx
Gentleness	xxxxxxx
Pleasantness	xxxxxxxxxxx

Masculine sounds/feelings are very high.
Feminine sounds/feelings are medium.
Pronunciation is easiest.

VICTORIA

Cheerfulness	xxxxxxxxx
Activity	xxxxxxxxxxx
Toughness	xxxxxxxxxxxxxxxx
Unpleasantness	xxxxxxxxxxxx
Sadness	x
Passivity	xxxxx
Gentleness	xxxxxxx
Pleasantness	xxxxxx

Masculine sounds/feelings are very high.
Feminine sounds/feelings are medium.
Pronunciation is most difficult.

VILMA

Cheerfulness	xxxxx
Activity	xxx
Toughness	xxxx
Unpleasantness	x
Sadness	xxxxx
Passivity	xxxxx
Gentleness	xxxxxxxxxx
Pleasantness	xxxxxxxxxxx

Masculine sounds/feelings are low.
Feminine sounds/feelings are very high.
Pronunciation is more difficult.

VIOLA

Cheerfulness	xxxxxxxxx
Activity	xxxxxx
Toughness	xxxx
Unpleasantness	x
Sadness	xxxxx
Passivity	xxx
Gentleness	xxxxxxx
Pleasantness	xxxxxxxxxxx

Masculine sounds/feelings are medium.
Feminine sounds/feelings are medium high.
Pronunciation is more difficult.

VIOLET

Cheerfulness	xxxxxxxxx
Activity	xxxxxx
Toughness	xxxxxxx
Unpleasantness	xxxxxxxxx
Sadness	xxxxxxxxx
Passivity	xxxxxxx
Gentleness	xxxxxxxxxx
Pleasantness	xxxxxxxxxxx

Masculine sounds/feelings are very high.
Feminine sounds/feelings are very high.
Pronunciation is more difficult.

VIRGIE

Cheerfulness	xxxxxxxxxxx
Activity	xxxxxx
Toughness	xxxx
Unpleasantness	x
Sadness	x
Passivity	x
Gentleness	xxxxxx
Pleasantness	xxxxxxxxxxx

Masculine sounds/feelings are high.
Feminine sounds/feelings are medium.
Pronunciation is average.

VIRGINIA

Cheerfulness	xxxxxxxxxxxxxx
Activity	xxxxxxxxxxx
Toughness	xxxxxxxxxx
Unpleasantness	x
Sadness	xxxxx
Passivity	xxx
Gentleness	xxxx
Pleasantness	xxxxx

Masculine sounds/feelings are very high.
Feminine sounds/feelings are medium low.
Pronunciation is most difficult.

VIVIAN

Cheerfulness	xxxxxxxxxxx
Activity	xxxxxx
Toughness	xxxxxxx
Unpleasantness	x
Sadness	xxxxx
Passivity	xxxxx
Gentleness	xxxxxxx
Pleasantness	xxxxxxxxxxx

Masculine sounds/feelings are medium high.
Feminine sounds/feelings are high.
Pronunciation is more difficult.

Women's And Girls' Names

WANDA

Cheerfulness	xxx
Activity	x
Toughness	xxxx
Unpleasantness	xxxxx
Sadness	xxxxxxxx
Passivity	xxxxxxx
Gentleness	x
Pleasantness	xxxxxx

Masculine sounds/feelings are low.
Feminine sounds/feelings are medium.
Pronunciation is average.

WENDI

Cheerfulness	xxxxxxxxx
Activity	xxx
Toughness	xxxxxxx
Unpleasantness	xxxxx
Sadness	xxxxxxxxx
Passivity	xxxxxxx
Gentleness	xxxx
Pleasantness	xxxxxx

Masculine sounds/feelings are medium.
Feminine sounds/feelings are medium high.
Pronunciation is easier.

WENDY

Cheerfulness	xxxxxxxxx
Activity	x
Toughness	xxxx
Unpleasantness	xxxxx
Sadness	xxxxxxxxx
Passivity	xxxxxxx
Gentleness	xxxxxxx
Pleasantness	xxxxxxxxxxx

Masculine sounds/feelings are medium.
Feminine sounds/feelings are very high.
Pronunciation is easier.

WHITNEY

Cheerfulness	xxxxxx
Activity	xxxxxx
Toughness	xxxxxxx
Unpleasantness	xxxxx
Sadness	xxxxx
Passivity	xxx
Gentleness	xxxx
Pleasantness	xxxxxx

Masculine sounds/feelings are medium.
Feminine sounds/feelings are medium low.
Pronunciation is easier.

WILLA

Cheerfulness	xxxxxx
Activity	xxx
Toughness	xxxx
Unpleasantness	x
Sadness	xxxxx
Passivity	xxx
Gentleness	xxxx
Pleasantness	xxxxxxxxxxx

Masculine sounds/feelings are medium.
Feminine sounds/feelings are medium.
Pronunciation is average.

WILLIE

Cheerfulness	xxxxxxxxx
Activity	xxx
Toughness	xxxx
Unpleasantness	x
Sadness	xxxxx
Passivity	xxx
Gentleness	xxxxxxx
Pleasantness	xxxxxxxxxxxxxxxx

Masculine sounds/feelings are medium.
Feminine sounds/feelings are very high.
Pronunciation is easiest.

WILMA

Cheerfulness	xxxxx
Activity	xxx
Toughness	xxxx
Unpleasantness	x
Sadness	xxxxx
Passivity	xxxxx
Gentleness	xxxxxx
Pleasantness	xxxxxxxxxxx

Masculine sounds/feelings are low.
Feminine sounds/feelings are high.
Pronunciation is more difficult.

WINIFRED

Cheerfulness	xxxxxxxxxxx
Activity	xxxxxxxxxxx
Toughness	xxxxxxxxxxxx
Unpleasantness	xxxxxxxxx
Sadness	xxxxxxxx
Passivity	xxxxx
Gentleness	x
Pleasantness	xxxxxx

Masculine sounds/feelings are very high.
Feminine sounds/feelings are medium.
Pronunciation is more difficult.

WINNIE

Cheerfulness	xxxxxxxx
Activity	xxx
Toughness	xxxx
Unpleasantness	x
Sadness	xxxxxxxx
Passivity	xxxxx
Gentleness	xxxx
Pleasantness	xxxxxxxxxxx

Masculine sounds/feelings are medium low.
Feminine sounds/feelings are high.
Pronunciation is easiest.

YESENIA

Cheerfulness	xxxxxxxxx
Activity	xxx
Toughness	xxxx
Unpleasantness	x
Sadness	xxxxx
Passivity	xxxxxx
Gentleness	xxxxxx
Pleasantness	x

Masculine sounds/feelings are medium low.
Feminine sounds/feelings are medium.
Pronunciation is most difficult.

YOLANDA

Cheerfulness	xxx
Activity	xxx
Toughness	xxxx
Unpleasantness	xxxxx
Sadness	xxxxxxxxxxxx
Passivity	xxxxxxxxx
Gentleness	xxxx
Pleasantness	xxxxx

Masculine sounds/feelings are low.
Feminine sounds/feelings are very high.
Pronunciation is most difficult.

YOUNG

Cheerfulness	xxx
Activity	xxx
Toughness	xxxx
Unpleasantness	x
Sadness	x
Passivity	xxx
Gentleness	x
Pleasantness	x

Masculine sounds/feelings are medium.
Feminine sounds/feelings are very low.
Pronunciation is easier.

Women's And Girls' Names

YVETTE

Cheerfulness	xxxxxx
Activity	xxxxxx
Toughness	xxxxxxx
Unpleasantness	xxxxxxxxx
Sadness	x
Passivity	xxx
Gentleness	xxxxxxx
Pleasantness	xxxxxx

Masculine sounds/feelings are high.
Feminine sounds/feelings are medium low.
Pronunciation is more difficult.

YVONNE

Cheerfulness	xxx
Activity	x
Toughness	x
Unpleasantness	x
Sadness	xxxxxxxxx
Passivity	xxxxxxx
Gentleness	xxxx
Pleasantness	xxxxxx

Masculine sounds/feelings are very low.
Feminine sounds/feelings are medium high.
Pronunciation is average.

ZELMA

Cheerfulness	xxx
Activity	x
Toughness	x
Unpleasantness	x
Sadness	xxxxx
Passivity	xxxxxxxxx
Gentleness	xxxxxxxxxxxxx
Pleasantness	xxxxxxxxxxxx

Masculine sounds/feelings are very low.
Feminine sounds/feelings are very high.
Pronunciation is more difficult.